CIVIC

TORRANCE PUBLIC LIBRARY

3 2111 00600 8434

S0-AXX-255

WITHDRAWN

HONOLULU
Crossroads of
the Pacific

Port of Honolulu, 1857 (Hawaii State Archives)

996.931
B414

CCL

HONOLULU
Crossroads of
the Pacific

Edward D. Beechert

University of South Carolina Press

William N. Still, Jr., Series Editor

Studies in Maritime History

Stoddert's War:
*Naval Operations During
the Quasi-War with France, 1798–1801*
by Michael A. Palmer

**The British Navy and
the American Revolution**
by John A. Tilley

Iron Afloat:
The Story of the Confederate Armorclads
by William N. Still, Jr.

**A Maritime History
of the United States:**
*The Role of America's Seas and
Waterways*
by K. Jack Bauer

Confederate Shipbuilding
by William N. Still, Jr.

Raid on America:
The Dutch Naval Campaign of 1672–1674
by Donald G. Shomette
and Robert D. Haslach

Lifeline of the Confederacy:
*Blockade Running During
the Civil War*
by Stephen R. Wise

Admiral Harold R. Stark:
Architect of Victory, 1939–1945
by B. Mitchell Simpson, III

History and the Sea:
Essays on Maritime Strategies
by Clark G. Reynolds

Predators and Prizes:
*American Privateering and Imperial
Warfare, 1739–1748*
by Carl E. Swanson

Copyright © 1991 University of South Carolina

Published in Columbia, South Carolina, by the
University of South Carolina Press

Manufactured in the United States of America

Library of Congress Cataloging-in-Publication Data

Beechert, Edward D.
    Honolulu : crossroads of the Pacific / Edward D. Beechert.
        p.   cm.—(Studies in maritime history)
    Includes bibliographical references.
    Includes index.
    ISBN 0-87249-719-4
    1. Honolulu (Hawaii)—History.   I. Title.   II. Series.
DU629.H7B44   1990
996.9'31—dc20   90-44328

Contents

Contents

Illustrations

Tables

Acknowledgments

Many people have contributed to the writing of this book. The research was facilitated by the talented and helpful archivists at such places as the National Archives, the Hawaii State Archives, and the Hawaii-Pacific Collection of the University of Hawaii.

Particular thanks are due to the staff at the G. W. Blount White Library of the Mystic Seaport Museum, as well as the Library of the Peabody Museum. The newly established Arthur Sewall Maritime Museum at Bath, Maine, opened its files to me in the midst of preparing to move into new and more efficient quarters. The Bernice P. Bishop Museum Library made its collection of the Dillingham Papers—the Oahu Railroad and Land Company and Hawaiian Dredging Company—available, as well as its vast photo collection.

Mabel Suzuki of the Map Room of the Hamilton Library, University of Hawaii, provided excellent help in selecting historical maps of Honolulu Harbor.

Alice Beechert contributed to all phases of this book, especially in her skillful editing and meticulous checking. Without her assistance, the book would not have been possible.

E. D. B.

HONOLULU
Crossroads of the Pacific

Introduction

Honolulu, now a tourist destination, state capital, center of Pacific commerce, and one of the world's largest military bases, began as an insignificant fishing village in ancient Hawaii. The sailing canoes of the Hawaiian people did not require a deep water harbor or a protected anchorage. Ancient Honolulu Harbor—the harbor of Kou—was a small collection of fishermen's houses. The important centers of activity on Oahu were elsewhere.

The discovery of the harbor in 1792 by Captain William Brown, some fourteen years after Captain James Cook sailed by the difficult entrance, marks the beginning of what became a modern port city, the center of a kingdom, the seat of territorial government, and the capital of the fiftieth state.

From 1792 until the first "improvement" was put in place in 1825, the harbor was a protected anchorage that could be entered only with difficulty to secure provisions and water. In 1825 an abandoned hulk was towed to the foot of Nuuanu Street and sunk to become the first wharf of the harbor, and regulations governing the use of the harbor promptly were issued. From that time on, Honolulu Harbor was in operation.

This meager beginning did not reflect the singular importance of Honolulu as the only deep water port in the vast area of the mid-Pacific. As a supply point, as a repair and maintenance center, and as a source of seamen, there was no other port to rival its advantages. These circumstances transformed the insignificant village of Honolulu into a major maritime center, as well as the political focus of the succeeding regimes of the Hawaiian Islands.

Traders in the Northwest Pacific, ships crossing to Asia, and those rounding Cape Horn needing repair and resupply congregated here in the early nineteenth century. Many contributed to the variegated, growing community of beachcombers, drifters, settlers, and merchants.

Honolulu Harbor quickly became the focus of an exotic triangular trade in Pacific Northwest furs, Hawaiian sandalwood, and Chinese tea. As that trade exhausted its resource bases, the Pacific whaling fleet moved in to supply the economic base. Honolulu was the most convenient and useful wintering refuge available to the North Pacific whaling fleet.

The collapse of the Pacific whaling industry in the 1860s seemed to leave Honolulu with an overly large harbor and few ships to take advantage of the improved facilities. Who would use the service when the whalers vanished?

The answer was found in the signing of the Reciprocity Treaty with the United States, which admitted Hawaiian sugar to the United States duty free. The boisterous whalers, with their demands for provisions, chandlery services, and entertainment, were replaced with an ever-increasing outflow of raw sugar, a steady, incoming stream of agricultural equipment and supplies, and, perhaps most important, a flood of immigrant workers. The harbor development reflected this shift in economic focus. Sugar lent itself to an unrelenting process of corporate concentration, pushing aside almost all activities not related to agriculture.

Sugar politics and American tariff uncertainties contributed to the overthrow of the Hawaiian monarchy and the subsequent annexation of Hawaii to the United States in 1898. The appearance of the U.S. Army Corps of Engineers brought a new element to the operation and design of Honolulu Harbor.

Although Pearl Harbor was the focal point of the controversy over renewal of the Reciprocity Treaty in 1886, nothing was done until well after annexation to develop the facility. Dredging of the entrance was completed by 1911 when the first naval warship entered the channel and anchored in the new naval base.

Staple exports and tourism continued to characterize the use of the harbor between 1918 and 1937. These activities placed minimal demands on the development of the harbor, which was reflected in the slow expansion of public and private piers and terminals. Kalihi Basin, a second entrance channel, a belt railroad, and a passenger terminal were the principal concerns of harbor authorities. Revenues based on the sugar and pineapple industries and the small tourist industry placed a limit on the expansive plans of the harbor commissioners.

The increasing militancy of maritime labor on the West Coast influenced working conditions in Honolulu. The steady flow of Hawaiian seamen and longshoremen to and from the chief ports of the coast generally meant a reaction, somewhat delayed, to larger disputes and developments there. The explosion of militancy in San Francisco and Seattle in the 1930s was soon reflected in Honolulu. When the Honolulu longshoremen's union brought the National Labor Relations Board (NLRB) to Hawaii in 1937, Hawaii's leaders were astonished, a reflection of the long isolation of Hawaii from the major trends on the mainland.

Close on the heels of militant labor and national law came the decision in 1938 to expand the military power of the United States to the Pacific. Central to Pacific strategy was Pearl Harbor, where the U.S. Navy began a day and night expansion of drydock berthing facilities. In 1939 Honolulu was treated to practice blackouts, which continued until May 1941, when the Navy was confident that the air defenses of Pearl Harbor were adequate.

Three years of intensive military buildup in Hawaii produced an air of confidence and optimism before 7 December. The tranquility and satisfaction of the era were blown sky-high by the Japanese attack on Pearl Harbor. Hawaii quickly gathered its resources and became the base of the Pacific war effort, but the heavily Asian population of Hawaii posed a dilemma. Who would provide the labor for the war effort if the military demand to ship out all persons of Japanese ancestry prevailed? Hawaiian-style logic won out. The Japanese remained, the war effort went on, and Hawaii was transformed into a modern community, fiercely proud and committed to winning the war.

The postwar period brought painful realignments to Hawaii. The familiar domination of the economy and political structure by the sugar companies was coming to an end. The new military role of the United States in the Pacific meant a continuation of major harbor activities as a support center. A modern labor movement and a significant level of competition from mainland business firms made important changes in Hawaii's maritime world necessary. Labor militancy was characteristic of Hawaiian history, making sailors and longshoremen the radicals of Hawaiian society. The climax of that militancy was displayed in the 1949 longshore strike that closed the port for 179 days. The experience transformed the waterfront and the Hawaiian political scene.

The role of sugar and pineapple in the economy began a sharp decline. Tourism, spurred by dramatic changes in air transport, was

promoted to replace the crops, and extravagant plans for the enlargement of Honolulu Harbor were put into place. Statehood in 1959
spurred these development plans. In 1963, an elaborate plan was put
forward to make Hawaii the transshipment and distribution center of
east-west trade. Elaborate calculations showed that with proper state
planning, Hawaii could be the focal point of the coming boom in
Pacific shipping.

Circumstances altered these plans. Container shipping and the jet
airplane had a dramatic impact. Hawaii's plans assumed an expansion of
American shipping lines as a product of increased U.S. military presence in the Pacific and Asia. The growth of the tourist trade naturally
would mean an expansion of ship arrivals, so a major passenger terminal
was projected. A second deep draft harbor at Barbers Point was deemed
essential to fulfill the transshipment and distribution role forecast.
Shifts in Pacific shipping patterns, the role of the jet plane, and the
decline of American shipping had major impacts on the future of
Honolulu Harbor.

The neighbor island ports, satellites of Honolulu, have changed
radically over the years. Lahaina and Hilo were early rivals to Honolulu
for patronage of the whaling trade. Despite their attractive shore ac-
commodations, neither could offer a secure anchorage for the wintering
whalers. Honolulu's protected harbor and ship services soon reduced
these ports to minor roles. The advent of sugar opened new requirements. Before 1930, the scattered plantations sent their sugar to Honolulu by off-loading at various coastal points, mostly using barges and in
some cases, wire rope transport slung from the high cliffs of the
Hamakua coast. Kahului on Maui, Hilo on Hawaii, and Nawiliwili on
Kauai were developed with breakwaters by the U.S. Army Corps of
Engineers, which afforded deep draft ships a protected anchorage. The
neighbor islands, caught in the monoculture of sugar, slowly declined
through the twentieth century. Population moved gradually to Oahu,
seeking better employment opportunities as the sugar plantations
mechanized their operations.

Harbor activities were further curtailed when the first of the bulk
sugar loading facilities was put into place at Kahului Harbor in 1941. By
1955, sugar sacks and their attendant longshoremen had vanished from
the scene. Fully automated container barges further depleted the maritime work force in all of the ports.

With statehood, the economic decline ended and the neighbor
islands began to expand, developing new agricultural industries and

becoming tourist destinations. Despite the jet airplane, shipping increased to reflect this new level of economic activity. Two Hawaii-based cruise ships now call at each island on a weekly schedule, recalling the early interisland steamers.

Future plans appear to present a mixture of ideas. Clearly shipping will continue to be a major activity, although not the transshipment trade envisioned in the 1960s. The community now discusses the possible interfacing of the city with the harbor. Honolulu's waterfront is likely to be developed along the lines of San Francisco's or Baltimore's—a mixture of a working port and tourist attraction. Honolulu Harbor differs significantly in two respects from the models of planning often suggested. It is small for the volume of vital traffic, and does not lend itself to expansion.

Shipping is shifting to the western end of the harbor at the Sand Island container station, and perhaps, in the future, to Barbers Point Harbor on the Ewa Plain. Whatever the future holds for Hawaii, the Port of Honolulu will continue to be the dominant factor in the economic life of the state. Although some cargo can and is being shipped by air, 96 percent of Hawaii's import requirements must come through Honolulu Harbor. Hawaii, unlike her sister states, has no alternative sources of supply.

1

Early Days

Volcanic Origins

The complex volcanic origins of the Hawaiian chain are difficult to comprehend. The awesome roar of the active volcano Kilauea is belied by the fact that one can approach the scene with relative impunity. The sight and sound of Kilauea remind us that what is before us now is only the current phase of the island process. The basaltic domes formed by the volcano quickly begin the process of decomposition and erosion. Until a sufficient layer of soil forms, rainfall is absorbed by the porous volcanic rock. When the layer of soil is sufficiently thick, the rainfall courses off into streams, speeding the process of erosion and cutting deep valleys. The islands have grown, divided, and subsided in a startling progression of the rise and fall of the shoreline. Both subsidence and fluctuating water levels have created what we see today.

Hawaii lies on the northern edge of the coral seas. Its reefs have grown slowly. Changes of the ocean level created a number of reefs around Oahu, some submerged, some high above the current level of the ocean. The slow growth of coral in Hawaiian waters makes them vulnerable to the impact of fresh water running off the slopes of the volcanos that make up the peaks of the islands.

The erosion of the slopes created a table-skirt for the island of Oahu, on which coral reefs developed. The reefs rest on shelves built with their own debris or on platforms of material deposited either by volcanic action or erosion. Streams from the island carry fresh rain water and significant quantities of silt and sediment to the ocean level. Where fresh water flows in sufficient volume, the growth of the fringing coral reefs is retarded, and an opening to the sea—the mouth of a harbor—is created.[1]

On the island of Oahu, two such harbors were formed, Puuloa

(mound of pearl) and Kou or Honolulu (fair haven), the alternative names depending upon the source. Puuloa is better known as Pearl Harbor. The mouth of the Nuuanu Stream deposited the fill that created a large, low-lying flatland that was largely mud-exposed at low tide, and at the same time kept open a narrow, meandering channel to the ocean (Figure 1.1). The great expanse of Puuloa (Pearl Harbor) has a somewhat different origin; it is a drowned valley, formed by the general subsidence of the island. The scouring action of the Waiakele Stream created the channel there. The formidable sand and coral bar at its mouth precluded all but the most shallow draft vessels from taking advantage of the great anchorage until the end of the nineteenth century. Although the vastness of the Puuloa Basin reduced the impact of the fresh water flow of Waiakele Stream, that was not the case at Honolulu. The Nuuanu Stream, working on a smaller plain area, was more effective in maintaining a channel to the sea. The large indentation in the shore line probably contributed to the dispersion of the sediment, creating what came to be known as Sand Island, around which the stream moves to the east and to the ocean, creating an opening in the coral barrier.

The name of Honolulu (fair haven) is of somewhat less certain origin than that of Puuloa. The present spelling did not come into common usage until approximately 1825. Early phonetic forms varied from that of Captain Vancouver, who transcribed the sounds as *Honununo*, to variants such as *Hanaroora*.[2] The nineteenth-century Hawaiian historian, Samuel Kamakau, placed the name *Hononuunu* in an ancient chant.[3] In ships' logs, the place names of Hawaii continued to be spelled phonetically and imaginatively. It was several years before the name Honolulu was generally accepted. Some twenty-eight variants of the name have been noted from 1793 to 1827, when the present spelling was used in missionary books. The first port regulations, issued in 1825, used the spelling *Honoruru*.[4] The name *Kou* appears to be a legendary figment for which there is little or no historical evidence. The name appears only in accounts published after 1827. Given the importance of place names in Hawaiian land tenure, the fact that it does not appear until used in a missionary geography of 1832 suggests that the name *Kou* was generated by the embroidery of Hawaiian legends.

The harbor and its environs did not attract early Hawaiian settlement. The harbor in its earliest phase was at most a fishing village and the site of man-made fish ponds located at the mouth of the Nuuanu

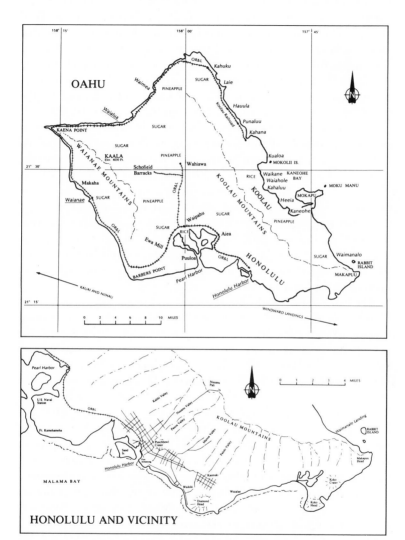

Figure 1.1 Oahu, Honolulu, and Vicinity (from Mifflin Thomas, *Schooner From Windward: Two Centuries of Hawaiian Interisland Shipping,* © University of Hawaii Press, 1983; used with permission).

Stream.[5] The narrow channel of the harbor and the mud flats offered few attractions in comparison to the area to the east. The hinterland of the harbor area was dry and dusty, while Waikiki, four miles to the east, was well-watered and fertile, offering shady groves and sandy beaches. The beaches were backed by a network of ponds and terraces that produced an abundant food supply, and the beach provided excellent surfing. In addition, the canoes of the Hawaiians were more easily landed through the many openings in the fringe reef and the sandy beaches of Waikiki. It was easily the favorite locale for the ruling class of Oahu.

The Elusive Harbor

Although Cook did not land at Oahu, the majority of ships immediately following him did call there, particularly at Waikiki, the residence of the ruling chiefs. Those ships failed to find the entrance to Honolulu Harbor, just a few miles west of Waikiki. In 1786 Captain Nathaniel Portlock anchored in Waialae Bay and sent a boat to explore the coast line to the west of Diamond Head. From the description in his journal, it is clear that the crew got no further in their exploration than Waikiki.

> [T]here was no convenient anchorage in any part of the bay; and that there was from sixty-six to seventy fathoms of water close in to shore. . . . He had found a small bay with very deep water, close to a sandy beach, where the natives generally landed their canoes, but no place for a ship to ride in safety; adjoining to the beach, in a beautiful valley, surrounded by a fine grove of cocoa-nut trees . . . there was a delightful town where . . . the king generally resided, and the district round it was called Whyteetee.[6]

One historian speculated that a Captain William Brown of the ship *Butterworth* might have told Vancouver about the harbor while they were together in the Pacific Northwest in 1792. Brown was in the islands in mid-1792 and with Vancouver at Nootka Sound in the later part of 1792.[7] Brown's description of Puuloa as a vast harbor naturally would attract Vancouver's attention. Captain Brown told Vancouver that Honolulu was "small, but commodious with regular soundings from seven to three fathoms . . . but the only means of getting in or out is by warping."[8] It was on this information that Vancouver sailed along the coast line of Oahu, guided by Kamohomoho, who had served as his navigator along the islands of Hawaii and Molokai. Vancouver noted two openings in the reef to the west of Waikiki, but did not examine either closely. One of these was certainly Honolulu Harbor, the other may have been nearby Kewalo Basin. Both would have shown a break in the surf. His journal describes what was apparently the opening to Honolulu Harbor: "The other opening to the eastward, called by the natives *Honoonoono*, Tomohomoho [Vancouver's guide] represented as being very much more shallow, and a smaller place; this induced me to pass it without examination."[9] Clearly, however attractive the opening might seem, the danger of approaching reefs given the prevailing brisk trade winds was a maneuver not to be undertaken lightly. The northeast trades made Honolulu Harbor impossible for a large ship to enter under sail and was a sore trial even for small sailing vessels.

Vancouver's guide took him farther west to Puuloa, which Vancouver's journal records as being superior to *Honoonoono*.[10] Puuloa (Pearl Harbor) was, indeed, much larger. It also had a shallow bar at the mouth of the harbor.[11]

Hawaiian Chiefs and Foreign Sailors

To the ships calling at Hawaii after Cook, Hawaii was a convenient and exotic place. Trade had grown dramatically from the simple iron nails traded for hogs by Captain Cook to demands for muskets, cannon, ammunition, and men to man those weapons.[12] The Hawaiians viewed the arrivals as an opportunity. "[T]he warring chiefs grasped every chance to strengthen their positions. The coming of the foreigners presented a golden opportunity, and foreign men, foreign weapons, and foreign ships were eagerly sought."[13] A few of the visitors, notably Cook and Vancouver, refused all requests for weapons and men to man them. Others were more than eager to trade guns for influence and supplies. One supplied Kamehameha with muskets, ammunition, and a swivel gun to mount on a double canoe. Vancouver was discouraged to find that a regular arms traffic had developed.[14] The maneuverability of the foreign ships was also noted by the marine-wise Hawaiians who sought to duplicate the vessels visiting their shores. By 1795, Kamehameha had built a forty-ton sloop for his invasion of Kauai.[15]

Unfortunately, the use of weapons was too often demonstrated for the Hawaiians. The ship *Eleanora*, commanded by Captain Simon Metcalfe, provided one of the bloodiest examples of the relationship between Hawaiians and foreigners. In late January or early February 1791, Metcalfe was at Honolua, Maui, to trade for supplies. At night Metcalfe moored his shore boat astern with a sailor to guard the boat.

Hawaiians came out, killed the sailor and took the boat. When the Hawaiians returned the next day to trade, Metcalfe carefully arranged a revenge that is best expressed in the rough language of the ship's log of the *Massachusetts*, which called at Olowalu some six months later.

> He [Metcalfe] had his Boat moored astern with one man in her to keep the Natives from Stealing her. The Natives swim off in the Night and killed the man and took the Boat onshore with them. The Nex Day they Brought Sum of the mans bons [bones] and Scrapes to Sell and Sume of the Boat. This unfortunate Man was a Portugea by the name of Antoney. This put Capt. Medcalf in a great Rage and [he] was resolved to [get] Satisfaction of them. he ordered all his guns to be Loaded with Grape Shot and the Hinges of the Ports greased after he got his Vessel all Clear for the Action. He got in with one of the Chiefes for to Tabboo his Vessel on one side of her, that he may have a good chance to Fullfill his Desire. Tabboing is Authority that the Chifes youse over the Lower Sort of P[e]ople and is the Death of Any one Douth Brack it of his Class. The Chife Tabbood one side of Capt. Medcalf Brig so that all the Natives were on the opersit Side. The Capt ordered all hands to heeve Beeds over Bord to Draw the Natives as Near as Possable. When he had corleckted upwards of three hundred Canoes a Long Sid the Capt called out the mans Name that was killed Anthoney as a Signnel for his men to Fire Thay did so and killed upwards of 200 Men Women and Childrin.[16]

The story is further complicated by the fact that Captain Metcalfe's son, Thomas Humphrey, was commanding a smaller vessel that arrived off the North Kona coast in February or March, trading and waiting for a rendezvous with his father's larger vessel. On a trading voyage the previous year, Metcalfe senior had been in the area and struck the local chief, Kameeiamoku, during a trading dispute. The schooner *Fair American*, commanded by Metcalfe's son, was the very next ship to call at North Kona. Kameeiamoku killed five crewmen and Thomas Metcalfe. One crewman, Isaac Davis, took to the rigging and was the lone survivor. Kamehameha took possession of the *Fair American*, and Isaac Davis became the first Englishman attached to Kamehameha's retinue.

Shortly after this event, Simon Metcalfe came to Kealakekua Bay to trade, unaware of his son's fate. John Young, boatswain of Metcalfe's ship, went ashore and was promptly captured by Kamehameha. After waiting for several days for John Young to return, Metcalfe sailed away. Kamehameha's motives apparently were to keep Metcalfe from learning of his son's fate and to obtain another experienced seaman. John Young joined Isaac Davis. Both men played important roles in Kamehameha's conquest of the remaining islands.[17]

Kamehameha took the schooner *Fair American* and, with his new English recruits in command of artillery, launched .a major attack against his opponents on the island of Hawaii in the spring of 1791. The resulting battle is remembered as the *Kepuwahaulaula*—the red-mouthed gun.[18]

On Oahu, the same sort of struggle was under way. The ruling chief of Oahu, Kahekili, had extended his rule from Maui to Molokai and Lanai. Kahekili, whom traders had described as a quarrelsome, ruthless individual, was anxious to enlist the aid of the powerful foreign visitors to complete his conquest by adding the island of Hawaii.[19]

Some time in 1792, certainly before March 1793, Kahekili showed the entrance of Honolulu Harbor to William Brown, captain of the ship *Butterworth*, the schooner *Jackall* and the sloop *Prince Lee Boo*. Brown returned to Oahu in 1794 and immediately played a major role in the chiefly wars. He eagerly agreed to lend his vessels and weapons in return for a cession of the island of Oahu and trading rights. He, like Vancouver, was thinking in English commercial terms.

Before Kahekili could launch his war of conquest, however, he sickened and died in Waikiki in June 1794, leaving his son and brother to divide the islands of Maui, Molokai, and Lanai. Kalanikupule, the son, almost immediately fought a battle with his uncle, Kaeokulani, for control of Oahu. Brown, with his ships and men, played a significant role in the battle on the side of the son. The battle was fought on the east bank of Puuloa, enabling Brown's small ships to sail into the East Loch and use his cannon to good advantage against Kaeokulani. Kaeokulani was killed, leaving Kalanikupule in control of the island. Brown and his ships returned to Honolulu Harbor to celebrate the victory. Firing a salute, a gun mistakenly loaded with grape shot killed Captain John Kendrick of the accompanying ship *Lady Washington* and some of his crew.[20]

The victory and the effectiveness of the weapons spurred Kalanikupule's ambitions to win control over all of the islands. With Brown's ships and weapons, he could effectively challenge Kamehameha for control. Brown sent his large ship, *Butterworth*, on a trading voyage, remaining behind with the schooner *Jackall* and the sloop *Prince Lee Boo* under Captain Robert Gordon.

On 1 January 1795, Kalanikupule and his men killed the two

captains, Brown and Gordon, and captured the crews of the vessels. On January 12, he moved the ships to Waikiki, where he prepared to sail for Hawaii and battle with Kamehameha. The mates of the two ships carefully prepared their plans. Shortly after getting underway, they overcame the Hawaiians, killed all but the chief, his wife, and a few attendants, and regained control of the vessels. The chief and his remaining retinue were put into a canoe and the two ships sailed to Hawaii. There they left a letter outlining the story with John Young and Isaac Davis and sailed on to China. [21]

Kamehameha immediately made preparations to attack Oahu, using the schooner *Fair American* and the services of Young and Davis. In the spring of 1795, he completed his conquest with the rout of the Oahu forces and the capture and sacrifice of Kalanikupule. [22]

Consolidation of Power

With the conquest of Oahu, the wars wound down, the bloodiest episodes now past. Only Kauai remained to be subdued. Kamehameha's use of western weapons and tactics made consolidation of power only a matter of time. In addition to canoes mounting small cannon, he ordered the building of a forty-ton sloop. There were sufficient foreign craftsmen in Honolulu to make that feasible and ships calling at Honolulu were able to supply the rigging and sails he needed.

Kamehameha returned to Hawaii in 1796 to consolidate his grip on that island, organizing the distribution of land to subordinate chiefs and carrying on a vigorous trade with visiting ships. In 1804, he returned to Oahu to prepare for the assault on Kauai. Before the fleet could be launched, an epidemic decimated his armada—the first of several devastating European diseases that would sweep the Hawaiian population. [23]

The epidemic signaled an end to the wars of conquest. Kamehameha settled down to the routine of maintaining his power and governing the islands. He was content to accept the acknowledgment of his sovereignty by Kauai's ruling chief, Kaumualii. Warfare ended but royal plotting continued. A scheme to murder Kaumualii on a visit to Waikiki was thwarted by Isaac Davis. For his trouble, Davis was murdered by the plotting Oahu chiefs in April 1810. Kamehameha returned to Kona in 1812, where he remained until his death in 1819. [24]

The prevalence of weapons, seamen, and gunners transformed the wars of the Hawaiian chiefs into bloody massacres. The arrival of manufactured goods and the trappings of wealth gave a new dimension to the ancient political power of the chiefly system. It is important to note that the Hawaiian notion of land tenure was substantially different from the English idea. When Kamehameha placed the island of Hawaii at George Vancouver's disposal, he intended to secure Vancouver's support in the form of weapons and men. To a Hawaiian chief, such an arrangement did not mean surrender of title or control, but was largely a grant of use or occupation of the land until such time as the cession was revoked. The notion of ownership of land apart from the chiefly role simply did not exist.

The consolidation of political power, carefully maintained by Kamehameha during his remaining years, set the stage for the development of Honolulu Harbor. Hawaiian oral tradition clearly makes the point that Honolulu was an inferior location to Waikiki. Even Hawaiians in canoes found the beaches of Waikiki a more reasonable place to land than in the narrow channel of the harbor and the mudflats that were exposed at low tide. The development of the harbor would come all too soon with the arrival of foreign traders.

Notes

1. The complex geology of the island of Oahu is best treated in Harold Stearns, *Geology of the State of Hawaii* (Palo Alto: Pacific Books, 1966), pp. 24–27, 79–102.

2. George Vancouver, *A Voyage of Discovery to the North Pacific Ocean and Round the World in the Years 1790, 1791, 1792, 1793, 1794 and 1795*, 6 vols. (London: Thomas and Andrews, 1801), vol. 3, p. 363.

3. Samuel Kamakau, *Ka Poe Kahiko: The People of Old*, Bernice P. Bishop Museum Special Publication No. 51 (Honolulu: Bishop Museum Press, 1964), p. 40; Abraham Fornander, *Collection of Hawaiian Antiquities and Folklore*, Bernice P. Bishop Museum Memoirs, 6 vols. (Honolulu: Bishop Museum Press, 1916), vol. 4, pp. 400–401.

4. John F. G. Stokes, "Honolulu and Some New Speculative Phases of Hawaiian History," *Hawaiian Historical Society 42nd Annual Report* (1933), pp. 51–53.

5. Stokes, "Honolulu," pp. 41–43; Fornander, *Collection of Hawaiian Antiquities*, vol. 4, p. 478; Abraham Fornander, *An Account of The Polynesian Race*, Bernice P. Bishop Museum Special Publication No. 4 (Honolulu: Bishop Museum Press, 1909), vol. 2, p. 164. The archaeological evidence reviewed by Fornander would suggest an occupation date of approximately A.D. 1100.

6. Nathaniel Portlock, *Voyage Around the World . . . 1785–1788* (London: J. Stockdale, 1789), p. 164.

7. Stokes, "Honolulu," pp. 71–72.

8. Vancouver, *Voyage of Discovery*, vol. 3, p. 363; Stokes, "Honolulu," p. 69. Given the dates of Vancouver's meeting with Brown on the Northwest Coast, it is clear that Brown must have explored the harbor in late 1792 or early 1793. Historian Stokes reached the conclusion that Vancouver had been deceived into bypassing Honolulu and was conducted by his guide to Pearl Harbor.

9. Vancouver, *Voyage of Discovery*, vol. 3, pp. 361–363.

10. Ibid., vol. 2, pp. 203–217.

11. Kamohomoho had supervised the examination of the bottoms of Vancouver's ships and so would have known of their draft. Stokes, "Honolulu," p. 70; Vancouver, *Voyage of Discovery*, vol. 3, pp. 293–294.

12. Ralph S. Kuykendall, *The Hawaiian Kingdom*, 3 vols. (Honolulu: University of Hawaii Press, 1938), vol. 1, pp. 22–23.

13. Kuykendall, *Hawaiian Kingdom*, vol. 1, p. 22.

14. Vancouver, *Voyage of Discovery*, vol. 1, p. 353, 355, 391–392; vol. 3, pp. 183–184; vol. 4, pp. 179–180.

15. Kuykendall, *Hawaiian Kingdom*, vol. 1, p. 23.

16. Log of ship *Massachusetts*, 22 August 1791. Log 656/1790M, Peabody Museum, Salem, Mass. For an account written by an officer of the *Eleanora*, see *Gentleman's Magazine*, (London, April 1794). See also a reprint of this account in the *Pacific Commercial Advertiser* (1 July 1906).

17. Kuykendall, *Hawaiian Kingdom*, vol. 1, p. 25. Metcalfe's career was marked by other episodes of violence toward native people. He was among the first to trade between China, Hawaii, and the Northwest, probably beginning in 1788. In 1794, on a voyage to China, Mauritius, and the Pacific Northwest, Metcalfe was killed by the Haida Indians at Houston Steward Channel in the Queen Charlotte Islands. Again, only one crew member survived. F. W. Howay, "Captain Simon Metcalfe and the Brig *Eleanora*," *Hawaiian Historical Society 34th Annual Report* (1926), pp. 33–39.

18. Kuykendall, *Hawaiian Kingdom*, vol. 1, p. 37.

19. See Portlock, *A Voyage Around the World, 1785–1778*, pp. 69–75, 161–163; James Colnett, "The Journal of Capt. James Colnett Aboard the Prince of Wales and Princess Royal," typescript in Hawaii Pacific Collection, University of Hawaii, Honolulu.

20. Kuykendall, *Hawaiian Kingdom*, vol. 1, p. 46.

21. Ralph S. Kuykendall, "A Northwest Trader at the Hawaiian Islands," *Oregon Historical Quarterly* 24 (1923):2; Gavan Daws, *Honolulu* (Ph.D. dissertation, University of Hawaii, Honolulu, 1966), pp. 23–24.

22. Kuykendall, *Hawaiian Kingdom*, vol. 1, p. 47; Sheldon Dibble, *A History of the Sandwich Islands* (Honolulu: T. H. Thrum, 1909), pp. 67–71; Samuel Kamakau, *The Ruling Chiefs of Hawaii* (Honolulu: Kamehameha School Press, 1961), pp. 170–171; John Boit, Jr., "Journal of a Voyage Round the Globe, 10 October 1795," typescript in Hawaii Pacific Collection, University of Hawaii, Honolulu.

23. Kamakau, *Ruling Chiefs*, pp. 188–189.

24. Kuykendall, *Hawaiian Kingdom*, vol. 1, pp. 50–51.

2

Fair Haven

Early Traders and Ports of Call

Ships seeking supplies called along the leeward side of each of the islands. Lahaina on the island of Maui, Honolulu on Oahu, Kealakekua on Hawaii, and Waimea on Kauai, were the favored supply points. Waimea soon became a favorite supplier of yams and taro, which were welcome substitutes for the often unpalatable bread shipped from New England. Kealakekua, Lahaina, and Waimea offered more in supplies and water than did Honolulu Harbor, which was located in a dry area of Oahu with water obtainable only at a distance.

In 1791, the ship *Massachusetts* recorded in her log these details of trading at the island of Hawaii:

> August 22, 1791: Nothing remarkable since the 15 of the mounth. This day saw a number of Birds and Sea Weeds and Sines of Land. Being the Latt. of Owyhee Bore away for it at 4 AM. Saw the land upon the bowsprit. Proved to be the Island of O-why-hee, hold in for it to roun Down the Lee Side of the Island. At 10 AM Several Canoes Came of[f] to us to Treade. They had plenty of Potators and Hogs. They craved nothing but Iron in Return for them. We bought theam Hogs at the rate of Two Spikes a Peace.[1]

The ship proceeded on to Oahu after two days of trading in Kealakekua Bay. Running to the leeward side, the ship came to anchor off Waikiki "in 20 fathoms of water. Great number of Natives came a Long Side to make Tread with Pleanty Hogs Potatoes Yams Bread Fruit Grass Lines Matts & Mother of Purl Beeds and a great Number of other Curignostes [curiosities?]"[2]

Iron and women proved to be an unbeatable combination. The laconic language of the log describes a common situation.

> Sunday, August 28, 1791: The King, Brother and Son Came onbord and made the Capt Present of three Head Feather'd Caps and sum Tapper [tapa]. Our Capt gave them a Musket and sum Powder for King. This day they sent all the handsomest Young Girls that they have on the Island onbord and the Every one thear Charge How to Behave at Night. When they gave a siginl for Every one of them Cling Fast to the Europan and to Devert them While they Cut our Cable. . . . At Night every man in the Ship tuck a Girl and Sent the Remainder onshore. At 10 oclock at Night the Watch on the upper Deck Persivd the Ship to Drift at the Same Time every Girl in the Ship clung fast to her man. . . . WE found the Cable cut about two fathoms from the Hawse Hole. We made sail Stood off and on the Bay all Night.[3]

Demanding the prompt return of the anchor, the captain threatened dire action. The Hawaiian chief offered to attempt to recover the anchor and went through a farcical routine of divers pretending to look for the anchor. After a day of great activity and no result, the captain resorted to an already familiar recourse—indiscriminate broadsides.

> At 11 am Got under Way and Fir'd four or five Broad Sides into the Villige. We could Sea thousands of Native Runing one uppon top of the other uppon the Beach. Saw a Great Numbr of Canoes off the Lee Bow, Made for them and fir'd a Broad Side at the Which Stove a Great many of them to Peaces . . . Seaing no Possibility of Gitting our Anchor Bore Away . . . At 6 pm Stearing NW by W for the Island of Otehy [Kauai].[4]

Behaving as they did in the Pacific Northwest, trading captains used whatever force they deemed appropriate against the Hawaiians.

On Hawaii, Kealakekua was perhaps the most visited, despite the unfavorable winds and currents. The example of the ship *Pearl* in 1805 was typical of the comments of captains seeking supplies here. From 26 February to 11 March 1805, the *Pearl* sailed up and drifted down the Kona coast, trying to come into the bay for supplies.

> *Feb. 26:* . . . The morning clear and pleasant. Load the Guns. At 9 A.M. blowing, reefed topsails. Latter part variable wind and strong current setting the ship off the shore. At Meridian the entrance to Karakakooa [Kealakekua] bore North distance 12 leagues. Two canoes alongside.

> *Feb. 27:* Throughout this 24 hours light variable winds and clear pleasant weather. At 12 Meridian the entrance of Karakakooa Bay bore North distance 7 leagues. Had several canoes alongside. Bought three hogs but they had no fruit.

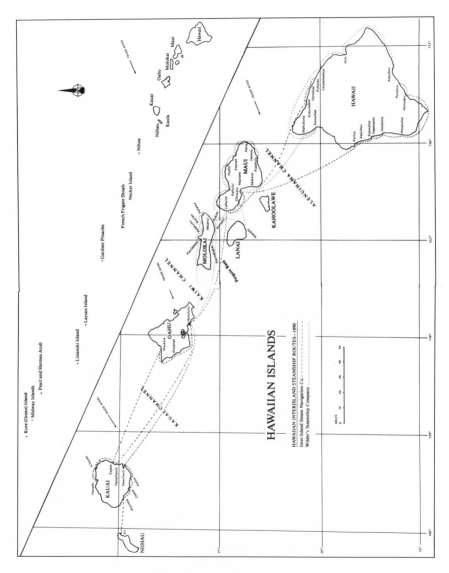

Figure 2.1 Hawaiian Islands (from Thomas, *Schooner From Windward*, © University of Hawaii Press; used with permission).

Feb. 28: Throughout these 24 hours light baffling winds and calm, the ship heading all round the compass . . .

Mar. 1: This 24 hours begins with calm weather and lofty swell from the Eastward. At 6 PM a light breeze from the East. Made all sail. . . . We thought the distance to be up with Karakakooa but found the ship to in the same place as the day before.

Finally, on 5 March, the ship entered the bay and began loading stores—hogs, vegetables, taro, and coconuts. When they cleared the Bay on 11 March, bound for the Pacific Northwest, the log records that they took John Young, Kamehameha's advisor, to Kawaihae and departed, giving "Mr Young three cheers, being happy to think we are leaving the islands being so long detained with baffling winds and contrary current."[5]

Beachcombers and Royal Aides

Each of the ruling chiefs managed to acquire one or more foreign seamen to handle the guns and cannons that became a part of the struggle for power after 1778. Some were valued for their mechanical skills, abilities to build boats, and repair and shape iron tools.[6]

The Hawaiians, operating in a wood-fiber-stone technology were excellent craftsmen. Able to construct canoes with a length of sixty feet and a draft of four feet, and to braid ropes of fiber capable of hauling ships into harbor, they had little difficulty in learning to use the new tools and techniques. A Hawaiian asked Vancouver's blacksmith how he shaped iron and was shown the forge. The next day the Hawaiian was observed on the beach heating a piece of iron in a coral-lined pit. The ship builders' adze and chisels quickly were appropriated by the skilled canoe builders.[7]

There was some fear expressed by the small foreign community that the Hawaiians were learning too rapidly and might reach a point where the services of the foreign beachcombers would no longer be needed. One sailor, Archibald Campbell, recounted his effort to have a loom made to weave cloth for sails at the request of the king. "Kamehameha's carpenter refused to help Campbell make his loom because he believed the Hawaiians would soon learn to make cloth and then European vessels would cease to visit."[8] Campbell had been a crew member on a Russian ship sent to Hawaii to secure a cargo of salt. Injured on the voyage, he was put ashore in 1809, and subsequently was retained to serve King Kamehameha.

Not all of the foreigners prospered. Early accounts describe a rather motley group for whom the name beachcomber is well suited. Some prospered in the service of the chiefs and Kamehameha; some moved too far into the arena of politics and paid the penalty. Isaac Davis, the sole survivor of the schooner *Fair American,* was named governor of Oahu and for twenty years was a thoroughly integrated foreigner. But he was poisoned by irate chiefs on Oahu when he informed the chief of Kauai of a plot to poison him.[9] Between 1804 and his death in 1810, Davis was the effective controller of trade in Honolulu, overseeing the king's control of that growing economy.

More astute was Francisco de Paula Marin, a Spaniard of uncertain background, but one of the closest advisors of Kamehameha and one of the successful foreigners in Honolulu. An enterprising man, Marin supplied ships with provisions, engaged in extensive trading activities, and energetically imported seeds and cuttings to plant on his various land holdings. As evidence of his stature, Marin was granted the rare privilege of building a stone house—after he built one for the king. House building was a privilege granted only to chiefs and Kamehameha generally refused permission to build permanent structures.[10]

Impact of Supplying Western Ships

The attraction of the Hawaiian chain was its location in relation to the growing fur trade of the Pacific Northwest. The voyage around Cape Horn was difficult at best and ships commonly incurred severe damage. The Spanish ports of South and Central America offered little in the way of support. Hawaii provided an attractive alternative; it was easy to reach, had a benign climate and friendly people, and seemed to have ample supplies of food and water.

The arrival of the Westerners created a severe strain on Hawaii's food production and distribution system. Hawaiian society had developed a complex political economy, based upon a chiefly system of power resting upon a large underclass of farmers and fishermen. Taro, fruits, sweet potatoes, and fish made up the bulk of the diet. Pork was a food primarily for the chiefly class and hence was not in general use. That food production was finely balanced seems clear from the number of legends having to do with famine and drought in Hawaiian history.[11]

Food was distributed through the system by collection in the form of rents and levies. The lowest level of chiefly authority apportioned land and water resources and passed on the food supplies through the chiefly clan. Surpluses at the chiefly level were redistributed at periodic intervals through festivals.

The problem of supplying ships that arrived in ever increasing numbers placed a strain on the production system and posed an equal threat to the political system of the chiefs. There was no concept of a market and the Hawaiians lacked any system of exchange beyond occasional barter between regions to obtain supplies of such things as basalt, wood, or foodstuffs from those regions of high productivity, such as Waipio on the island of Hawaii. The land distribution system generally was arranged to make available to each group a range of resources from sea to mountains for the necessities of life.[12]

The increasing number of ships to be supplied raised two important questions: the amount of food to be taken out and the method of collection and payment. Local chiefs still wielded their authority in the period before the consolidation of political power under Kamehameha. There was little uniformity in the patterns of trade and supply until after the final triumph of Kamehameha and the development of the sandalwood trade. In practice, as well as in theory, the chiefs exercised absolute control over the actions of their people. They could be commanded to perform any and all tasks, and could be restricted in whatever fashion the orders decreed. There should have been no difficulty in regularizing the extraction of supplies from Hawaii. The casual approach of the foreigners and the fact that they possessed items of great value to Hawaiians weakened the authority of the rulers. The chance to obtain pieces of iron, cotton cloth, and tools was almost irresistible to the Hawaiian, commoner and chief alike.

The political authority of the Hawaiian system was supported by a system of taboos or prohibitions laid down by the ruling and lesser chiefs. Some foods, such as pork and certain types of fish, were restricted to particular groups or individuals and denied to the general population. An especially strong emphasis was placed upon sexual roles. Women were not permitted to eat bananas, pork, or certain types of fish, and were forbidden to eat with men. Men performed all of the limited cooking routines of the Hawaiians. The arrival of the Europeans and the easy sexual relations that developed contributed greatly to the breakdown of these institutional rules and roles. Ships' logs reveal that women frequently ate with the sailors. The delivery of foodstuffs for payment, however trivial, likewise undermined the traditional pattern of tribute and distribution. These circumstances probably were as disruptive of the Hawaiian system as were western weaponry and military tactics that were used to force consolidation of the islands under one ruler.

Another factor contributing to the breakdown of the old system was the number of Hawaiians recruited as crew members for the visiting ships. Few ships calling between 1790 and 1825 failed to sign on a number of Hawaiian sailors. The Hawaiians were seen as valuable crewmen, at home in or on the water, strong, and sea-wise. Judging from the numbers signed on, there was no lack of eager volunteers. The hazards of the Pacific Northwest trade, both maritime and Indian trade, placed a premium on full crews. The first recorded crew recruitment was a woman who was signed on in 1787 as a maid to the wife of Captain Charles Barkley.[13] The lure of foreign travel attracted even the ruling chiefs, who traveled more as tourists than as crewmen. High chief Kaiana used his foreign experiences on behalf of Kamehameha's campaign when he returned to Hawaii in 1788 and became one of Kamehameha's more important lieutenants.[14]

Triangle Trade

Hawaii was a crucial element in maintaining the triangular trade that developed in this period between the Pacific Northwest fur trade, China, and New England. The route that Captain Cook surveyed, hoping to find the Northwest Passage to get the furs of Hudson's Bay to China, did not at first envision a role for Hawaii. Cook's successor, Captain Nathaniel King, proposed a route that omitted Hawaii. Leaving China in the April monsoon, the ships would go north along Japan, the Kurile Islands, and the Aleutians, arriving on the coast of North America in late May or early June. Collecting furs along the coast, the ship would depart for China in October. The flaw in this neat scheme was that there were no provisions to be had along this coast. Abundant provisions available at astoundingly low prices in the early years made Hawaii an important supply point. The pigs, fowls, yams, fruits and vegetables, water, and firewood made the voyage to and from China much easier.

Salt for curing the furs was also in great demand and the Hawaiians produced a considerable quantity of salt, particularly at Kawaihae and on Oahu. The rapid development after 1800 of the fur trade in the Pacific Northwest made salt a premium commodity. The only supplies, other than Hawaii, were in Spanish hands—difficult to obtain and expensive. Salt was Hawaii's first export commodity and, until the development of sandalwood, the only such item of trade.[15]

The prices charged for these commodities changed rapidly as the supply of goods grew with the increasing number of ships. The novelty of iron in various forms wore off as the Hawaiians incorporated the metal in their handicrafts. From simple iron the demand escalated to tools—chisels, knives, axes, guns, and ammunition. In those places where ships called frequently, as at Kealakekua and Waimea, prices escalated. "By 1795, a 'Muskett' was required in one case to purchase nine large hogs; and a 'few chisels' to buy six pigs."[16] By 1809, exchange had settled to established rates: a fathom pig for 2 axes; a pair of fowls for a knife, a pair of scissors, or a small mirror.[17]

The experiences of the English schooner, *Columbia*, provide an example of the triangular trade between the Pacific Coast, Hawaii, and China. Belonging to three London companies, the schooner left London on 26 November 1813 and arrived off the Columbia River in June 1814. After repairing the ship, the captain took on a cargo of bar-iron, rum, shot, and gunpowder for the Russian settlement at New Archangel (Sitka), sailing in August. The cargo was exchanged for furs at New Archangel on 5 September. Returning to the Columbia River, a cargo of furs was assembled for China, as well as "goods for the Spanish Main." *Columbia* sailed, arriving in Monterey on 24 November. There, all trade except through the governor was prohibited. The plan was to leave an agent to collect provisions for the company station at the Columbia River. The *Columbia* was allowed to land its goods and barter for beef, but was denied the privilege of leaving the agent. The Spanish authorities did permit the ship's cooper to remain to supervise the curing of the purchased beef.

On 25 December, the ship sailed for Hawaii, after first visiting the Russians at Bodega Bay, arriving at Kealakekua on 16 January. After replenishing supplies, the schooner sailed for Canton on 18 January, arriving on 8 March. Changing captains, the schooner took on sixteen Hawaiians who had been left behind by the ship *Isaac Todd* at Macao. On 2 May, they sailed for the Columbia River, arriving on 1 July, and from there the *Columbia* went to Monterey to retrieve the cooper and, it was hoped, the beef. In addition, flour, beans, corn, and peas were loaded.

At the Columbia River, the cargo was discharged and a new one loaded for Norfolk Sound, the ship sailing on 16 September 1817. On 25 October, the *Columbia* was back at the Columbia River station with a cargo of furs to make ready for another trip to Canton. The ship left on 13 November, and was at Kailua, Hawaii, from 10 December to 4 January 1816, where the captain noted the presence of the American ship *Millwood* buying sandalwood, and the presence of the Russian agent, Dr. Georg Anton Schaeffer. Taking on pork and "a large amount of island rope, with a large number of passangers, [the *Columbia*] sailed for Oahu where the ship was repaird." After a visit to Kauai for vegetables, it departed on 4 January for Canton, arriving on 11 February and leaving on 30 April for New Archangel, returning to the Columbia River with furs in August.

On 10 January, the *Columbia* sailed for Oahu to refit, cure pork, "and get Sandwich Islanders for Columbia River." On 21 January, off the island of Hawaii, canoes brought out "pigs, taro and yams." At Kailua, the following day, Kamehameha arranged for additional supplies of pork. Sailing to Maalaea Bay, Maui, the ship "took in hogs, salt, and vegetables. At Lahaina, hogs and passengers." On 13 February, at Oahu, *Columbia* found the ship *Forester* loading for Canton. A party was put ashore to cure pork; another cut wood. "Took on 60 natives for Columbia River. Visited Kauai, without landing. Dr. Schaeffer was there."

Between 10 May and 10 October, the schooner sailed to Norfolk Sound, New Albion, and returned loaded with furs. On 10 November, the schooner sailed for the Sandwich Islands "to sell the vessel. If not there then to go to Norfolk Sound for same purpose." Arriving in Kailua on the island of Hawaii on 6 December, the captain visited the king who agreed to buy the *Columbia* at Oahu, subject to inspection. On 24 December, the governor, Kalanimoku, on the advice of John Young, "agreed to buy the vessel, giving twice the full of the vessel of sandalwood for her in not more than six months, possession when paid for." The captain sailed among the islands, trading and collecting sandalwood until 1 May 1818, when the payment was completed and the vessel turned over to Kalanimoku.[18]

The Russian Episode

Some sporadic trade had taken place between Hawaii and New Archangel, Alaska, in 1804. In 1807, the Russian ship *Neva* was sent to Hawaii to secure a cargo of salt, but did not return to Hawaii until 1814 to obtain supplies. The ship was wrecked off Waimea, Kauai, but the cargo was salvaged and stored. The governor of New Archangel sent another ship in 1815 to retrieve the cargo and make more permanent arrangements for supplies. The expedition was put in the charge of Georg Anton Schaeffer, a German surgeon on one of the ships of the Russian American Company.

Schaeffer was among the adventurers who saw great opportunity in Hawaii. Like many before and after, he thought in terms of seizing Hawaii, literally. Going to Kailua, he ingratiated himself with Kamehameha and secured an order directing Chief Kaumualii of Kauai to surrender the *Neva* cargo. When the Russian ships arrived to retrieve the cargo some months later, Schaeffer went to Kauai and launched his scheme. He persuaded Kaumualii to sign a document placing the island of Kauai under Russian sovereignty. He also obtained a signature on a plan granting him exclusive right to export sandalwood from Kauai and to build factories on the island. Further, Kaumualii gave Schaeffer control over the harbors of Oahu and the promise of 500 troops to enforce this provision.

Schaeffer went to Honolulu with his document and proceeded to erect a primitive fortification at the harbor and to run up the Russian flag. Kamehameha sent John Young and troops to put a stop to the Russian's activities. Schaeffer's actions were disavowed by Lieutenant Otto von Kotzebue, a Russian naval officer who arrived in Kailua, Hawaii, on an exploring mission in November 1816. Told about Schaeffer's moves, he denounced them as being contrary to the express wishes of the czar. With this loss of support, Schaeffer had no option but to withdraw, and sailed for Canton only a few days before the arrival of von Kotzebue on Oahu.[19]

It was Schaeffer's building of a rudimentary fort at Honolulu Harbor that led Kamehameha to order the building of a substantial coral-block fort, manned with sufficient cannon to protect the harbor. John Young was sent to supervise the construction. The fort was completed just in time to welcome von Kotzebue and the ship, *Rurick*.[20]

The Sandalwood Trade

Traders quickly discovered the value of the sandalwood of the islands. As early as 1790, a schooner captain, William Douglas, is reported to have left two men on Kauai to collect sandalwood while his ship went on to the Pacific Northwest.[21] Efforts to utilize the wood in the China trade were apparently made, to little avail. It seems that the first cargos sent were of inferior quality and not acceptable to the Chinese traders.

The turning point in the trade came with the agreement to carry a cargo of sandalwood to Canton for King Kamehameha. Three captains, brothers Nathan and Jonathan Winship and William H. Davis, carried their furs and the king's wood to Canton, returning with merchandise for Kamehameha.[22] Marin recorded this transaction for the king in his accounts for 12 July 1812. "I received the statement of King Tameamea's [Kamehameha] account from Capt. Guinciep [Winship] in the year 1812, in the month of July on the returns from the sandalwood which he carried to China in the month of December, 1811."[23]

As often happened with traders in the Pacific, when outright annexation or expropriation was not feasible, the discovery of this lucrative item of trade or exchange brought forth the notion of a monopoly. The captains Winship signed a contract giving them the exclusive right for ten years to export sandalwood from Hawaii, through the agency of the king. Curiously, the contract included cotton as well as sandalwood, although no cotton had been planted in Hawaii. Kamehameha was to receive one-fourth of the net proceeds, either in specie or Chinese merchandise.[24]

Due to the outbreak of the War of 1812, the more lucrative trade in furs, or the attraction of selling to others at higher prices, only one or two cargos were collected under this agreement. The effect of the war was more psychological than real. Both British and American ships captured vessels, but trading voyages continued with little noticeable effect.[25]

The volume of the trade escalated rapidly in the last years of Kamehameha's reign. The chiefs and Kamehameha used their traditional authority to command the work of their subjects. The log of the schooner *Columbia* describes the loading of sandalwood:

> We lay in Honolulu harbour until the 17th of March, 1818 without anything in particular occurring until that day, when we received orders from Tamehameha to proceed to [Kauai] for a cargo of sandalwood. Teymotoo, or Cox, with several other chiefs came on board. We made sail, and on the following day came too in Whymea Roads. Our chiefs landed and were well received by Tamooree; and the next they commenced sending wood on board. About 500 canoes were employed in bringing it off, and by the 25th of March we had the ship quite full. We weighed anchor and made sail for Woahoo.[26]

One of the king's greatest passions was the purchase of ships. By 1810 he had amassed a sizeable fleet of small schooners and sloops, some built to order, most purchased. Archibald Campbell reported more than thirty sloops and schooners pulled up on the beach at Waikiki, in addition to a dozen or more at anchor in the harbor. Most of these were purchased at high prices paid in sandalwood.[27] John Jacob Astor quickly cashed in on this propensity when one of his captains informed him of Kamehameha's refusal to sell sandalwood for anything but a ship. Astor then sent two vessels to Hawaii in 1816 and sold them to the king to gain access to the sandalwood trade.[28]

Sandalwood brought the first large influx of capital to Honolulu. The harbor, providing not only safe anchorage but the possibility of making repairs, quickly became the focal point of development. Boston and New York mercantile firms sent agents to Honolulu to tap the trade. James Hunnewell of Massachusetts set up as the resident agent for Bryant and Sturgis in 1817. His task was to dispose of the cargo of the ship *Bordeaux Packet*, which had been sold to Kamehameha. This task lasted until September 1818. The brief journal entries give a vivid picture of early Honolulu trade. He explained: "All trade was in barter, as there was no money in circulation among the natives and this detained us until September, 1818. . . . We were the only traders on shore at Honolulu that had any goods to sell. All our cash sales amounted to $104, and this was from an English Captain and officers."

On 14 May 1818, he reported: "Sold 40 looking-glasses for 4 piculs of wood." On 15 May, "Sold the remainder of the muslin, 2 pieces, for 31 piculs wood received." Illustrating the role of the chiefs in controlling the trade, he noted on 15 January 1818, "The principal chiefs left here in the *Columbia*. We have had no business, as it is tabooed until their return."[29]

Honolulu and the Royal Monopoly

Kamehameha's ability as a trader undoubtedly did much to strengthen his regime against the incessant threats to his rule. Almost as soon as he added such people as John Young and Isaac Davis to his retinue, he used them not only for their knowledge of weaponry and naval skills but as emissaries in trade with the increasing numbers of ships arriving at the island of Hawaii. Recognizing the importance of controlling access to these ships, John Young and Isaac Davis were given the primary tasks of granting permission to ships' captains to trade or to take on provisions.

Trade items for Hawaii were rudimentary—ships refitting, clothing and tools, and merchandise for the Hawaiian community. "The articles of trade which are customarily carried to the Sandwich Islands consist of naval stores and ammunition, cloth, spirituous liquors, and some dollars (piastres)."[30]

Money was in short supply and did not seem to be valued as highly as certain trade goods. Campbell, in 1809 reported

Almost all their dealings are conducted by barter; they know the value of dollars, and are willing to take them in exchange, but they seldom appear again in circulation, being always carefully hoarded up. . . . Vessels are supplied with fresh provisions, live-stock, salt and and other articles of outfit, for which they give in return cloth, fire-wood, arms and ammunition, the teeth of sea-lion, carpenters tools, hardware, and, in general, articles of everyday description.[31]

Campbell remarked that "He [Kamehameha] has amassed a considerable treasure in dollars, and possesses a large stock of European articles."

King Kamehameha and others of the chiefly class soon favored payment in Spanish dollars when they were available. This tendency to adopt a monetary standard is a measure of how much change had occurred in the Hawaiian traditional political economy. The problem was well stated by a Polynesian chief in Tonga on the problems posed by the use of money:

Certainly money is much handier, and more convenient, but then, as it will not spoil by being kept, people will store it up, instead of sharing it out, as a chief ought to do, and thus become selfish; whereas if provisions were the principal property of man, . . . he could not store it up, for it would spoil . . . so he would be obliged to share it out to his neighbors, and inferior chiefs and dependents, for nothing.[32]

Kamehameha moved back from Kailua to Oahu in 1804 to prepare for the invasion of Kauai. He may also have wanted to be able to assess more accurately his royal monopoly on the supply of provisions and trade in general. It is difficult to determine the extent of the king's authority, who was in residence in Kailua, Waikiki, or Honolulu, depending upon the year. Ships' logs indicated that much trading took place outside the royal purview. Ships generally stopped at Kailua or Waikiki to pick up an agent of Kamehameha before proceeding to Honolulu to avoid difficulty.[33] Certainly the accounts of travelers indicate that Kamehameha took an active interest in the coming and going of the vessels engaged in the triangular trade between the Pacific Northwest, China, and New England.[34]

After consolidation of his rule, Kamehameha's appointment of governors on each of the major islands was connected with the appointment of foreigners to oversee such matters as providing a harbor pilot for Honolulu, the collection of fees and the royal share of trade. He had already imposed a control system over the provisioning of the visiting ships, levying a tax on all transactions and attempting to funnel all supplies through his agents.

The return to Oahu moved Honolulu into the central role formerly played by Kealakekua Bay. The advantages of Honolulu, once a ship was towed safely into the anchorage, were obvious. The good shelter from the frequent, strong on-shore winds, and the facilities for hoving down and repairing ships quickly attracted the foreign vessels. The importance of Honolulu Harbor grew after King Kamehameha moved from Waikiki in 1809 to Pakaka Point, close by the Nuuanu Stream, where the Robinson shipyard would be built in a few years. Campbell noted (1809–1810) that the sloop *Leila Byrd* had been repaired by Kamehameha's carpenters "and laid up at Honaroora, along side a wharf built for the purpose."[35] The wharf was present when the missionaries arrived in Honolulu. One journal keeper made a record of being received at King's Wharf, where he was met by Mr. Bingham and Mr. Harwood.[36] This remained the only pier in the harbor for a number of years. By 1824 it was known as King's Wharf and in 1825, Lt. Malden described it as "a small pier for facilitating the unloading of vessels."[37] Some accounts described this wharf as being built on a hulk sunk at the foot of Nuuanu Street. This makeshift wharf remained in use until 1842, when it was removed and replaced with a proper pier by the harbormaster.

Kamehameha returned to Kailua in 1812. He left Oahu with a functioning, if rudimentary, apparatus of municipal government. He appointed a governor and later a harbor pilot to collect the landing fees he imposed. He discovered this attribute of civilization when he sent his newly purchased ship *Kaahumanu* (ex-*Forester*) to Canton in 1817 with a load of sandalwood. The captain, Alexander Adams, reported that the harbor dues and wharf fees largely had consumed the profits of the voyage. Kamehameha promptly installed the system in Honolulu to augment the growing need for revenue. Although not given to the kind of display and behavior of other high chiefs, Kamehameha had a strong acquisitive urge.[38]

Increasing enlightenment about the outside world led to sharp increases in the prices of commodities, as compared with the halcyon days of a hog for a nail.

Besides the control exercised by the law of supply and demand, prices rose as a result of general enlightenment, from observation and the information imparted by foreigners who settled in the islands. After a time, when Kamehameha had completed his conquest, we find prices and the course of trade affected by royal monopoly.[39]

By 1811, traders reported that Kamehameha had made the sale of hogs a royal monopoly on the advice of John Young. "Kamehameha seems to have kept a close oversight of all trade and his Yankee-like shrewdness and his honesty and fairness, were characteristics often mentioned."[40]

Even before the development of the sandalwood trade, Honolulu was clearly the important harbor at which ships could collect cargoes and distribute trade goods.[41] Honolulu thus became one of the Pacific ports whose location was dictated by both geographical factors and political circumstances. Papeete, Levusia, and Apia were, with Honolulu, the principal port towns of the Pacific, as distinguished from colonial administrative ports such as Noumea, Suva, and Auckland.[42]

Forces of Change

While Kamehameha exercised his chiefly control over the islands, there was little apparent change in the traditional Hawaiian political economy. Structural changes appeared only after his death, followed by the imposition of very different ideas about society, culture, and authority.

The gap between western and Hawaiian thinking on such issues as property rights, sovereignty, and the rights of non-Europeans had been an issue since the arrival of Captain Cook. When an Hawaiian chief granted a privilege, it was for the duration of his pleasure and no more. To the western mind, the action was interpreted as an irrevocable right, but a moment's reflection would demonstrate that such a conclusion was a convenient but historically inaccurate one.

Land tenure was held in Hawaii only at the pleasure of the granting chief and could be revoked at any time.[43] Political favors in the European tradition were easily revoked by a variety of means so long as political power was available. More to the point, western thinking was geared to the idea that people of the Pacific were "natives" and therefore without rights as compared to the "civilized." With varying intensity, each of the representatives of the west who came to Hawaii after Cook's arrival recommended the annexation, conquest, or subjection of the islands.

The political structure put together by Kamehameha was at best a fragile one, threatened by three revolts and constant pressure from adventurers. His ability in focusing trade and power in his person and his skillful use of foreign advisors kept power seekers at bay. The observation of Russian naval officer, Captain V. M. Golovnin, summed up the difference between Hawaii and other Pacific Island nations:

> The petty faults we may find in the old King will not obscure his great merits. He will always be considered as an enlightener and reformer of his people. One fact which shows his good sense is this. None of the foreigners visiting his country enjoy any exclusive privileges, but all can trade with his subjects with equal freedom. Europeans are not allowed to own land. They receive it on condition that after death it shall be returned to the King, and during their lifetime it is not transferable from one to another.[44]

Kamehameha I managed through skill and good judgment in selecting lieutenants to retain a good measure of control over the rapidly changing scene. He was able to exercise the traditional, absolute authority of the ruling chief as in the days before the arrival of westerners, maintaining the *kapu* system, which reinforced both the chiefly status and the religion. By the time of his death in 1819, the pressure for change probably could not have been held back much longer.

Too many Hawaiians had gone out into the world and returned, experienced and aware that the outside world did not operate through the terrible power of the Hawaiian gods and chiefs. The prohibitions governing women in regard to certain foods or being present when men were eating, to name only two, were eroded severely by the many opportunities to socialize with visiting ships. There were too many ships and too many opportunities to eat pork, and eat it with men, to be able to maintain the old ways. The greed of foreigners hoping to seize a prize, as they had in other parts of the Pacific, would generate destructive pressures on the old Hawaiian system.

At Kamehameha's death, Hawaii had a burgeoning trade—supplying provisions, ships' chandlery, and sandalwood—with which to pay for an escalating consumption of imported goods. Without the control and restraint of the king, this would bring Hawaii near destruction.[45]

The Hawaiian political structure outwardly resembled the traditional culture. The ruling chief, working through subordinate chiefs, down to the level of the local *konohiki,* or district official, at first glance seemed to represent a smooth continuity with the past. Beneath this surface a quite different reality lurked, operating in ways that would shortly transform Hawaiian society.

The difference lay precisely in the rapidly expanding maritime economy that Kamehameha so carefully cultivated. The well-being of the system had, in the past, depended upon an intricate production of subsistence products and a small amount of nonsubsistence materials, such as ornaments and trappings of office. The foodstuffs, agricultural and maritime, were the responsibility of the commoner, under the guidance of local chiefs. The combination of an escalation in warfare for political consolidation and the arrival of foreign ships transformed this relationship. Products such as hogs, yams, taro, and, importantly, salt, took on very different roles in this new economy. The focus of the chiefs was now to secure the wealth and the artifacts of a new civilization in the form of manufactured goods, ships, and weaponry. What had been a communal society, without a medium of exchange or means of wealth accumulation, was transformed at the top into a mercantile economy.

A serious disruption occurred in the roles of commoners. They were expected to continue as in the past to serve without question the demands of the ruling class. The system conferred on the chiefs absolute authority, reinforced by a religion that supported that authority with swift and awful vengeance. The role of the commoner was to obey. Yet the chiefs now exercised that authority to obtain wealth that was not redistributed and came at a tragic cost to the general populace.

Other changes also occurred in the lives of the common people. These changes were not just in the incredible burdens of the chiefly wars and the sandalwood exactions, but also in the form of significant numbers going out of Hawaii as seamen and travelers and returning with new ideas and new skills. It was the presence of these Hawaiian travelers that first attracted the New England churches to the possibility of establishing a mission in the Sandwich Islands. Opukahaia, who went to Boston in 1809, came to the attention of clergymen at Yale. He became the focal point of the effort that resulted in the establishment of the Foreign Mission School at Cornwall, Connecticut. Opukahaia died in 1818, before he could realize his hope of returning home to convert his people to Christianity. The first missionaries left for Hawaii in 1820.[46]

The death of Kamehameha I on 8 May 1819 unleashed these forces of change. The force of his personality and his shrewdness in picking his way among the many competing interests for the wealth of Hawaii could not carry over to his successors. The arrival of whaling ships in 1819 and the influx of missionaries by 1821 brought additional pressures. The changes probably would have overwhelmed Kamehameha's abilities in a short time, for an essential ingredient in the Hawaiian social structure was rapidly vanishing. The demoralization or loss of confidence in the basic social order was the inevitable consequence of the appearance of the trader.[47]

Notes

1. Log of ship *Massachusetts*, 656/1790M, Peabody Museum, Salem, Mass.

2. Ibid., 27 August 1791.

3. Ibid.

4. Ibid., 30 August 1791.

5. F. W. Howay, "The Ship *Pearl* in Hawaii in 1805 and 1806," *Hawaiian Historical Society 16th Annual Report* (1937), pp. 29–33.

6. Ralph S. Kuykendall, *The Hawaiian Kingdom*, (Honolulu: University of Hawaii Press, 1938), vol. 1, chaps. 2, 3, gives a detailed account of this period and provides rich documentation. Gavan Daws, *A Shoal of Time*, (New York: Macmillan, 1968), chap. 2, gives an excellent summary of the military-political struggle. A shorter treatment is in Daws, Honolulu (Ph.D. dissertation, University of Hawaii, Honolulu, 1966), pp. 21–46. A comparative treatment of foreigners in the Pacific in the early nineteenth century is Carolyn Ralston, *Grass Huts and Warehouses: Pacific Beach Communities in the Nineteenth Century* (Honolulu: University of Hawaii Press, 1978).

7. Edward Beechert, *Working In Hawaii: A Labor History* (Honolulu: University of Hawaii Press, 1985), chap. 1; George Vancouver, *A Voyage of Discovery to the North Pacific Ocean and Round the World in the Years 1790, 1791, 1792, 1793, 1794 and 1795*, 6 vols. (London: Thomas and Andrews, 1801), vol. 1, p. 295.

8. Ralston, *Grass Huts*, p. 32; Daws, "Honolulu," pp. 44–45; Kuykendall, *Hawaiian Kingdom*, vol. 1, p. 27.

9. See chap. 1, p. 12, 14; Kuykendall, *Hawaiian Kingdom*, vol. 1, p. 51; Daws, *Honolulu*, p. 41.

10. Ross H. Gast, *Don Francisco de Paula Marin: A Biography*, (Honolulu: Hawaiian Historical Society, 1973), pp. 29–30.

11. E. S. C. Handy and Elizabeth G. Handy, "Native Planters in Old Hawaii: Their Life, Lore, and Environment," *Bernice P. Bishop Museum Bulletin No. 233* (1972), pp. 74–75; David Malo, *Hawaiian Antiquities* (Moolelo Hawaii), trans. by Nathaniel B. Emerson, Bernice P. Bishop Museum Special Publication No. 2 (Honolulu: Bishop Museum Press, 1951), pp. 16–18.

12. Marshall D. Sahlins, *Social Stratification in Polynesia* (Seattle: University of Washington Press, 1958), pp. 14–15.

13. Frederick W. Howay, "Early Relations between the Hawaiian Islands and the Northwest Coast," in *The Hawaiian Islands . . . Papers Read during the Captain Cook Sesquicentennial Celebration, Honolulu, August 17, 1928*, Albert Taylor & Ralph Kuykendall (eds.), Archives of Hawaii Publication No. 5 (Honolulu, 1930).

14. Kuykendall, *Hawaiian Kingdom*, vol. 1, pp. 22, 35–36; John Meares, *Voyages Made in the Years 1788 and 1789, from China to the Northwest Coast of America* (London: Logographic Press, 1790), p. xxxix.

15. Theodore Morgan, *Hawaii: A Century of Economic Change, 1776–1876* (Cambridge: Harvard University Press, 1948), pp. 57–58, 60–61.

16. Ibid., pp. 60–61; Charles S. Stewart, *Journal of a Residence in the Sandwich Islands* (Boston: H. Fisher & Son, 1839) p. 199.

17. Archibald Campbell, *A Voyage Round The World, From 1806 to 1812*, 4th American ed. (Roxbury, Mass.: Charleston, Duke and Brown, 1822), p. 201.

18. Peter Corney, *Voyages in the Northern Pacific: Narrative of several trading voyages from 1813 to 1818, between the Northwest Coast of America, the Hawaiian Islands and China, with a description of the Russian Establishment on the Northwest Coast.* (Honolulu, T. H. Thrum, 1896), pp. 31–40.

19. Ralston, *Grass Huts*, pp. 98–99; Daws, *Honolulu*, pp. 51–57; Glynn Barratt, *The Russian Discovery of Hawaii: The Journals of Eight Russian Explorers* (Honolulu: Editions Limited, 1987), pp. 190, 248.

20. Otto von Kotzebue, *A Voyage of Discovery to the South Sea and to Behring's Straits Undertaken in the Years 1815–1818*, 3 vols. (London: Longman, Hurst & Brown, 1821), vol. 2, pp. 196–198. Kuykendall, *Hawaiian Kingdom*, vol. 1, pp. 55–59, provides excellent documentation of the Russian connection with Hawaii.

21. Samuel E. Morison, "Boston Traders in the Hawaiian Islands," *Massachusetts Historical Society Proceedings*, (October–November) 1920, p. 13.

22. Kuykendall, *Hawaiian Kingdom*, vol. 1, p. 87.

23. Hawaii State Archives, *Marin Papers*, Historical and Miscellaneous File. "Quenta de lo que Recibio el Rey Tameamea de quento del Capitan Guinciep en el año 1812 en el mes de Julio en Retorno del Palo Olorozo que llevó a China en el mes de Diziembre de 1811."

24. "Solid Men of Boston in the Northwest," manuscript in Bancroft Library, University of California, Berkeley; Kuykendall, *Hawaiian Kingdom*, vol. 1, p. 87; *The Letters and Journal Of Francicso de Paula Marin*, edited by Agnes Conrad (Honolulu: University of Hawaii Press for Hawaiian Historical Society, 1973), 4 August 1812, p. 207.

25. F. W. Howay, "A List of Trading Vessels in the Maritime Fur Trade," *Royal Society of Canada Transactions*, 3d series, Sec. 2 (1932), pp. 85–86.

26. Corney, *Voyages in the Northern Pacific*, p. 36.

27. Campbell, *Voyage Around the World*, pp. 109–110.

28. Ralston, *Grass Huts*, pp. 82–83.

29. James Hunnewell. "Honolulu in 1817 and 1818." *Hawaiian Historical Society Papers*, No. 8 (1895), pp. 15, 19.

30. Louis de Freycinet, *Voyage Autour Du Monde Pendant Les Annees 1817, 1819, Et 1820*, 2 vols. (Paris: Impremerie Royale, 1824), vol. 2, p. 617, cited in Kuykendall, *Hawaiian Kingdom*, vol. 1, p. 84.

31. Campbell, *Voyage Round the World*, pp. 199–200.

32. Handy and Handy, *Native Planters*, pp. 17–18.

33. Ralston, *Grass Huts*, p. 50; Daws, *Honolulu*, p. 37, contains excellent references to travel accounts and voyages in this period, 1804–1816.

34. Isaac Iselin, *Journal Of A Trading Voyage Around The World, 1805–1808*, 3 vols. (London: McIlroy & Emmet, n.d.), vol. 2, pp. 64–65; Gabriel Franchère, *Narrative of a Voyage to the Northwest Coast of America, 1811–1814* (New York: The Lakeside Press, 1854), pp. 63–65; Howay, "The Ship *Pearl*," p. 37.

35. Campbell, *Voyage Round the World*, p. 120.

36. Levi Chamberlain Journal, 6 February 1824, manuscript in the Hawaiian Mission Children's Society Library, Honolulu.

37. Maria Graham Calcott, *Voyage of the H. M. S. Blonde to the Sandwich Islands: 1824–1925*, (London: J. Murray, 1826), p. 121.

38. Alexander Adams, "Journal of Captain Alexander Adams," 4 November 1817, Hawaii State Archives; "Golovnin's Visit to Hawaii in 1818," in *The Friend*, 52 (1894): 52–53.

39. Kuykendall, *Hawaiian Kingdom*, vol. 1, p. 83.

40. See also Franchere, *Narrative of a Voyage*, pp. 59–60; von Kotzebue, *Voyage of Discovery*, vol. 1, p. 293.

41. Ralston, *Grass Huts*, pp. 49–50.

42. Alexander Spoehr, "Port Towns and Hinterlands in the Pacific Islands," *American Anthropologist*, 62 Series 2 (1960): 586–587; Ralston, *Grass Huts*, 47.

43. Ibid., pp. 88, 98–99.

44. Quoted in Kuykendall, *Hawaiian Kingdom*, vol. 1, p. 60.

45. See Ibid., vol. 1, p. 67 for a succinct statement on the problems. The overthrow of the *kapu* and religious system in the Society Islands by King Pomare was known to the Hawaiians. See also Gavan Daws, *Honolulu*, pp. 63–65, and M. C. Webb, "The Abolition of the Taboo System in Hawaii," *Journal of the Polynesian Society*, 74(1) March 1965: 21–39. It is important to note that the collapse of the religious system came two years before the arrival of the missionaries.

46. See Edwin W. Dwight, *Memoirs of Henry Obookiah, a Native of Owyhee, and a Member of the Foreign Mission School* (New Haven: Edison, Hart, 1819); Rufus Anderson, *History of the Sandwich Island Mission* (Boston: Congregational Publication Society, 1870); Bradford Smith, *Yankees in Paradise: The New England Impact on Hawaii* (Philadelphia: Lippincott, 1956).

47. Andrew Lind, *An Island Community: Ecological Succession in Hawaii*, (Chicago: University of Chicago Press, 1938), p. 143. See also E. S. C. Handy, "Polynesian Religion," *Bernice P. Bishop Museum Bulletin* No. 34 (1927), pp. 87–88.

3

A New Era

The Changing Village

The death of Kamehameha, the arrival of the whalers, and the overthrow of the system of *kapu* combined to complete the destruction of the Hawaiian socioeconomic system. Civil war, which was quickly put down, broke out on Kauai, occasioned by the death of Chief Kaumualii. Normally in such circumstances, the lands of Kauai would have been redistributed by the ruling chief. In a departure from ancient custom, Kaumualii left his kingdom to King Kamehameha II (Liholiho).

The traditional Hawaiian community was not concentrated geographically and the culture rigidly separated male and female roles. Hawaiian houses were special-function units, with houses for women and their activities, for men, for young people, for chiefs, and so on. Houses were small, and living took place largely out-of-doors. Nor did Hawaiians live in village complexes. Chiefs had their retinues, while commoners tended to arrange themselves in extended families, focused around particular area resources. Identity was through alliance to a chief, not to a locality. Commoners could and did change that identity occasionally, moving to a new jurisdiction.[1]

These cultural traditions were behind the fact that there was no significant settlement around Honolulu Harbor before the arrival of western commerce. When the king moved to the harbor from Waikiki in 1809, only those in his retinue set up housekeeping near his residence. Yet, inevitably, the attraction of the constant arrival of ships brought the commoners to settle there in large numbers. The village of Honolulu began to grow slowly. The preemption of space by the chiefly retinue kept the *maka'ainana*, the commoners, at a distance.[2]

Without the sanctions imposed by the system of *kapu*, there was no need to follow the system of "exploded housing," each dedicated to a particular function. The old style of living "dictated that [Kamehameha's] complex of houses be built close to the water. Chiefs and specialists—kahunas, warriors, boatbuilders and fishermen—were clustered along a mile and half of beachfront between Nuuanu and Kakaako."[3] Now the western idea of housing began to prevail—to shelter a particular family unit—a notion that resulted in overcrowding.

After 1816, when Kamehameha had his fort built on the site of the Russian fort, it logically became the focus of the increasingly numerous mercantile interests. This early settlement was notably haphazard. "The streets are formed without order or regularity. . . . The streets or lanes are far from being clean."[4]

Another visitor described Honolulu in this way:

> A few years since, Honolulu was a mere collection of straw hovels interspersed with a few buildings of a little better character, occupied by the chiefs or foreign residents. The whole were arranged much after the plan of the Dutch settlers of Manhatten; although, in this instance, cows were not the authorized surveyors of the streets, the waywardness of the tastes and disposition of the builders effected a corresponding confusion, and narrow streets or foot paths, was a result.[5]

Lord Byron and Malden's Map

In 1824, King Liholiho (Kamehameha II) and his queen, Kamamalu, sailed to England. The English crown had been asked by Kamehameha I, through Vancouver, to agree to protect Hawaiian sovereignty from other nations. In the midst of their state visit to George IV, the king and queen contracted measles and died. British Foreign Secretary George Canning asked permission for a warship, the H.M.S. *Blonde,* to return the bodies to Hawaii. He suggested that some attention should be paid to the islands: "An Attention perhaps the more advisable as the Government of both Russia and the United States of America are known to have their Eyes upon those Islands; which may ere long become a very important Station in the trade between the N.W. Coast of America and the China Seas."[6]

According to Boki, the governor of Oahu, who had accompanied the royal pair to London, one of the purposes of the H.M.S. *Blonde's* visit was to confirm the commitment of England to the independence of Hawaii in the face of threats from other powers. George IV said to Boki that "I will watch over your country, I will not take possession of it for mine, but I will watch over it, lest evils should come from others to the Kingdom."[7]

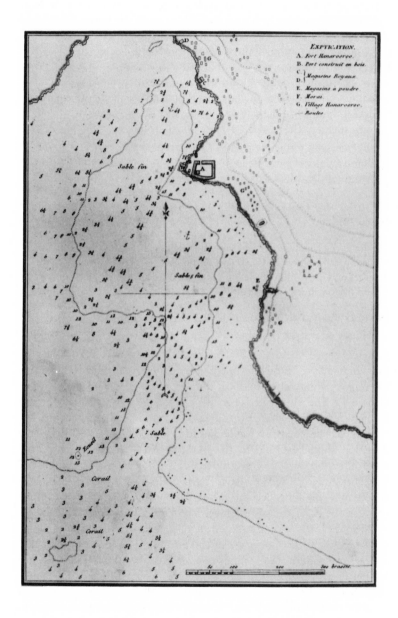

Figure 3.1   Golovnin Map, 1817 (University of Hawaii Map Collection)

Lord Byron was named the official emissary of the crown to accompany the bodies of the royal couple to Hawaii. His visit proved to be one of the most decisive events in the history of Hawaii. A council of high chiefs was convened after the funeral, with Lord Byron in attendance. Kauikeaouli was appointed king, with Kalanimoku as regent. The regent proclaimed that the desire of Kamehameha had been to establish hereditary occupation of the land (as Kaumualii had done in leaving his land to Liholiho) and that land would no longer revert to the local ruling chief on the death of the holder. The chiefs approved this change—a significant step away from the traditional land tenure system of Hawaii and the first step toward the western concept of fee simple ownership of land.[8]

The next question to be resolved was the need for law—something more than the traditional rule of Hawaiian custom. On the island of Hawaii, Kapiolani, as governor, had tried to establish laws prohibiting robbery, murder, adultery, drunkenness, and infanticide. She suggested that these be extended to all of the islands. When asked to speak to the subject, Lord Byron presented a short list of suggestions—comments that codified the several ideas put into practice by Kamehameha and his successors. Lord Byron added the notion of trial by jury for capital offenses. The last suggestion in his list was redundant, "that a port duty be laid on all foreign vessels."

The missionaries had proposed that a code should be enacted that would establish Christianity as the state religion. Byron, while approving of the idea of establishing education and Christianity, was of the view that the missionaries should not be permitted to intervene in the political and economic affairs of the nation.[9]

Byron had been given a careful set of instructions. He was to avoid any discussion of the surrender of Hawaiian sovereignty. He was to assert British rights of sovereignty only if it was apparent that other powers were about to seize the kingdom. He was to "pay the greatest Regard to the Comfort, the Feelings, and even the Prejudices of the Natives," and to show moderation to the representatives of "other Powers."

It was in this spirit that Byron ordered a survey of the harbor and town. The haphazard pattern of Honolulu's development can be seen in a comparison of Golovnin's map of 1817 with the map produced in 1825 by Lt. C. R. Malden of the ship HMS *Blonde.* There are no fixed streets that can be identified today. Trails to Nuuanu Valley and the Pali were well-marked, as was a trail to Waikiki to the west, and a trail to

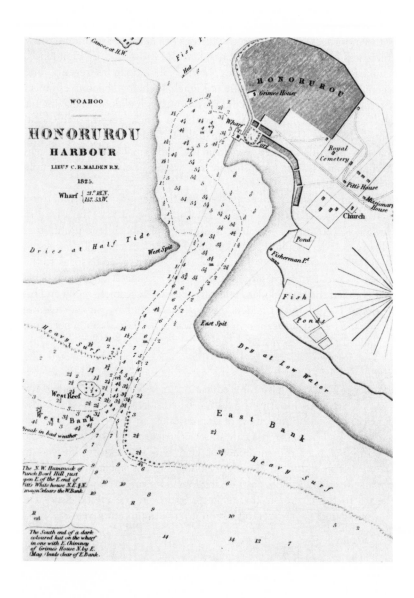

Figure 3.2 Malden Survey, 1825, by Lt. C.R. Malden, R. N., Hydrographic Department, British Admiralty, 1825.

the east, toward Kalihi on Malden's map. The small size of the harbor
and the limited anchorage are readily apparent from Malden's map. He
marked the only wharf as an old hulk sunk at the foot of what became
Nuuanu Street. "There is a small pier for facilitating the unloading of
vessels."[10]

A rapid increase in the resident population in the early 1830s and
the prevalence of horses in the streets created new municipal problems.
Queen Kaahumanu II issued a proclamation in 1838, pointing out that
"[b]ecause of the lack of streets some people were almost killed by
horseback riders and the rulers of the kingdom barely escaped in 1834."
An even more serious problem was that of sewage and garbage. "Because the streets lack yards, therefore, that may be the reason for the
filth and stench and the too close living that cause people of the city to
be sick." In 1838, Kaahumanu II decreed the laying out of streets. Her
proclamation declared, in part, "I shall widen the streets in our city and
break up some new places to make five streets on the length of the land
and six streets on the breadth of the land.[11] The effect of the order is
clearly illustrated in the Wilkes expedition map of 1840.

Harbor Pilots and Sailing Conditions

The reef on the eastern side of the harbor was put to good use in
hauling ships into the harbor. This could be done only if the wind and
current conditions were satisfactory. A current set across the mouth of
the harbor to the northwest and the northeast trades made hauling into
the harbor difficult. Early morning and evening calms were the times
most frequently used for towing in—by ships' boats or with Hawaiians
engaged to tow in ships with their canoes. Ox teams were used occasionally after the missionaries introduced them. Sailing in was virtually
impossible. Current, wind, and a sharp turn in the harbor put the
maneuver out of bounds for all but the smallest craft—schooners and
sloops.

Since 1816, there had been an official pilot for Honolulu Harbor, to
escort ships into the harbor, assign anchorage, and control the limited
wharf space. The first pilots, John Young and Isaac Davis, acted primarily as agents of Kamehameha. John Harbottle, who was probably
appointed in 1820, was the first of a succession of regular pilots.

The informal procedures and nature of harbor pilots' work in the
early period is well illustrated in Chamisso's journal of a voyage made by
Russian ship *Rurick* in 1816.

> We reached the harbor of Hana-ruru during the midday hours of the 27th
> of November. Manuja went on shore in the first canoe which showed up,

and soon a royal pilot came out, an Englishman—Mr. Herbottel [Harbottle], who had us anchor outside of the reef, as each entering ship must be towed in during the calm which regularly preceeds sunrise. . . . At 4 AM, in accordance with a prearranged gun signal, we called the canoes alongside that were to row us into the harbor. The pilot and eight double canoes, each its owner with sixteen to twenty men, came out. Mr. Young was in a smaller canoe. . . . The anchor was got up and playfully, laughing the while and noisily, the Sandwich Islanders towed the *Rurik* into the harbor in fine style, with a power that surprised our crew. We were making three knots by the log. We dropped anchor under the walls of the Fort and Mr Young came on board to demand payment for the services, which were not performed by the King's men.[12]

The ship *Mayflower* arrived at Honolulu on 28 October 1835 and employed what was probably a very common method of entering the anchorage: "At 5 a.m. came to anchor off Honolulu. At 6 a.m. sent three boats to tow the *Stonendlas* in the harbor and went on shore. No pertickler news were to be found. . . . *October 29.* Towed in Harbor and came to anchor in 5 fathoms, mud bottom."[13]

Whalers and Missionaries

The rapid demise of the sandalwood trade in the early 1820s was not as drastic for Honolulu as it might seem. Honolulu, unlike other Pacific island ports, was able to function without the sandalwood trade, thanks to its strategic location for ships plying the fur trade to China that still needed a place to refit and resupply after the trip around Cape Horn. These in turn were succeeded by whalers going to the Japanese whaling grounds and then to Arctic grounds. It was the whaling industry's arrival in 1820 that permanently altered the port town and touched off its commercial development.

The exhaustion of the sandalwood trade had little visible effect upon the port or the community surrounding it. The primary effect was on the habits and life style of the chiefs. Faced with large debts, an exhausted population, and growing pressure from the United States to pay up on existing debts, there was little opportunity to continue to run up the astronomical debts that had been incurred after the death of Kamehameha I in 1819.

Table 3.1 gives an indication of the impact of the whaling industry on Hawaii. Although the data are shaky, they do present a clear picture of the fluctuating fortunes of the whaling industry and its undoubted importance to the commercial life of Honolulu.

Equally important was the rising number of traders coming to Hawaii

Table 3.1. Whalingships at Honolulu and Lahaina, 1824–1861, and for All Ports after
1861. Data before 1841 are uncertain and often conflicting. Entries are for
the number of times ships entered the ports, whaleships often entering twice
in each calendar year. Morgan estimates a deduction of approximately one-
third for the number of ships calling.

Year	Honolulu	Lahaina	Other Ports	Traders	Total
1824	87	17		17	121
1825	36	42		18	96
1826	107	31		37	175
1827	82	16		23	121
1828	112	45		37	194
1829	111	62		32	205
1830	95	62		39	196
1831	81	78		37	196
1832	118	80		37	235
1833	197	82		35	189
1834	111	—		31	
1835	76	—		33	
1836	73	—		39	
1837	67	62		32	161
1838	76	72		23	171
1839	60	56		33	149
1840	47	39		31	117
1841	60	73		31	164
1842	74	98		46	218
1843	136	247		37	420
1844	165	325		42	532
1845	163	379		41	583
1846	167	429		53	649
1847	167	239		67	473
1848	148	161		90	399
1849	120	154		180	454
1850	125	112		469	706
1851	90	103	27	446	666
1852	226	189	104	235	754
1853	246	177	110	211	744
1854	189	224	112	125	650
1855	171	184	113	123	591

Table 3.1. continued

Year	Honolulu	Lahaina	Other Ports	Traders	Total
1856	150	121	95	82	448
1857	142	122	123	115	502
1858	224	141	161	139	665
1859	249	116	184	117	666
1860	179	62	84	93	418
1861	110	24	56	—	190
1862	73[a]			113	186
1863	102			88	190
1864	130			157	287
1865	180			151	331
1866	229			150	379
1867	243			113	356
1868	253			113	366
1869	102			127	229
1870	118			159	277
1871	47			171	218
1872	47			146	193
1873	63			109	365
1874	43			120	163
1875	41			120	161
1876	37			141	178
1877	33			168	201
1878	27			232	259
1879	25			251	276
1880	16			239	255

[a] partial year

Sources: Kuykendall, Hawaiian Kingdom, vol. 1, p. 307, compiled from private journals before 1844, from Custom House Statistics, published annually in Pacific Commercial Advertiser; Morgan, Hawaii, app. 2, pp. 225–226.

Note: It has been suggested that the raising of port fees by Liholiho shifted the traffic from Honolulu to Lahaina (Daws, Honolulu, p. 235.) The figures suggest that other factors may have been at work. The period 1824 to 1835 was one in which the numbers of whalers coming to Hawaii was fairly constant, with the single exception of 1825 when only 36 whale ships were recorded at Honolulu as compared to 42 at Lahaina.

to share in both the whaling trade and the re-export trade from Hawaii to California, the Russian settlements, and to the Pacific region. In 1840, it was estimated that something approaching one-half of the goods landed in Honolulu were re-exported.[14] Trade in sea otter fur and horses was the big attraction for Hawaiian trade with California. Horses brought a premium in Hawaii, where they were the most prized possessions of the Hawaiian people.[15]

Whaling ships probably accounted for one-third to one-half of the listed exports of Hawaii. Salt was a principal export before 1861; after that date, sugar and molasses assumed the leading role. As the logs of ships indicate, whaling ships found it easy to visit several locations to complete their supply needs; thus there are many gaps in the data. In most instances, Lahaina Roads offered a somewhat protected anchorage, was easy to approach, and provided easy departure. Honolulu was often difficult to enter, even by towing-in, because of the northeast trades, and occasionally difficult to leave when the southerly (*kona*) wind blew. These same *kona* winds forced the ships to sail off and on the Lahaina Roads until they subsided. Honolulu's greatest advantage was the protected anchorage that allowed ships to refit and load and unload cargo without regard to the weather. In Honolulu, many whalers took the opportunity to send their oil and bone home via the trading ships that frequented the port. They were thus able to extend their cruise while satisfying the business end in New England.

The bark *Pantheon* was a typical example. Returning from the Arctic in November 1843, the bark called at Lahaina for supplies and then went on to Oahu.

> November 19, 1843: Dropped anchor outside the bar three miles from the Harbour. Took Captain ashore, the wind blows right out the harbor so that we can't get in. The *William and Elizabeth* is lying near waiting for cargo to take home. We are going to send home 1,000 bbls of oil and all of our bone by her and then go back to the Northwest and fill up which will make us about 3,500 bbls. Tuesday. Nov 23. Light winds, warped into the harbour, got inside the harbour by 10 oclock.[16]

In the effort to regularize the landing of goods and the flow of ships, several changes were instituted. Whalers were permitted both to purchase supplies and to barter for those supplies, provided no more than $200 in barter value was involved. If the amounts per ship were greater, ad valorem duties of 3 percent and merchant vessel's fees were exacted, regardless of the basic purpose of the ship. It is clear from the logs that some ships engaged in whaling also engaged in trade, selling bread, barrel staves, oil, and other commodities.

Lahaina and Honolulu were declared in 1844 the only legal ports of entry and the only points at which seamen could be discharged or shipped, including Hawaiian seamen. Goods could not be landed at any of the other ports.

Inexperienced port personnel had difficulty interpreting the many situations that arose. Seamen discharged from whaling vessels were customarily given their portion of the "lay"—the share in the proceeds. The question that arose immediately was how to establish the value of the share—was the sailor landing cargo or personal property? At what price was the oil or bone to be valued? The problem arose frequently with the Hawaiian seamen who were discharged following a cruise. Charles Bishop, Collector of Customs, tried to deal with the question in an even-handed manner when queried by the harbormaster at Lahaina:

> respecting the prices which are paid for oil and bone to native seamen discharged at Lahaina. . . . You are aware that there is nothing in the shipping articles . . . that establishes the prices at which the oil and bone shall be valued at settlement. . . . All seamen serving on American vessels [regardless of nationality] must get their discharge from the United States Consul and have their accounts inspected by and settled before him. . . . But neither the Consul nor the Captain can oblige a seaman who is entitled to his discharge, to settle for the prices which either of them may make, nor can any local authority compel the Captain to pay any price which they may state.[17]

Regulations not ordinarily found in harbor rules reflected the importance of the whaling fleet sojourning in Hawaii. Whaling ships were forbidden to sell, barter, or dispense "spiritous liquors." Any traffic in liquor subjected the whaler to full commercial duties and penalties. "Rapid riding in the streets is prohibited under a penalty of five dollars." Ship masters were required to give notice of the desertion of any of their sailors within forty-eight hours, under penalty of $100.[18]

Law and Order

It was not only the visit of Lord Byron and the push of the missionaries that led to the promulgation of laws. The burgeoning of commerce and the rapid increase of the whaling fleet made some order mandatory. In response to the disorders occasioned by drunken sailors, the first printed laws were issued on 9 March 1822, entitled "Some Laws for the Port of Honoruru, Oahu." Published in both English and Hawaiian, the regulations required each ship's captain to furnish a list of crew, a certificate of registry and a signed statement that no crewman would be left in Hawaii without permission. A fine of $30.00 was imposed for each deserting seaman left in Honolulu; deserting seamen were to be punished with six months at hard labor and captains were required to pay $6.00 for each returned crewman. Drunk or rioting sailors were to be confined in the fort and kept there until a fine of $30.00 had been paid.

The 1822 rules also included the first regular port charges. Ships entering for "refreshing or refitting" paid a fee of six cents per ton; those coming to trade paid fifty cents per ton. A towing fee of $1.00 per foot of draft was levied.[19]

A second notice published at the same time proclaimed that any foreigner "molesting strangers, or in any way disturbing the peace," would be confined in the fort and sent out of the kingdom on the first available vessel. Some confusion exists as to the date of these regulations. The Minister of Public Instruction in his Biennial Report to the Legislature, 1 August 1846, said, "The first law ever promulgated by the press in the hawaiian language related to the harbor of Honolulu and was printed in June, 1825." This likely refers to the fact that the rules were printed in a pamphlet form in 1825, having been merely posted as notices in 1822.[20]

As the Hawaiian chiefs increasingly came under the influence of the missionaries after 1825, the conflict with seamen in Lahaina and Honolulu produced some tense situations. British and American merchants and captains complained about the vagueness of the posted laws. The reliance on oral traditions of the Hawaiians made these foreigners uneasy and they argued that the king and the chiefs had no authority to make arbitrary laws applicable to foreigners. In response to these complaints, Governor Kauikeaouli issued what amounted to a penal code in December 1827. This incorporated most of the rules laid down in 1824 by Queen Kaahumanu. Murder was declared to be a capital offense; fornication, adultery, theft, prostitution, and gambling were forbidden.[21]

The confusion of proclamations, laws, and ad hoc attempts to deal with the growing problem of the maritime community reflected, in part, the general attitude of the foreign community that they were beyond the authority of the Hawaiians. British Consul Richard Charlton insisted that Hawaii had been surrendered to the sovereignty of Great Britain and the Hawaiians could make no laws without the approval of the British government, arguing that the cession given Vancouver by Kamehameha was final. Charlton was quite fond of asserting the authority of the British government and continued to do so until removed from office.

Riots and armed demonstrations of sailors demanding access to prostitutes and alcohol occurred several times between 1825 and 1827. Although no serious physical damage was committed in these episodes, the effect was a toleration of liquor and prostitution in the vicinity of Honolulu Harbor, and also at the Lahaina Roadstead. [22]

The conversion to Christianity of Queen Kaahumanu in her last years brought vigorous attempts to enforce a rigid, puritanical code. On her death in 1832, there was a considerable division of opinion among the high chiefs. Many preferred a more relaxed approach to drinking, sexual mores, and gambling—the principal sources of contention among the Hawaiian rulers and the merchant community. Most of the resentment focused on the missionary group as obvious targets and the source of the puritanical impulses. [23]

Efforts to control the growing number of crews coming to Honolulu between whaling seasons was made difficult by the actions of some captains. One spectacular episode involved the U.S. Navy schooner *Dolphin*, commanded by John (Mad Jack) Percival, on a voyage in 1825 to pick up mutineers who had holed up in the Mulgrave Islands and to check on the overdue debts of the Hawaiian chiefs. Captain Percival, while meeting with the chiefs, asked them to remove the *kapu* on women consorting with the sailors. Kaahumanu had ordered that no women were to be permitted to visit the ship or its crew. Percival took immediate issue with the order and charged it was discrimination against the United States, arguing that both England and the United States tolerated the traffic in women. He threatened violence if the ban were not lifted. Percival offered to "beat the head" of Hiram Bingham if he did not recommend the lifting of the ban. [24]

The wife of the leading missionary put the matter quite directly, if in subdued language:

> The unprovoked attack upon the houses and persons of the defenseless missionaries, was approved by some of the foreigners already gathered in

our little metropolis, with some honorable exceptions, but, I am sorry to say the foreign officials were not of this excepted number. They treat the magnates of the land with rudeness and indignity.[25]

The continuing conflict between the missionaries and the commercial community was reflected in two events in 1852. The governor of Oahu increased the number of drinking house licenses from two to twelve, selling them at auction. The twelve licenses brought a total of $9,860. *The Friend* blasted this sale in an editorial.

[Seamen and mechanics] will be compelled to support twelve drinking houses, with their retinue of landlords, bartenders, and bottle washers. Merchants, mechanics, and sailors, you must spend your hard earned money freely to meet this enormous expense. . . . Beware ye spirit-drinkers, touch not, taste not, handle not. Death is in the bowl.[26]

The curfew law of Honolulu (7:30 P.M. for sailors) was a frequent source of trouble in the 1840s when visits of French, British and American warships were frequent. One such episode was the riot of the British sailors from the HMS *Junco* on 28 September 1846. The riot apparently began when police tried to remove a sailor from a grog shop at 7:30. This blew up into a full scale riot. The British commander felt his men had been abused and allowed his men to parade through town in the nights following the riot. The matter remained an issue at the diplomatic level for more than a year.[27]

The most notable disturbance occurred in 1852 when rioting sailors from the whaling ships burned down the Honolulu police station, stormed through the streets for the better part of a day, and tried to break into the fort to release the prisoners.[28] Only with the decline of the whaling industry did the problems subside to manageable levels.

When the "foreign residents" of Honolulu—largely the American community—became alarmed at the disturbances caused by the growing number of sailors ashore, they did what citizens always do; they petitioned the government to spend more money. When the citizens petitioned the Honolulu marshal for more police protection, the Minister of Interior answered:

I am instructed by His Excellency the Acting Minister of Interior, to inform you that the petition signed by the Foreign residents of Honolulu praying that the Police force be raised to its former standard during the shipping season has been referred from the Privy Council to him for consideration. . . . [H]e directs me to say, that in view of the report

made by you and Mr. Swinton [Lahaina] in October last, . . . there is no
need to increase the Police Force.[29]

The petition was no doubt occasioned by the cuts made in the
previous year, "in consequence of the scarcity of funds in the Treasury,
it has been found necessary to reduce the expenses of Government in all
its departments." The police force of Honolulu was reduced to "six
white men and two lunas [supervisors], 2 deputy lunas, 20 native
constables and 2 station house men." Lahaina would have "1 white-
man, 2 native lunas. 2 native constables and 1 jailor." During the off
season, these forces were to be reduced.[30]

Deserters and Eager Crew

If one accepted the extreme view of John C. Jones, the first U.S.
Commercial Agent to be sent to Hawaii (1821), the numbers of crew
stranded in Honolulu and Lahaina were very large. This was not
entirely due to the attractions of Hawaii—climate and women—but to
the machinations of the whaling captains. Jones reported in his first
dispatch to the State Department a drastic situation.

A practice has for many years existed with the commanders of ships
touching the Sandwich Islands either for supplies or trade, to turn on
shore all seamen against whom they could allege any trivial misconduct,
and employ in their lieu natives of the Islands, by this means lessening
their passage bills, but depriving their country of valuable subjects.
American vessels have been sold to the natives and their crews discharged, without any means of support, thus left to the protection and
mercy of the rude savage. . . . These abuses of the laws of the United
States I have been able to remedy.[31]

The concern over the rising number of seamen living in Lahaina and
Honolulu was felt not only in Hawaii but in New England. A petition
was dispatched to President Monroe at the request of some 137 signers
in December 1824, asking that a warship be stationed in the Pacific to
prevent mutinies such as that of the whaling ship Globe and the
frequent desertion of seamen. A later petition claimed that there were
"over one hundred fifty seamen, prowling about the country, naked and
destitute, associating themselves with the natives, assuming their habits
and acquiring their vices."[32]

In 1845, to cope with desertions, the governor of Oahu ordered the
harbormaster to search vessels for deserting seamen when requested by

consular agents.[33] In 1855, the United States consul at Honolulu estimated that of the eight to ten thousand men engaged in the Pacific whaling industry, approximately half were discharged and reshipped from Hawaii.[34]

The issue of Hawaiians shipping out was never satisfactorily resolved. The rapid decimation of the Hawaiian population from the epidemics of measles and cholera in the first half of the nineteenth century raised serious questions about the viability of the Hawaiian Kingdom. The effort to restrict the departure of healthy young men was largely a response to this threat to sovereignty. Efforts were made early to prevent the wholesale departure of Hawaiian men but there was little possibility of effectively enforcing any regulations. Many Hawaiians were picked up by ships at places other than Honolulu and Lahaina, and even in those ports there was no means of enforcing any restrictions. With the establishment of a constitutional government in 1842, continuous efforts were made to enact legislation to deal with the problem.

One estimate made in 1846 put the number of Hawaiians at 700 employed during the 1845 whaling season.[35] This was close to the peak of the whaling fleet, which numbered 542 vessels in Hawaii during two seasons that year. It is likely that approximately 5 percent of the whaling fleet was made up of Hawaiian seamen in 1845.[36]

In 1858, the legislature enacted a requirement that a bond be obtained from the harbormaster at Lahaina or Honolulu for each Hawaiian shipped. A fee of $2.00 was collected if the voyage lasted less than twelve months and $4.00 if longer than one year.[37]

Another estimate of the numbers of Hawaiians outside Hawaii or serving as seamen was made in 1868 during a controversy over the Masters and Servants Act. Some five to six thousand Hawaiians were estimated to be living and working on the Pacific coast.[38] A later Department of Finance report in 1872 estimated the number of Hawaiians serving on ships in the Pacific at an annual average of 560 for the period 1806 to 1872.[39]

The Mercantile Community

As long as the source of authority was Kamehameha I, Hawaiians dominated the relationships with the increasing number of visitors. But the foreigners gradually attached themselves to the various Hawaiian chiefs. Isaac Davis and John Young were only the first and most notable of that community. In the decade of the 1820s, the situation changed rapidly.

As the beach communities became established and began to attract more foreign residents they underwent several changes. Old beach community settlers, many of whom had lived or worked quite closely with the islanders, were gradually outnumbered by foreigners who settled at once in the small port areas and had minimum contact with their island hosts.[40]

Informal, casual trading arrangements quickly gave way as more organized, permanent firms came to Honolulu. James Hunnewell arrived in Hawaii in 1817 as the resident agent for Bryant and Sturgis. Dropped off from the ship *Bordeaux Packet,* after successful voyages to the Pacific Northwest and California, Hunnewell remained in Honolulu. "By request of Capt. Blanchard I agree to stop and assist in selling the remainder of our goods, and for my services to have two per cent, and monthly wages as before."[41] Hunnewell returned to Hawaii in 1826 to open a mercantile house, one that evolved into the agency of C. Brewer and Company, one of the Big Five of later years.

In 1821, a U.S. Commercial Agent was appointed at Honolulu. The appointment was the lowest category of diplomatic post. John C. Jones was also an agent for Marshall and Wildes, one of the more successful Northwest trading companies. The second diplomatic representative, Richard Charlton from England, was also the agent for Palmer, Wilson and Company. Jones and Charlton were the first such representatives in Hawaii. Both quickly earned reputations for hard dealing in business and as troublesome personalities who expressed loud disdain for the Hawaiian rulers and the missionaries.[42]

These and other trading companies were able to secure the appointment of their employees in this early period "largely due to the dearth of suitable candidates. Even in the beach communities it was difficult to find hard-working men who wanted to take on a post which entailed much time-consuming and often acrimonious business, rewarded by a meager salary."[43]

By 1823 four American mercantile houses were established, two of Boston, one of New York and one of Bristol, Rhode Island. "The whole trade of the four, probably, amounts to one hundred thousand dollars a year, sandalwood, principally, and specie, being the returns for imported manufactures."[44]

In 1827, two shipwrecked sailors opened a shipyard and promptly did a thriving business in building and repairing ships. James Robinson and Robert G. Lawrence signed on an English whaler for their first cruise.

After a stop in Honolulu, the ship departed for the Japanese whaling grounds. Their ship *Hermes* and an accompanying vessel struck a reef twenty days to the east. Robinson and Lawrence proceeded to build a small schooner from the wreckage and with eleven crew members set sail for Honolulu—a ten-week journey. On arrival in Honolulu, the two sold the schooner and used the proceeds to set up in the ship repair business at Pakaka Point near the site of Kamehameha's 1812 residence.[45]

The Hudson's Bay Company arrived in Honolulu in 1834 and quickly became a major factor in the port's business.[46] By 1844, British vice-consul Robert C. Wyllie listed six general merchants and fifteen shopkeepers in Honolulu. The list was predominately American, although the competition of the British firms was keenly felt. The tendency of the Hawaiian chiefs to identify with the British aggravated the tension between the rival merchants.[47]

The decline in the sandalwood trade coincided with the sharp decline in the fur trade. The depletion of the seal and otter herds drastically lowered the profits to be expected. The major traders such as John Jacob Astor, Marshall and Wildes, and Bryant and Sturgis discontinued their operations in the Pacific Northwest and Hawaii. Although this resulted in a decline in business activity, other Pacific Coast developments brought new trade opportunities.[48]

A rapid diversification occurred at this point, stimulated in good part by the independence of the Spanish colonies. California became an important trading partner for Hawaii and Honolulu became a distribution center for the Pacific. Cargoes brought to Honolulu were reshipped to California, China, and Manila. Stephen Reynolds' journal listed seventeen ports trading with Hawaii.[49]

After 1841, sugar and molasses reached respectable levels, averaging approximately 200 tons of sugar per year. Salt was a principal export, going to California for meat curing. Hides and provisions (potatoes, onions, fruit) also were traded actively.[50]

England Seizes Hawaii

Harbormaster William Paty complained in his journal for 25 January 1843 of boredom, with little activity. He noted: "During the past eight days we have nothing of importance. . . . The season has been very dry until the 24th. . . . The rain will have an excellent effect on the trees which have lately been set out in all the streets of the village."[51]

But by the end of February, he was no longer bored. A long

simmering dispute over a land claim by the former British Consul, Richard Charlton, boiled over into a seizure of Hawaii by Lord George Paulet, captain of the HMS *Carysfort*. Paulet arrived in Honolulu Harbor on 10 February 1843. The acting British Consul, Alexander Simpson, immediately enlisted the naval officer in the ongoing disputes. The consul had a long list of demands to present to the king, backed by the authority of the British Navy. These included immediate granting of Charlton's claim, reversal of several court decisions adverse to British citizens, the acknowledgment of Simpson as acting British Consul, immediate action to insure half of each jury involving British subjects in court would be British subjects selected by the acting consul, and, finally, "A direct communication between His Majesty King Kamehameha III and her Britannic Majesty's Consul, for the immediate settlement of all cases of grievance and complaint on the part of British subjects against the Sandwich Island Government."[52] Paulet refused to receive the French and American consuls on arrival in the harbor, claiming that they had not recognized Alexander Simpson. "Lord Paulet informed him [Dr. Judd] that he would hold communication with no one but the King."

American merchants alarmed over the possible seizure of Hawaii urged a joint American-French protectorate. Matters were complicated by the arrival of an American warship in the harbor, the USS *Boston* on 13 February. The king arrived from Lahaina on the 16th. Paulet demanded a private audience with the king and was refused. Paulet then issued a warning that he would take "immediate coercive steps" if the demands were not met. It was thought that a joint American-French protectorate would likely result in French control and the absorption of Hawaii as had happened in Tahiti. The alternative the king selected was to "throw himself into the arms of England, trusting in the justice of his cause, and hoping still for independence."[53]

Paty recorded this sad event: "The Piratical proceedings of H.R. Majesty's Ship *Carysfort*, comenced on the 11th inst. and continued by bullying and threats of violence on the 18th inst. have been this day [25 February] consumated by taking formal possession of these Islands."[54] Summoned before the newly appointed Board of Commissioners—Paulet, two officers and the Acting British Consul—Paty, Collector of the Customs, submitted his books, which were found in order by the three Navy men, but not by Mr. Simpson. Paulet ordered him to collect an additional 1 percent import duty henceforth (in addition to the 3 percent levy on imports established in 1842) and questioned the fees for seamen coming ashore. By the laws of 1842, seamen coming ashore had to post a bond of $60.00 guaranteeing they would depart within sixty days. The harbormaster collected a fee of $6.00 for issuing and canceling the bonds. Consul Simpson argued that this revenue should go to the government but was overruled.

On the same day, Paty was appointed by Judd as his assistant at the Treasury Board. Paty now served as Harbormaster, Collector of Customs, and Director of Finance. This was only one of the many maneuvers that took place. The whole farce came to an end in July when the British commanding officer in the Pacific, Rear Admiral Thomas arrived from Valparaiso. Admiral Thomas immediately set about restoring the sovereignty of Hawaii. In a joint statement that offered safeguards for British subjects, the commander in chief of the British Navy in the Pacific, "as the highest Local Representative of Her Majesty Queen Victoria. . . . Hereby declares and makes manifest that he does not accept the Provisional Cession of the Hawaiian Islands made on the 25th Day of February 1843."[55]

California Gold

The discovery of gold in California had a significant impact on the maritime activities of Hawaii. Shortly before the gold rush, Sir George Simpson described Hawaii's strategic location. "For all practical purposes, the Sandwich Islanders are on the direct route from Cape Horn to all the coasts of the Northern Pacific . . . with respect to California and the northwest coast, the apparently inconvenient deviation to the left is rendered not only expedient but almost necessary by the prevailing breeze."[56]

The first reaction in Hawaii to the gold rush was an outpouring of people, followed by a veritable boom in business. Food, clothing, and tools were scarce commodities in California. The number of trading ships coming to Honolulu increased significantly at the same time the number of whalers began to drop. The short-lived nature of the boom is also evident in the traffic figures (table 3.2).

Hopes were high in Honolulu that the rush of business would result in permanent advantages. A land rush to plant potatoes on Maui developed. Other produce, although in demand, could not respond as readily, although efforts were made in sugar, coffee, and poultry.

Another response to the gold rush was an emigration of Hawaiians. Although the number was not large compared to the numbers going to California from all sources, it had a significant impact on Hawaii,

Table 3.2. Trading and Whaling Ships Calling at Hawaii from 1847 to 1854.

Year	Whalers	Traders
1847	406	67
1848	309	90 a
1849	274	180
1850	237	469
1851	220	446
1852	519	235
1853	533	211
1854	525	154

Source: Morgan, *Hawaii*, p. 226.
a. All ports after 1847.

where the native population was declining rapidly. This exacerbated a situation in which Hawaiians had already developed a reputation for demanding high wages. Perhaps more exasperating than the numbers migrating to the gold fields were the numbers who refused to be employed by enterprising agriculturists, preferring instead to produce their own crops for sale to the eager ships from California.[57]

The hoped-for permanent rise in business was doomed by the short-lived nature of the California gold rush, a rising supply of food and merchandise from California suppliers, and a rapid increase in the supply of potatoes coming from Oregon. For some, the gold rush produced little more than frustrations, but for a few, there was indeed gold at the end of the rainbow. Six Hawaiians from Kauai returned to Hawaii in 1854 with "savings of $52,000 among them . . . not a very great sum for five years of labor, but they were an envied *hui* [group]."[58]

Harbor Regulations and Improvements

The harbor meanwhile was beginning to display signs of wear and tear. In 1841 the chiefs put in place a law that forbade the throwing of stones and heavy rubbish into the harbor.[59] In 1846, the Minister of Foreign Affairs asked Admiral Hamelin of the French Navy to make a survey of the harbor. Hamelin was in Honolulu to restore $20,000 seized by another French naval officer in 1839, in one of the several instances of challenges to Hawaiian sovereignty.[60]

The survey, not completed until July 1847, presented a dismal picture. At the Robinson wharf, built in 1827, the water at low tide was only fourteen feet. Loaded vessels were grounded in the mud at low tide. The other wharfs were little better.[61] Strapped for funds and struggling with threats to Hawaiian sovereignty, the government made few improvements.

Complaints about the poorly marked channel entrance led to a request for channel buoys and new lights in 1851, but little was done to resolve the problem.[62] An editorial in the government publication, *The Polynesian,* called for dredging the harbor from Robinson's wharf to the First Jetty (Fort site) to a depth of twenty-four feet. The area was now sand and mud, with loaded vessels still grounding with the tide.[63]

The initial 1825 wharf built on a hulk sunk at the foot of Nuuanu, was gradually joined by other wharves built by private parties. The hulk was followed by the wharf of the Robinson & Company in 1827 at nearby Pakaka Point to serve Robinson's ship repair business (Figure 3.3). According to the map of the city in 1843, there was another wharf built to the east of those two. A landing was built into the fort in 1817 that provided a shallow landing site, suitable largely for ships' boats and small vessels.[64]

A further development was the sale of a site for a wharf by the Minister of Finance. This was likely at the foot of Mauna Kea Street. A harbor description in 1844 lists the Charlton-French wharf and the wharf of Ladd and Company.[65]

As late as 1855, passengers were likely to be landed on the beach if the few wharves were busy during the whaling season. Charles de Varigny, French Consul, was one such passenger. "The newcomer landed on the beach where the whaleboats ran aground, and seldom did he depart with dry feet."[66]

Charges at the wharves varied. Robinson charged $1.00 per day for schooners, $2.00 for brigs, and $3.00 for ships. Ladd and Company's fee in 1844 was sixteen cents per ton of goods landed or shipped, but "no charge for a vessel laying alongside unless for repairs or exceeding the reasonable time for discharging or embarking cargo." Harbor fees had changed considerably from the early days of 1816 when pilotage was negotiable and flat fees were collected, regardless of size. The dues were set in 1844:

> The harbor dues at this port are the following, viz: 20 cents per ton on merchant vessels; 6 cents per ton on whale ships and merchant vessels entering for the purpose of obtaining refreshment only; $2 for the use of the buoys; $1 for certificate of clearance; $1 per foot [of draft] pilotage for taking a vessel in or out.[67]

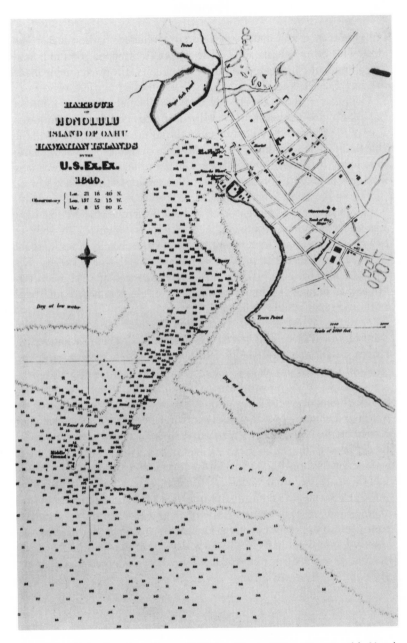

Figure 3.3   Wilkes Expedition Survey, 1840 (from Charles Wilkes, *Narrative of the United States Exploring Expedition during the years 1838, 1839, 1840, 1841, 1842,* 5 vols. (Philadelphia: C. Sherman & Sons, 1844).

In 1850, new and lower fees were established for harbor duties and Hilo, Kawaihae, Kealakekua, and Waimea were declared ports of entry. Since Honolulu and Lahaina were the ports with consular representation, discharging and shipping crews were confined to those two.[68]

The outport issue had been raised by the Collector General, Charles Bishop. He pointed out to the Minister of Finance that merchantmen were inconvenienced by being unable to use the outports, particularly Hilo and Kealakekua. He urged the opening of the outports as a means of stopping illegal trading. "Allow me to call your attention to the fact that merchant vessels lying outside the harbor of Honolulu when at anchor or not may land merchandise or passengers to any number or take on board cargo without being liable according to Laws to pay any charges for anchorage, tonnage, or buoys."[69] The outports were opened in July, August, and September and new, lower fees were established and made uniform for all ports.

The harbor system of the kingdom was regularized in 1852 when the Minister of the Interior made comprehensive rules for all of the harbors and roadsteads. Tonnage dues were set at fifteen cents per ton register. Pilotage was $1.00 per foot of draft for Honolulu and Hilo. Health certificates and clearance certificates were $1.00 each at all ports. At Lahaina, Kealakekua, Waimea, and Kawaihae, a $5 boarding fee was charged. Payment at one port sufficed for all other ports visited on the same voyage. Whaling ships touching for "repairs, supplies or refreshments, shipment or discharge of crew, and neither lading, unlading, or transhipping any cargo or passengers" were exempted from tonnage dues. Whaling vessels were permitted to land goods up to $200 in value, free of duty and up to an additional $1,000 for a duty of 5 percent ad valorem.[70]

The arrival in 1844 of Robert C. Wyllie as assistant to the new British Consul General, William Miller, set in motion a movement for improvement of the harbor. The sharp increase in traffic and the increasing size of ships calling at Honolulu made dredging imperative. The removal of the harbor bar was desirable but not urgent. Dredging the harbor was only one of the many projects urged by the ubiquitous Wyllie. In a series of articles in *The Friend* in 1844, he outlined a variety of projects. In particular he urged the removal of the now decrepit fort and filling in the area to the southeast, toward the entrance, creating valuable waterfront property. Since 1817, the fort, largely symbolic in its career, had served as a little more than a convenient prison for errant seamen and a base for the tiny military force of the government.[71]

Wyllie was appointed Minister of Foreign Affairs in 1845. He planned to dismantle the fort and use the material for the construction of a new prison and the rubble for filling in Waikahalulu reef, an area that was dry at low tide. The plan was approved by the legislature in 1852, but could not be implemented until a new prison could be constructed. Wyllie's enthusiastic plan included the building of "a small steam tug, so constructed as to be available for a dredge for cleaning out the harbor, to tow vessels out of or into the harbor, and when necessary, to bear two long guns, so as to oppose any vessel or vessels breaking the quarantine laws, that might be at anchor outside."[72]

The rapid expansion of the town of Honolulu was creating a silt problem and the Nuuanu Stream was carrying a heavy burden. A wall was proposed at the northern end of the harbor to divert the flow of the stream to the west-southwest, toward Kalihi Basin.[73] A 940-foot wall was built from the Emmes Wharf, near the lime kiln, west-southwest across the inner harbor. Wyllie's plans for developing the harbor he had proposed in 1844 and 1850 were again brought to notice in 1853. Wyllie strongly urged that the harbor lands be made public lands. As if to emphasize that need, the owners of a reef in the harbor proposed to build a causeway to connect the reef on the western side of the harbor with the shore land to the north of Nuuanu Stream. The privy council appointed an engineer to survey the harbor and determine if owners Sumner and Sea would sell their land to the government. A factor in setting these plans in motion was the organization of a steamship line to run between San Francisco and China—the Oriental and Pacific Steam Navigation Company. William Webster, an engineer, was hired to make the survey and develop a plan for the harbor. His completed plan was estimated to cost approximately $500,000. It included dredging the harbor, building wharves, removing the bar, and widening the entrance.[74] The report agreed with Wyllie's recommendation to purchase the reef land of Sumner and Sea. The privy council was unable to make an agreement and the matter lapsed. It would return as an issue much later and at high cost.[75]

Progress was made on dredging. Chief Justice William Lee traveled to New York on two missions—to negotiate a reciprocity treaty with the United States and to purchase a dredger and steam tugboat for the harbor. Lee failed to secure a treaty but did return with the machinery and equipment to build the dredger and tugboat. The principal aim was to deepen the entrance in anticipation of steamship service. The bar proved to be beyond the capacity of the dredge and it was used to improve the harbor beginning in April 1856. The Minister of Interior reported in 1860 that it would be necessary "to make some alterations in the machinery of the present dredge and to procure another hull in which to place the machinery. The steam tug *Pele* began a long career of towing in and out of the harbor and assisting the dredge.[76]

The shaky financial condition of the government delayed the completion of these plans. In 1854 the Superintendent of Public Improvements reported on the effects of the financial bind:

> Nearly all the Public Works were stopped in October last, as a large decrease in the revenue, . . . was then anticipated and the salary of the Superintendent was also suspended at the same time. . . . The appropriation of $1,000 for wharves having been insufficient to keep them in proper repair, I have in addition expended for this purpose the sum of $1,384.49; which I trust you will sanction, since without it, the most valuable wharf would have been almost entirely useless, during the entire shipping season.[77]

It had become increasingly difficult to get fresh water from Nuuanu Stream as the population—and pollution—had increased dramatically. Laundry done in the stream, cattle pastured higher in the Nuuanu Valley, and taro patches drawing and returning water to the main stream made the water unpalatable and even dangerous. Household needs were supplied by backyard wells—all too often located adjacent to the pit toilet.

In 1847 a one-inch pipe was laid from a taro patch to the harbormaster's office. This was replaced in 1850 with a four-inch pipe from a spring in Nuuanu Valley to the waterfront.[78] The harbormaster was in charge of the system and gradually extended it to other areas of the downtown section, although the quality of water left much to be desired.

Perhaps the best sign of the transformation into a modern port community was the arrival in Honolulu of the first shipment of ice in the bark *Harriet J. Bartlett.* The ice was sold at auction. For several years thereafter, ice was imported regularly and then discontinued as unprofitable.[79]

Gradually, the missing elements were fitted together. Dredging continued fitfully but progress was made. A new harbor light was put in place in 1859. Other elements such as warehouses, additional water facilities, and channel markers were slowly put in place. The fort was not demolished until 1857 and the building of the sea wall and the filling in of the causeway was not completed until 1870. The 1854 Legislature authorized the borrowing of amounts up to $150,000 for public improvement. The government's poor financial condition, however, resulted in only a portion of this authorization being used.[80] The harbor remained the number one priority of the government and work continued slowly as funds were made available.

Notes

1. E. S. C. Handy and Elizabeth G. Handy, "Native Planters in Old Hawaii: Their Life, Lore, and Environment," *Bernice P. Bishop Museum Bulletin* No. 233 (1972), p. 52. See also Irving Goldman, *Ancient Polynesian Society* (Chicago: University of Chicago Press, 1970), pp. 301–302.

2. The term means, literally, the people living on the land, reflecting the agrarian basis of common Hawaiian society. Handy and Handy, "Native Planters," pp. 322–326; David Malo, *Hawaiian Antiquities* (Moolelo Hawaii), trans. by Nathaniel B. Emerson, Bernice P. Bishop Museum Special Publications No. 2 (Honolulu: Bishop Museum Press, 1951), pp. 60–61.

3. Gavan Daws, *Honolulu* (Ph.D. dissertation, University of Hawaii, Honolulu), p. 68.

4. Andrew Bloxham, *Diary of Andrew Bloxham, Naturalist on the Blonde*, Bernice P. Bishop Museum Special Publications No. 10 (Honolulu: Bishop Museum Press, 1925), p. 32.

5. James Jackson Jarves, *Scenes and Scenery in the Sandwich Islands During the Years 1837–1842* (Boston: J. Munroe, 1843), pp. 19–20.

6. Great Britain, Foreign Office 58/3, printed in *Report of The Historical Commission Of The Territory Of Hawaii* (Honolulu: 1924), p. 33.

7. Statement of Governor Kekuanoa, written probably in 1839, in Kuykendall, *The Hawaiian Kingdom* (Honolulu: University of Hawaii Press, 1938), vol. 1, p. 79.

8. Ibid., pp. 118–120.

9. Ibid., pp. 120–121.

10. Maria Graham Calcott, *Voyage of the H.M.S. Blonde to the Sandwich Islands: 1824–1825* (London: J. Murray, 1826), p. 121; John Healy, *Mapping of the Hawaiian Islands* (Master's thesis, University of Hawaii, Honolulu, 1959).

11. T. Blake Clark, "Honolulu's Streets," *Hawaiian Historical Society 20th Annual Report* (1938), p. 5.

12. Victor S. K. Houston, transl., "Chamisso in Hawaii,: *Hawaiian Historical Society 48th Annual Report* (1939), p. 70–71, (trans. from *The Collected Works of Adelbert*

Von Chamisso). John Young was Kamehameha's governor of Oahu and had just completed construction of the fort.

13. Mystic Seaport Museum, G. W. Blunt White Library, Mystic, Connecticut, Ship Log 669, ship *Mayflower,* 10-14-1834 to 4-23-38; see Log 769, bark *Pantheon,* 11-16-42 to 5-25-45; log 41, bark *Shepardess,* 9-3-1844 to 6-3-47. See also Howay, "The Ship *Pearl* in Hawaii in 1805 and 1806," *Hawaiian Historical Society 16th Annual Report* (1937), pp. 29–33.

14. *The Polynesian* (12 September 1840).

15. Kuykendall, *Hawaiian Kingdom,* vol. 1, p. 303; Harold W. Bradley, *The American Frontier in Hawaii: The Pioneers, 1789–1843* (Palo Alto: Stanford University Press, 1942), p. 76.

16. Mystic Seaport Museum, G. W. Blunt White Library, Log 769, bark *Pantheon,* Fall River, 11-16-42 to 5-25-45; see also Log 55 bark *Oscar,* 11-28-1854 to 5-1-57; Log 146, ship *Charles Morgan,* 11-1-1866.

17. Charles Bishop, Collector of Customs to H. S. Swinton, Lahaina, 12 November 1850, Collector of Customs Letter Book, Hawaii State Archives.

18. Hawaii State Archives, Minister of Interior, Harbor Regulations, 20 August 1852; *The Friend* (September 1852), pp. 2–43.

19. W. D. Westervelt, "Printed Laws Before the Constitution," *Hawaiian Historical Society 16th Annual Report* (1908), p. 41.

20. W. D. Frear, "Hawaiian Statute Law." *Hawaiian Historical Society 13th Annual Report* (1906), p. 26.

21. Kuykendall, *Hawaiian Kingdom,* vol. 1, p. 121.

22. Ibid., vol. 1, pp. 129–132.

23. See Hiram Bingham, *A Residence Of Twenty-one Years In The Sandwich Islands,* 1st ed. (Hartford: H. Huntington, 1847), pp. 350–352.

24. Ibid., pp. 283–289; Laura Fish Judd, *Honolulu: Sketches of Life in the Hawaiian Islands from 1828–1861,* Dale L. Morgan (ed.) (Chicago: Lakeside Press, 1966), pp. 55–56.

25. Judd, *Honolulu,* p. 56. See also, Bradford Smith, *Yankees in Paradise: The New England Impact on Hawaii* (Philadelphia: Lippincott, 1956), pp. 130–134.

26. *The Friend* (July 1852): 20.

27. *The Polynesian* (3, 17 October 1846); Daws, *Honolulu,* pp. 357–259.

28. W. C. Parke, *Personal Reminiscences of William Cooper Parke, Marshall of the Hawaiian Islands, from 1850 To 1884* (Cambridge: Harvard University Press, 1891), pp. 34–44; *Thrum's Annual* (1921), pp. 62–68.

29. *Minister of Interior to W. C. Parke, Marshall, 30 December 1857,* Hawaii State Archives, Interior Department, Letter Book No. 6, p. 435.

30. Ibid., 6 November 1856, p. 417.

31. Dispatch of John C. Jones, U.S. Agent for Commerce, to John Quincy Adams, Secretary of State, 31 December 1821, cited in Theodore Morgan, *Hawaii: A Century of Economic Change, 1776–1876* (Cambridge: Harvard University Press, 1948), p. 69n. The dispatch clearly had more to do with illustrating the work of Mr. Jones than describing the state of affairs in Honolulu in 1821. There is no evidence that the problem was that extensive. See also Carolyn Ralston, *Grass Huts and Warehouses: Pacific Beach Communities in the Nineteenth Century* (Honolulu: University of Hawaii Press, 1978), p. 66. 79, 101–102.

32. U.S. Congress, 28th Cong., 2d Sess., Doc. No. 92, *House Reports*, pp. 9–10; Bradley, *American Frontier*, pp. 105–106. Harold W. Bradley, "Thomas Ap Catesby Jones and the Hawaiian Islands, 1826–1827," *Hawaiian Historical Society Annual Report* (1930), pp. 17–30, is a detailed examination of the visit of the USS *Peacock* and the issue of deserting seamen.

33. Directive to Harbor Master, 4 March 1845, Hawaii State Archives, Foreign Office and Executive, Foreign Office Letter Book No. 10, p. 9.

34. Morgan, *Century of Change*, p. 148.

35. *The Polynesian* (4 April 1846).

36. Morgan, *Century of Change*, pp. 147–148.

37. Hawaii State Archives, Kingdom of Hawaii. *Session Laws of 1859*, pp. 35–36; Bradley, *American Frontier*, p. 227; Sir George Simpson, *Narrative of a Journey Around the World During the Years 1841 and 1842* (London: Henry Colburn, 1847) vol. 2, pp. 132–135. Simpson estimates that fully half those leaving Hawaii did not return, p. 135.

38. *Pacific Commercial Advertiser* (28 November 1868).

39. Hawaii State Archives, Kingdom of Hawaii, Department of Finance, *Biannual Report* (1872), p. 71. The report gives no indication of the source of the information before 1850 when a reporting requirement and bond was established for the recruitment of Hawaiian seamen.

40. Ralston, *Grass Huts*, p. 101.

41. James Hunnewell, "Honolulu in 1817 and 1818." *Hawaiian Historical Society Papers* No. 8 (1895), p. 9.

42. Jean I. Brookes, *International Rivalry In The Pacific Islands, 1800–1875*, (Berkeley: University of California Press, 1941), pp. 49–50; Ralston, *Grass Huts*, p. 102.

43. Ralston, *Grass Huts*, p. 105.

44. Charles S. Stewart, *Journal Of A Residence in the Sandwich Islands* (Boston: H. Fisher & Son, 1839), pp. 154–155.

45. *Pacific Commercial Advertiser* (10 August 1867); "Streets of Honolulu in the 1840s," *Thrum's Hawaiian Almanac* (1904), p. 81.

46. Morgan, *Century of Change*, pp. 99–100.

47. James Jackson Jarves, *History of the Hawaiian or Sandwich Islands* (Boston: J. Munroe, 1843), pp. 366–367; R. C. Wyllie, *The Friend* (August 1844).

48. Bradley, *American Frontier*, pp. 117–118.

49. Stephen Reynolds, "Journal," *Thrum's Hawaiian Almanac* (1909), pp. 153–159.

50. *Thrum's Hawaiian Almanac* (1876), p. 56.

51. *Journal of William Paty,* January 1, 1842; January 25, 1845, Honolulu, Hawaii State Archives.

52. Kuykendall, *Hawaiian Kingdom,* vol. 1, pp. 210–215; Journal of William Paty, 11 February 1843.

53. Kuykendall, *Hawaiian Kingdom,* vol. 1, p. 216; Bradley, *American Frontier,* pp. 430–431.

54. *Journal of William Paty,* 8 February 1843.

55. Kuykendall, *Hawaiian Kingdom,* vol. 1, p. 220; Bradley, *American Frontier,* pp. 440–441, describes the events as reflecting the schism between missionaries and merchants. The merchants regarded Paulet as a welcome antidote.

56. Simpson, *Narrative of a Journey,* vol. 2, pp. 132–135.

57. Edward Beechert, *Working in Hawaii: A Labor History* (Honolulu: University of Hawaii Press, 1985), p. 37.

58. *Pacific Commercial Advertiser* (4 August 1854).

59. Hawaii State Archives, Kingdom of Hawaii, *Fundamental Laws of the Kingdom,* (1841), p. 87.

60. Kuykendall, *Hawaiian Kingdom,* vol. 1, p. 370; Minister for Foreign Affairs to Admiral Hamelin, Hawaii State Archives, Foreign Office Letter Book No. 4, 24 March 1846, p. 176.

61. Hawaii State Archives, "Filling of the Harbor," Foreign Office and Executive, Letter Books, 1 July 1847.

62. Hawaii State Archives, Interior Department Letter Book No. 4, 10 April 1851, p. 3.

63. *The Polynesian* (23 September 1854): 78.

64. Clark, "Honolulu's Streets," p. 6.

65. Wyllie, *The Friend* (2 September 1844): 51.

66. Charles de Varigny, *Fourteen Years in the Sandwich Islands, 1855–1868* (Honolulu: University of Hawaii Press, 1981), pp. 4–5.

67. Laws of 1850, published in *The Polynesian* (20 July 1850).

68. *The Polynesian* (20 July, 31 August, 5 September 1850); fees, (20 July 1850): 96, 101–103.

69. Hawaii State Archives, Minister of Finance, Letter Book, 28 March 1850, p. 90.

70. Hawaii State Archives, *Minister of Interior Report* (1852), p. 10.

71. The Fort was demolished in 1857. See Kuykendall, *Hawaiian Kingdom,* vol. 2, p. 21. W. D. Alexander prints Wyllie's proposal in full, "Early Improvements In Honolulu Harbor," *Hawaiian Historical Society Annual Report* (1907), pp. 16–18.

72. Hawaii State Archives, *Privy Council Record,* 4 (29 June 1847): 23; Alexander, "Early Improvements," p. 15.

73. The plan to eventually fill in the area to the north of the wall was frustrated in later years by the award of the fifteen-acre area by the Land Claims Commission to an applicant. Alexander, "Early Improvements," p. 15.

74. Kuykendall, *Hawaiian Kingdom* (1957), vol. 2, p. 22. No copy of the report survives in the Archives. *The Report of the Secretary of War, in Charge of Bureau of Public Improvements*, 1858, pp. 24–28, Hawaii State Archives, contains only a portion of the report. See *The Polynesian* (4 February 1854), for comments and details on the report.

75. Hawaii State Archives, *Minister of the Interior, Biennial Report* (1860), pp. 6–7.

76. Alexander, "Early Improvements," pp. 25–26.

77. Hawaii State Archives, Minister of the Interior, *Report of the Superintendent of the Bureau of Internal Improvements* (1854), p. 6.

78. Daws, *Honolulu*, pp. 527–528; *The Polynesian* (18 May, 1 June 1850).

79. *The Polynesian* (26 June 1852).

80. Kuykendall, *Hawaiian Kingdom*, vol. 2, p. 23.

4

Between Mercantile and Agricultural Economies

The End of Whaling

The heady days of the whaling boom in the 1840s seemed to assure Hawaii a permanent place in the New England-based whaling fleet. Who could argue with the "natural advantages" of Hawaii in the pursuit of whale oil? As with most economic forecasts, the not-included variables proved to be the most significant in the long run. The rapid depletion of the whale stock, just as the otter and seal population had been depleted on the Pacific Northwest coast, began to raise the cost of voyages by the end of the decade.

Most significant was the steady increase in the length of time required to fill a ship with oil. Severe depletion of the whale stock in the Sea of Japan meant that the time required to fill a ship with 2,000 barrels of oil jumped sharply. Before 1830 a two-year cruise in the Pacific would produce 2,000 barrels of sperm oil. By the 1850s, the time required for a whale oil cargo had increased to four years and then to six years. [1]

Clearly one of the inhibiting factors for Hawaii's fortunes was the sharply increased capital costs of a whaling expedition. The expansion of New England's industrial economy and the rapid spread of gas lighting after the Civil War offered more attractive opportunities for capital investment than the increasingly risky whaling business. [2]

Another depressing factor for Hawaii was the increasing popularity after the Civil War of San Francisco as a base for the whale fleet. The sharply reduced Arctic whaling fleet of 1872 was divided, with twenty-one ships going to San Francisco in the fall of that year and only eight going to Honolulu. [3] A minor factor to be considered was the adoption of a new American Seaman's law in June of 1872. This reform legislation aimed to curb the worst abuses in the notoriously bad conditions faced by American seamen under the Seaman's Act of 1790. A shipping commissioner was appointed in each of the relevant circuit court districts of the United States. Crews were required to be shipped before the commissioner and the contracts had to conform to the standards laid down in the law. This made it more difficult to recruit seamen in ports such as Honolulu, which were served only by United States' consuls who had earned a poor reputation for protecting seamen. Although the law was a step in the direction of reform, abuses remained until the reform act of 1914 brought the American sailor under the full protection of the Constitution.[4]

Robert Wyllie in 1844 expressed the fear that "[w]ere the whale fishery to fall off, the Islands would relapse back into their primitive insignificance."[5] Not everyone agreed. There were those who were convinced that the whaling would end one day. At the time of the first shrinkage in the fleet, 1848, the editor of the Hawaiian government publication, *The Polynesian,* argued, "It is evident that no permanent reliance can be placed upon the whaling enterprises as a source of business for this kingdom. . . . Agriculture is the only sure reliance for the country."[6]

The steady decline in the number of whalers moved the *Pacific Commercial Advertiser* in 1857 in a lead editorial to conclude that the "Whaling Fleet Is Declining." The number of ships expected, they said,

> will be smaller than for fifteen years past. . . . The annual visits of whaleships have heretofore been considered a main reliance of the business of our principal ports. . . . We must produce for [foreign countries] what they want. . . . They want our sugar, molasses, coffee, wool, cotton, and hides, to an indefinite amount, far beyond our ability to supply them.[7]

Interest in agriculture was always high and continued without regard to the whale industry. Prior to 1860, the principal commodity, other than produce, exported from Hawaii had been salt. Sugar entered the list of exports in 1837, with a total of two tons of raw sugar and three thousand gallons of molasses. In the 1840s, coffee was added to the list of exports. Not until the Civil War created a new market for Hawaiian products did these commodities reach sizeable proportions, but once entered in the stream of export activity, the amounts grew steadily.

Land and Labor

Two problems—capital and secure land titles—beset the early efforts in agriculture. Capital tended to be in the hands of mercantile firms that were tied to the whale fishery. Most early agricultural ventures foundered for lack of working capital. Land titles in the Hawaiian system were not conducive to large-scale investment. The system of holding land at the whim and wish of a ruling chief changed in the 1840s to a system of offering long term leases, which still fell short of what the British and American holders of capital desired. The transformation of the land-holding system in 1848 (The Great *Mahele*) removed the last of these problems. The decline of the whaling industry freed capital for investment in agriculture.[8]

Beyond the issue of access to land was the question of labor. The New England missionaries held firmly to the notion that work was a necessary element in salvation. The Hawaiian communal life style did not require incessant labor, and the frequent pauses for sport, relaxation, or amusement were seen as evidence of Hawaiian paganism. From their arrival in 1821, the missionaries exerted great effort to bring the Hawaiian commoner into the Calvinist world of work. Elaborate plans to foster agriculture and various cottage industries such as spinning and weaving were made in the 1830s. In 1836 the American Board of Commissioners for Foreign Missions rejected an elaborate plan to convert the Hawaiians into industrious workers and farmers on the grounds that the plan was too far from the mission of conversion.[9] Most of the plans put forward featured very low pay for the Hawaiians and consequently were not received with any enthusiasm by those for whom the "salvation" was designed.

In contrast to the rejection of these plans was the enthusiastic acceptance by Hawaiians of jobs paying a decent wage. There was no lack of Hawaiian young men to sign on for whaling cruises or as deck hands on merchant ships. After 1860, Honolulu became a primary supplier of seamen. "The principal reservoir from which [seamen] were obtained was the youth of Hawaii. Thousands of these young men were employed as seamen on whaleships and some also on ordinary merchant vessels."[10] Many Hawaiians worked as longshoremen or draymen in Honolulu and Lahaina. Judging from the complaints of businessmen about the exorbitant wages demanded by these workers, there was no lack of entrepreneurial spirit among these Hawaiians. The majority of Hawaiians, living away from the commercial centers, continued their age-old life style, engaging in subsistence agriculture, fishing, and providing for their extended families' needs.[11] The comment of the U.S. Commissioner in Honolulu in 1844 summed up the issue: "[The Hawaiians] are a well clothed, civilized, and well paid class of natives."[12]

More important than any question of willingness to work or wage levels was the decreasing number of Hawaiians due to epidemics and outmigration. The population declined to approximately 84,000 in 1850, which represented a 65 percent decline from 1832. In an effort to stop the decline, the government in 1850 forbade Hawaiians to leave the kingdom without permission of the government.[13] Undoubtedly this inhibited a few from leaving but the act was easier to pass than to enforce, particularly with young men signing on ships and then leaving those ships outside of Hawaii.

Agricultural promoters, having secured access to the land with the Great *Mahele* of 1848, now turned their attention to the question of labor. The Hawaiian Legislature enacted a sweeping apprentice and laborer's statute in 1850 that permitted the importation of indentured laborers. All that was required to unleash the agricultural bonanza was cheap and dependable labor. Henceforth the focus of the Hawaiian economy would be on agriculture.[14] This sweeping solution to economic development conveniently omitted discussion of capital and possible crops.

Transition in the Harbor

The harbor, its capacity and facilities, was the focus of most of the concern over economic development—whether the center of that development was to be whaling, agriculture, or warehousing for the Pacific region. The *Pacific Commercial Advertiser* reviewed the government's effort to improve the harbor in 1856 and found much wanting. The newspaper charged that the water depth at the piers was decreasing at the rate of two feet per year, "and no vessel of one thousand tons can now come within ten to fifteen feet of either pier to discharge."[15] Two years after the legislature voted to demolish the fort to make way for new wharves and to create waterfront land behind a seawall built from the blocks of the now useless fort, no progress had been made.

The people have been anxiously looking for months and even years for the first step to be taken. . . . [T]wo years ago they were told that the work must wait till the new prison was completed. This has now been so far completed as to allow for its occupancy, but the first steps toward improving the wharf lots remains to be taken. . . . Commerce with its true instincts always alights upon the best [harbor] and converts it to a metropolis. . . . We think it would be well . . . to make the [harbor] the center of that wide commerce for which it is favorably situated.[16]

The 600 feet of wharf space available at the five wharves could be expanded easily by the creation of the planned waterfront lots to provide an additional 1,000 feet of space. The newspaper feared, however, that "not a single additional foot of wharfage will be provided by the government in the next five years, unless there is a radical change in the administration of the department [Ministry of the Interior]." Within the year, the new wharfs were under construction and the dredge was busy deepening the harbor and filling in what came to be called the Esplanade.

In 1855, the water system, installed in 1847, was opened to people paying an annual fee of $25.00 through half-inch pipes or buying water from a water carrier. Within two years, the system was overburdened and water restrictions had to be put in place. The shortage became aggravated and presented serious problems of sanitation and fire safety, not to mention the inconvenience to ships seeking to fill their casks. Finally, in 1859, the legislature directed the establishment of a "water supply system for the city of Honolulu," including a reservoir and pipe system.[17] For the two years ending March 1861, the harbormaster reported a commission collected for water of $605.00 (7.5 percent of the charge).[18]

More than a convenient supply of water was involved now. Rapid development of the valley above Honolulu led to serious soil erosion and increased water run-off.

> Denuded hillsides gave up water as fast as it fell, and . . . flowed quickly, uselessly, and sometimes dangerously to the sea . . . down Nuuanu valley to the harbor, [carrying] big logs from timber-yards, flimsy bath houses and laundries from the sides of the stream, occasional drowned livestock, and—most bizzare—coffins of natives buried in houseyards fronting on Nuuanu stream.[19]

Even with the wall built to deflect the Nuuanu Stream from flowing directly into the harbor, much debris still came into the already overburdened harbor.

The shift in the economy is reflected in the activities of the harbor. Merchant ships began to outnumber whale ships. Interisland trade assumed a new importance as sugar and coffee plantations developed on the outer islands. The shift to agriculture also changed the pattern of usage of the ports of Hawaii. Opening the outports as ports of entry in the 1850s was based on their use by whaling ships coming in the spring and fall off-seasons for refreshment and refitting. As the whaling fleet declined, so did the commerce of such ports as Hilo, Waimea, Ka-waihae, and Kealakekua. Lahaina continued to receive whale ships, but that number also declined and the port was transformed into an agricultural service center.

Honolulu Harbor would have different demands made upon it. To accommodate as many as 249 whaling ships as Honolulu did in 1859 meant the harbor capacity was strained to the maximum. Beyond the physical facilities needed for such an influx, the business mixture required to service the ships and men was quite different than that required for an agricultural exporting economy.

Sugar Factors

As the whaling industry was reaching a climax in 1859, the sugar industry was working its way through the complex problems of capital, technology, and support services. The capital came, in part, from the firms that had dominated the maritime trades. Two of the earliest mercantile houses, Castle and Cooke and C. Brewer, took an early part in the financing of sugar expansion. Beginning by supplying credit the planters needed for the purchase of supplies, these factors moved to act as agents for plantations. The first to do so was C. Brewer, which by 1866 was acting as the agent for four plantations, managing, lending money, and directing sales and imports of machinery and fertilizer.[20]

The isolation of Hawaii's early sugar plantations created great difficulties in shipping their product. For most of the nineteenth century, sugar was shipped from landings—loaded onto lighters or in ships' boats, which went through heavy surf. On the Hamakua coast, cables were run from the 100-foot high cliffs to ships anchored perilously close to the surf. There was a constant danger from sudden winds blowing them on shore, or calms after weighing anchor combined with heavy swells would quickly set the ship on the beach. Ships calling for sugar at the north end of the island of Hawaii's Hamakua coast faced fearsome conditions. A captain described the process:

> To load sugar, a ship moored 200 yards offshore, parallel to the cliffs, with two bow anchors down and stern lines to a fixed buoy, picking up the end of a seawire running up to and over the cliff to a donkey engine. . . . A block in the loop of an endless loading wire then was sent down. . . . For ship captains it was a nervous business . . . captains tended to pace the decks, consult watches, and run for sea room the minute the wind started to blow, which was frequently.[21]

A lack of roads or railroads on the island of Hawaii meant that sugar cargoes could not be consolidated in Hilo for larger ships. On Oahu, similarly located plantations, such as Kahuku and Waialua, had to resort to off-shore loading until the completion of the Oahu Railway and Land Company line in 1899, which linked these plantations to Honolulu.[22]

Spurred by the Civil War, the sugar industry expanded rapidly—too rapidly for the size of the post-war market. Some of the more inexperienced and unwise operators were absorbed by the more soundly based. This process of absorption and consolidation was one that continues to the present time; the over sixty plantations of the early period have been reduced to fewer than twelve, which produce as much sugar as modern quotas and market conditions will permit—roughly 1 million tons per year.

The development of a few other crops added to Hawaii's export totals. Rice, the other principal crop, began as an experiment in 1857. With the arrival of South Carolina seed in 1860, a veritable craze of rice planting began that exceeded the enthusiasm shown for sugar just ten years earlier and replaced the growing of taro on a wide scale.[23]

The rising interest in agricultural commodities turned attention toward markets. Clearly Hawaii had to have a market for any serious production. The triangular trade of the early days was no longer viable. Of the most promising commodities, sugar was a difficult one. A highly political commodity, everywhere taxed or protected with tariffs, Hawaiians found it difficult to compete with United States' producers operating behind the tariff walls. The California market, once so promising, changed with the admission of California as a state in 1850. Except for the boom period produced by the Civil War and the loss of Louisiana sugar to northern markets, Hawaiian producers had problems. Competition from Cuban and Philippine sugars and overproduction by the two San Francisco refineries sharply depressed prices in 1866. The serious depression that followed in Hawaii, which lasted through 1867, drained the small kingdom of financial resources and sharply limited its ability to finance needed public improvements, such as the harbor.[24]

Sail versus Steam

Sugar, like wheat, coal, lumber, and a few other bulk cargoes, seemed ideally suited to sailing ships. Compact and without a particular time value, these crops were attractive cargoes for sailing ships, which were dwindling in the face of the more time-efficient and economical steamships. The declining fleet of sailing vessels carried these cargoes into the 1920s before being displaced by steamers.

Steamer service for Hawaii took some time to become firmly established. A California promoter was able to secure a promise of an exclusive charter for interisland service in 1851, to run for five years. The charter was conditioned on the arrival of a steamer in Honolulu by November 1851. After considerable delay, William A. Howard arrived in the Pacific Mail Steamship Company steamer *Constitution* on 24 January 1852 to meet the terms of the contract.

The government agreed to allow the use of its wharves free of charge and coal could be imported duty free. The financially strapped treasury could do no more. The *Constitution*, a twin screw steamer, made one round trip to Lahaina and then departed for San Francisco. This was the only and final trip of the company. The promoter, William A. Howard, offered many reasons for the failure to establish the line. The principal problem was the difficulty of competing with schooners plying between the two ports and the relatively low volume of imports available. Howard argued that the chartered Pacific Mail Steamship Company vessel was too large and too expensive for the relatively small Hawaiian trade and asked for an extension of his charter.[25] The Privy Council refused to alter or extend the agreement and Howard passed out of the picture.

A new group entered the competition for the exclusive charter in 1853, bringing a side-wheel steamer, the *Susan B. Wheeler*, to Honolulu. The small vessel of 114 tons and a length of 106 feet, had difficulty in the rough Molokai Channel. Armed with the Howard experience, the Council was more cautious this time. They took a trip to Lahaina and back on the small steamer. A creditable voyage of thirteen hours down to Lahaina and eleven hours return convinced the Council and they chartered the Hawaiian Steam Navigation Company. A second steamer was to be added within one year. Government business and mail were to be carried free. In addition to the use of government wharves, the company was to have free water for five years and duty-free importation of coal and machinery. Rates were to be regulated by the Hawaii Supreme Court.[26]

Beginning service in November 1853, the small steamer, *Akamai* (formerly the *Susan B. Wheeler*), sailed between Honolulu and Lahaina, with an occasional visit to Kauai. Eleven months later the small steamer reached the end of the line. Her last voyage to Lahaina was in 1854.

> She started for Lahaina, having on board between four and five hundred passengers [sic] and nineteen horses. Among the passengers were Princes Alexander and Lot. . . . When she left her guards were under water, and apprehensions were expressed that she might meet with some disaster. With calm weather she might have made the passage to Lahaina in safety, but about 10 o'clock she was struck by a heavy squall . . . and she sprung a leak. She was fortunately got about and kept afloat into the harbor.[27]

The *Akamai* was laid up for repairs. She finished out her days assisting the tug *Pele* in towing, before being broken up.

The company promptly brought two steamers to Honolulu, *Sea Bird* and *West Point;* the first was a vessel of 440 tons and the second, an older ship of 209 tons. Renamed the *Kamehameha* and the *Kalama,* respectively, they were put into interisland service, with the *Kamehameha* running to Lahaina and the older, smaller vessel to Kauai, in October 1854. The *Kamehameha* was withdrawn from the Lahaina run in April 1855 and returned to San Francisco as it was too expensive to operate and there was insufficient business for two steamers. The *Kalama* had to be laid up in May 1855 with a poor hull and corroded boiler. Repaired and put back into service in November, the vessel lasted only until 5 January 1856, when she went ashore in a southerly wind at Koloa. The old *Akamai* was pulled out and refitted and pressed into service as a tugboat. Apparently the syndicate in San Francisco had invested heavily on the expectation that Hawaii would be annexed in 1854 and they would then be on the scene with a lucrative monopoly.[28]

Enthusiasm died hard. Applications continued to be made for exclusive charters. When the Minister of Finance submitted a request to the legislature for the building of a government steamer, the legislature complied, authorizing the purchase or building of a vessel with the cost not to exceed $60,000. No funds could be found for the project.[29] In the spring of 1858, another proposal was passed by the legislature for a six year charter to operate steamers in interisland service.

The Honolulu firm of C. A. Williams was given the charter for the Hawaiian Steam Navigation Company on their proposal to put a screw steamer of 400 tons in service. The steamer *Kilauea* was put into service on 28 June 1860, launching a fitful, frequently interrupted fifteen-year career of interisland service, and as a wholly government-operated service after 1870. The operation was primarily a passenger service. The bulk of freight continued to be carried by the schooner fleet.[30]

The prospect of trans-Pacific service presented more problems for Hawaii. Reliable sailing ships of moderate cost provided swift transportation to Hawaii. Two sailing lines and numerous independent ships competed for this service. When the U.S. Congress established an ocean mail service to China in 1865, the contract was awarded to the Pacific Mail Steamship Company. Honolulu was specified as a port of call and service was to begin in 1867. Hawaii's location operated against her at this point. The company simply omitted Honolulu. They argued that Hawaii was too far off the great-circle route and calling there would increase the cost of the service. A clinching argument was that the harbor at Honolulu was inadequate to handle the large steamers in that service. Congress amended the contract to omit Hawaii.[31]

Congress subsequently authorized a monthly mail service to Hawaii with a subsidy of $75,000 annually. A contract service was established with the California, Oregon, and Mexico Steamship Company and service was inaugurated in September 1867. A subsidy for a Hawaiian mail service was enacted after considerable controversy. Apart from partisan politics, the issue involved the threat to the sailing ships of the various mercantile firms in Honolulu. They feared the loss of the passenger traffic to the faster steamers.

> For years on end, the numerous sailing vessels providing this service [San Francisco–Honolulu] had been owned by the leading merchants of Honolulu, and they understood perfectly well that the establishment of a steamship line would present them with some stiff competition . . . and then, in the very near future, deprive them of their business as carriers for the sugar planters.[32]

The subsidy, involving bonds, was never paid. Instead an agreement granting free use of the harbor facilities and tax exemption in return for the carrying of mail was reached in 1867.[33]

Despite the arrival of the steamships and the increase in sugar and agricultural exports, the revenues coming to the harbor declined as the annual influx of whaling ships declined. The resignation of the assistant harbormaster in 1874 put the matter succinctly:

> The proceeds of the Harbor Master's Office, arising from the following services, viz., 10 per cent on gross receipts of wharfage, storage on

wharves and esplanade; mooring and unmooring and hauling vessels, shipping and discharging native seamen, previous to 1871 used to average $3,600 nett or $1,800 for an each. . . . Now in 1874 it is barely $2,400 or $1,200 for an nett. . . . I am sorry to inform you that I cannot live on this amount and have at the end of the quarter to give up my situation as Deputy Harbor Master.[34]

Annexation versus Reciprocity

The experience of the 1840s, the declining population of Hawaii, and the rising spirit of intervention so prevalent in the 1850s were seen as serious threats to continued Hawaiian independence. In 1853, Judge William Lee, acting for the king, negotiated a treaty with the United States. "At the moment of his death [Kamehameha III], a treaty of annexation needed only his approval for its signature by the negotiators."[35]

The arrival of a new United States Commissioner in 1854 restimulated the fears. David Lawrence Gregg took up his new post on 6 January 1854, determined to bring about the annexation of Hawaii to the United States. His observations on his first day in Hawaii were to be typical of his stay of four years.

7 January 1854: Among the great mass of the natives there is a strong conviction of the superior abilities of white men for government. They are daily losing respect for the chiefs and would welcome the rule of republican institutions under the guaranty of the United States.

There is in the minds of all classes an apprehension, of revolution from within, and filibustering operations from without. The chiefs fear for their position and authority, and are inclined, in view of the probability of their loss, to arrange terms which will secure them most advantages. . . . It is apparent that no great effort would be necessary to induce the government to make an offer of annexation. . . .

The true policy to be pursued is to keep the fears of the chiefs and people thoroughly excited. They already apprehend domestic disturbances, and "filibustering" expeditions from California, and by the aid of inducements skilfully held out in an indirect way, an exigency could be precipitat[ed], and annexation speedily consumated.[36]

Kamehameha III, who was eager for annexation, was a most willing audience for Gregg. The financial problems of Hawaii were mounting. The unstable nature of the whaling economy and the high tariff barriers to the only logical market for Hawaiian products made either outright annexation or a reciprocity treaty the only reasonable solutions.

The death of Kamehameha III ended the negotiations of Judge Lee and Gregg. With the failure to obtain the king's signature on the 1853 treaty, the discussion shifted from annexation to the possibility of a trade treaty with the cession of Pearl Harbor as the bait. Kamehameha IV, strongly anti-missionary, was not opposed to American interests so much as he was fearful of a loss of Hawaiian sovereignty and the extinction of the Hawaiian race.

The most pressing problem was how to restore the finances of the government. Trade was an obvious approach, but there was little agreement as to how to expand in that area. Some urged a reduction in the duties on liquor, hoping for a corresponding increase in the volume imported. Gregg correctly pointed out in 1855 that if a reciprocity treaty was negotiated, "most of the class of articles now subject to a duty of five per cent would be free. . . . The present sources of revenue would be so cut-off that the government could not raise enough to meet its ordinary expenditures."[37]

In March 1855, Hawaii made a valiant effort to resolve its continuing fears of annexation or conquest from France, the United States, or Great Britain. Supreme Court Justice Lee was appointed envoy extraordinary and minister plenipotentiary to the United States, Great Britain, France, and Russia to negotiate a guarantee of Hawaiian independence through a joint treaty. Enroute to Washington, Lee was able to win the support of California Senator William Gwin for a reciprocity treaty. Meeting with President Pierce, Lee found him agreeable to a reciprocity treaty. Pierce told him, "I incline to the opinion that the wisest policy for countries is that of independence, and free interchange of products."[38]

A general free trade agreement would have required a shifting of the Hawaiian revenue base from trade to property—a move politically impossible given the dominance of Hawaiian chiefs in the legislature. A limited treaty was negotiated, which admitted the principal exports of Hawaii—sugar, coffee, molasses and a few other products—duty free into the United States, in exchange for a limited number of U.S. products such as wheat, flour, coal, fish, and lumber products. Lee returned to Hawaii with the draft treaty. He was unable to secure the multination agreement, which he had sought, but was well satisfied with the trade agreement.

The treaty was promptly ratified by the Hawaiians. Opposition

developed quickly in the U.S. Senate, led by Senator Slidell of Louisiana—the cane sugar producing state. Vermont joined the list of
objectors, fearing for its wool trade if Hawaii should export its wool.
The treaty was debated and tabled in August 1856. Some relief was
afforded Hawaii when the duty of sugar was lowered from 30 percent to
24 percent in the general tariff revision of 1857.

The continuing decline in the Hawaiian economy renewed the effort
to obtain a reciprocity treaty. The Civil War proved to be the stumbling
block on this occasion. Secretary of State Seward vetoed the idea as
"inconvenient and inexpedient" during wartime.[39] The loss of the
Arctic whaling fleet in the winter of 1871 when 33 ships, staying too
late in the year trying to bolster their meager catches, were trapped and
lost in the ice, and the diversion of whaling ships to San Francisco in
the off seasons were further blows to the already shaky economy.
Agricultural exporting was the only possibility. The harbor had to
assume a new role in the changing economy.

The Reciprocity Treaty

The final passage of the Reciprocity Treaty of 1876 and its renewal in
1886 completed the transition of Hawaii from a mercantile-maritime
center to an agricultural economy on a large scale. In a way that none of
the previous experiences had, sugar transformed not only the economy
but the Hawaiian nation itself, leading directly to the abolition of the
Hawaiian monarchy and ending with the annexation of Hawaii to the
United States.

The transfer of Hawaiian sovereignty in 1898 climaxed more than
seventy years of struggle to preserve that sovereignty. Beginning when
U.S. Commercial Agent John C. Jones took up his position in Honolulu in 1821, the British, French, and American residents of Hawaii
had all promoted the notion of at least a protectorate, if not outright
annexation. Hawaiian leaders had often seen these devices as a means
of guaranteeing the conservation of their sovereignty. The dominating
fact of Hawaiian life was the strong and unbroken economic chain that
bound Hawaii to the U.S. mainland from the earliest days of the Pacific
Northwest fur trade to the now burgeoning sugar industry.[40]

For the United States, clearly the main importance of Hawaii was as
a naval outpost and coaling station to support the larger Asian and
Pacific interests, which were developing rapidly. This interest was
revealed in the mission of General Schofield, who was sent in 1873 to

survey Pearl Harbor with Colonel B. S. Alexander of the Corps of Engineers. Their mission, laid out in a secret order, was "for the purpose of ascertaining the defensive capabilities of the different ports and their commercial facilities, and to examine into any other subjects that may occur to you . . . in order to collect all information that would be of service to the country in the event of a war with a powerful maritime nation."[41]

The surveyors declared Honolulu Harbor to be a poor risk, difficult to defend from attack. Pearl Harbor they found had a great potential as a military base, easily defended from land, the only large, natural harbor in the Pacific region. It would require great effort to bring it into usable condition. The formidable bar at the entrance, the long passage through the coral reef, and dredging were all needed as preliminaries to creating a naval base.[42]

Pearl Harbor would remain a topic of discussion for many years before it was developed into a Pacific naval base. The harbor issue became a vehicle for opponents of annexation and rising Hawaiian nationalism. Paradoxically, the advocates of American annexation used the harbor as a strategic plum to offer to American expansionists. Sugar production expanded so feverishly that a shortage of capital funds developed, forcing the Hawaiian government to lend money for a season to the eager planters. By the end of the Hawaiian period, sugar exports had risen some 72 percent, from approximately 13,000 tons in 1874 to 165,000 tons in 1893.[43]

The Harbor from Reciprocity to Republic

The economic boom resulting from the Reciprocity Treaty brought problems along with economic growth. While the commissions for the harbormasters were declining, the tonnage going through the harbor was increasing with the new size of vessels. In 1870, a short-lived steamship service from Australia to Hawaii was put into operation.

In 1877, the old *Kilauea* was joined by a newly built steamer named the *Likelike.* The government quickly put the two ships up for sale and they were sold to the only bidder, Samuel G. Wilder, the man most responsible for the government deciding to build the *Likelike.*[44]

The new steamer and increasing traffic in the port put a considerable strain on harbor facilities. Coaling facilities had to be established and wharf space was largely inadequate for the size of the steamers. The harbor entrance had only twenty-three feet of water at low tide and the heavily loaded Australian steamers and Pacific Mail steamers came close to that mark. Wharves designed for smaller sailing ships were inadequate in this new era.[45]

The wharves by 1880 had been "taxed to their full capacity in the past two years." The Bureau of Public Improvements could note with some pride that despite that heavy usage, "they are in fair order, having been properly cared for."[46]

The major concern at this point was to install an adequate marine railway or floating dock to attract and hold ship repair business. Samuel Wilder was contracted to build a railway for $90,000. Completed in 1882, the marine railway was to be the property of the government, but it was agreed that Wilder would take a lease to operate the facility for a term of fifteen years, paying a rental of 5 percent of the total cost per year.[47]

In the same year, the steam tug Pele reached the end of her towing career. "The steam tug Pele is now almost useless. Unless steps are taken to replace it with a new one, there will be no means for towing in or out of the harbor." A new one was estimated to cost $50,000.[48] The tug Pele had entered service some three months after the dredge in 1856, and functioned until 1882 as a towboat.

The dredge put into service in 1856 had been unable to work in the channel entrance due to wave and current action. Some work was done in dredging and enlarging the harbor basin and expanding the waterfront acreage with the resulting fill. While work progressed slowly because of the limitation of funds in the 1860s, the steady nature of the work resulted in considerable improvements. Stone wharves were built with a depth of twenty-two feet of water. They were small, however, being less than sixty feet in length. The channel and bar resisted all efforts to enlarge and deepen the entrance.[49]

One exotic technique was employed in an attempt to remove the bar at the harbor entrance. A visiting Russian naval commander in 1879 offered to fire torpedoes at the bar as a way of eliminating the hard coral reef. Several were fired with little effect, other than producing a large fish kill.[50]

The availability of funds was an ever-present limitation. The Minister of Interior patiently explained to the harbormaster in 1878 that the department recognized the condition of the wharves and the need for resurfacing and the continuing need for dredging. The budget for the next two years, however, could not be expanded.[51]

In 1889 the Ministry of the Interior began to tackle the harbor entrance problem in earnest. It was a long-held view that the harbor bar was a solid coral reef, but a diver examining the reef could find no solid barrier. Pipes were used to force water down to a depth of thirty feet. The conclusion was "the entire bar consisted of loose coral sand, with a few small and scattering pieces of coral. Previous estimates based on blasting through the coral are worthless. A new report will be made."[52]

A new program of dredging began in January 1889 and continued until winter storms put an end to the work in November. Some 24,000 cubic yards of material were removed. The solid coral base of the bar was uncovered. The harbormaster projected the cost of removing the material at the entrance to a depth of thirty feet at $50,000.[53]

The work on expanding wharf space also continued. The Esplanade was to be extended to the west to reach to the Pacific Mail dock at the foot of Fort Street, extending the seawall and filling the area with the dredge material. This was to be done "by building two wharves from the Pacific Mail dock, and excavating between them back to the line of the makai (seaward) side of the Esplanade, making the wharves 300 feet long and 100 feet wide."[54]

Two smaller wharves were constructed—one at the foot of Kekuanoa Street, 200 feet long and 80 feet wide, and one as a triangular extension of the Inter-Island Steam Navigation Company (IISN) wharf, which gave an additional length of 140 feet.

The Minister of the Interior reminded the legislature that the "prosperity of the Kingdom is greatly dependent upon our commerce. . . . It is wise to provide ships with every facility for the taking and discharge of cargo. The largest source of revenue is through the Port of Honolulu." To that end, the Bureau of Public Improvements had completed the building of a new, large wharf at the foot of Fort Street, with covered storage space for it and the adjacent Brewer Wharf, making it possible to protect cargoes and passengers in all weathers. That improvement was countered by the report that marine borer damage meant that the wooden piles of most other wharves would shortly have to be replaced.

Money had been saved in this two-year period by suspending dredging. The 1880 report had declared that in the judgment of the harbor captain, "It will not be necessary to dredge the harbor; a survey and soundings show but little change in the last two years." In 1882, the report stated: "There has been no dredging done in this period. . . . The Harbor Master is of the opinion that a good deal of work in this direction has now to be done."

The conflicting statements as to the condition of the harbor likely are due to the need to juggle expenditures in a rapidly changing political situation. Revenues, based upon an old system of customs revenue, were proving inadequate for the growing size of the government and the development of its economy. The harbormaster's report for 1882 obviously reflects conditions that were present in 1880, when the optimistic report was rendered. Now the conditions were presented in a different light.

> The water in our harbor is shoaling. We have three wharves for vessels drawing 20 feet. One is the Pacific Mail Steamship Co.'s wharf, the entire length, including the coal wharf. Another is the wharf opposite the Custom House, and the third is the end of the Market Wharf. At the Iwalani Wharf, the water is 14 feet and in one place opposite the drain to Fort Street the water has shoaled to 10 feet. On a line from the end of Market Wharf to the buoy in mid-harbor, we have a depth of 19 feet at half tide. . . . As the commerce of the port has increased, I have been sometimes put to my wits end to accommodate the shipping with the wharves.[55]

The reports seem to have accomplished a part of their purpose. In the next biennium, there is no report on the harbor facilities, only a reported increase in the amount spent for dredging and resurfacing of piers.

A new steam tug contracted for in 1884 arrived in February, 1885. The *Eleu* was a seventy-ton wooden vessel, "with powerful, compound engines of the latest pattern, with powerful steam pumps and fire apparatus for use in case of fire on shipboard, as well as a steam winch of the latest patent."[56]

The next major project recommended was the lengthening of five of the more heavily used wharves by some sixty feet each and the building of two new wharves, 300 feet long, "projecting from the PMSS Co. wharf, and one 180 feet long, between the *Kinau* [steamship] and IISN Co. wharves."[57] These ambitious extensions were scaled down radically in the appropriation of the legislature. The new wharves were not built and the old wharf extensions were changed. An extension was made to the Oceanic wharf to join it with the IISN wharf, "so that the outer line of the Oceanic wharf is continued to a junction with the IISN's wharf, making it long enough for the California mail steamer or two sailing vessels. An extension to Brewer's wharf gives a frontage of 100

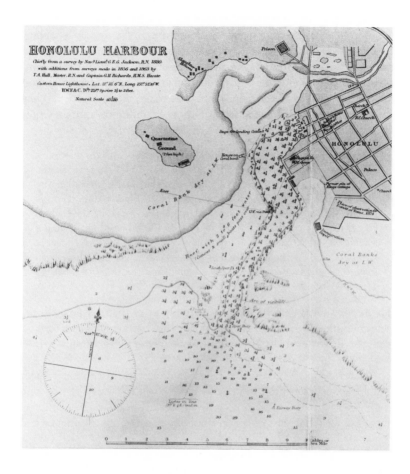

Figure 4.1 Honolulu Harbor, 1880, from a trigonometrical survey by the Hawaiian government.

feet on the end and 200 feet on the west side. This gives room for two large vessels where formerly [there] was only room for one."[58]

This 1886 report also faced the fact that dredging needed to be an ongoing operation. Although "a considerable amount of dredging [had] been done in the harbor . . . the deposits have been accumulating during the five months that have elapsed since, that it will be necessary

to go over the ground again within a year . . . strongly advise that
provision be made for dredging during at least three months each year."
The Bureau also recommended that three small piers at the foot of
Nuuanu Street and the Fish Market be removed and "two large ones
constructed in lieu thereof."

The average size of vessels using the harbor increased as more
transoceanic steamers called at Honolulu. In 1888 the Minister of the
Interior reported, "In the near future we will be in the direct line of
travel of a larger class of vessels than have been coming here, and it is
the better part of prudence to prepare for that time."[59]

The expansion of the harbor raised once again the question of title
to the lands surrounding the harbor. The government suddenly was
confronted with a claim from the Bishop Estate, the heir to much of the
crown land, to a majority of the harbor. The Minister of the Interior
summarized the issue in 1890:

> This question is one of the most vital importance to the whole country.
> The fact that there is, in good faith, an existing claim on the part of the
> Bishop estate, to the title of Honolulu Harbor, in opposition to the
> Government thereto, is probably not known to the general public, but
> such is the fact, and there are now on file in the Interior Department
> claims for damages for the unauthorized use thereof. This claim involves
> not only the title to the deep water of the harbor; but to the site occupied
> by the Pacific Mail Dock; the Likelike, the Kinau, the Kekuanaoa, the
> Inter-Island Steamship Co., the Brewer, the Old Custom House, and the
> New O. R. and L. wharves and should no longer remain in suspense.[60]

The Bishop Estate was claiming, in effect, the whole of the western
portion of the harbor. There was also a claim for the mudflats on the
western side of the harbor entrance, extending from the lighthouse at
the entrance to the shore adjoining the prison. The latter claim was
filed by Dowsett and Sumner and was considered somewhat dubious.
The attorney appointed to investigate argued that the title of Dowsett
and Sumner referred only to fishing rights.[61]

The source of the problem arose from the procedure used to divide
the land in the Great Mahele of 1848. The act provided that recipients
of land patents were required to pay a commutation fee to extinguish
government interest. The fee was set at one-third of the appraised value
of the land. In many cases, where the claimants were in occupation of
the land, the fee was not paid and the act provided no means of
enforcement. As the investigator reported, "a large number of them

took their chances as to what would happen, and failed to pay the Treasury the amount due the Government, while keeping all the proceeds of the land."[62] Mandatory registration laws were enacted in 1868, 1872, 1880, and 1888, again with no penalties, and many ignored the procedure. Some of those complying with the registration laws offered the unique solution of paying at the original 1848 appraised value, rather than the current value. The settlement reached with the Bishop Estate conceded a portion of the claim of 350 acres "of reef, channel, and harbor" described in the original Royal Patent. The Patent offered no further description of the boundaries, leaving ample room for differing views as to how much of the harbor was included.

The proposed improvements to the harbor and the need to fill in the shoreline with the dredged material from the harbor bar, "made prompt settlement of this disputed question a matter of urgent public necessity."[63] In the southeastern portion, the government surrendered about 100 acres of Kaakaukukui Reef (at the east side of the harbor entrance), a lot on the west end of the harbor known as Emmes Wharf lot, the site of the marine railway, the adjacent boat club, and the Immigration Depot wharf, approximately thirteen acres. This latter grant provided that "no wharf or obstruction of any kind could be built without the consent of the Hawaiian Government, so as to, in any way, obstruct or interfere with the navigation of the Harbor." All of the Kaakaukukui Reef adjoining the channel and harbor, extending along the southeast side of the main channel and extending to the outer reef, were included. In return the government received "all of the Harbor and Channel, except the Waikahalulu tract (already owned by the Government, purchased in 1825 from the Queen) and the site of the marine railway."[64] The government portion added up to approximately 157 acres of harbor and channel. Some of these issues remained unresolved for many years and it would be 1947 before the government would assume full title to these harbor lands.

The optimism generated by the Reciprocity Treaty extension in 1886 was quickly extinguished in 1891 when a Democratic administration removed the tariff on sugar. This free trade period lasted from 1891 to 1894. The loss of the subsidy produced a mild depression in Hawaii's sugar industry. The Minister's 1892 report, although saying, "It is evident, even to the most casual observer, that the wharfage facilities are wholly inadequate to meet the commercial demands," went on to agree that some of the proposed new slips could be postponed, "providing that those adjoining the Pacific Mail Wharf are made."[65] Funds remained chronically short over the next several years, limiting the ambitious plans.

Development of the entrance had to await the construction of a dredger that could operate in turbulent conditions of the harbor en-trance. A coral block wall had been constructed on Kaakaukukui Reef to receive the dredge material. The wall, 5.5 feet wide at the base and 3 feet wide at the top, was 3,272 feet long. This filled area became the basis for what is known as Sand Island.

By the time of the next report, 1894, the Hawaiian monarchy had been overthrown and replaced by a provisional government, awaiting the long hoped-for annexation. Work continued on the projects under-way.

The dredger, built in San Francisco at a cost of $49,000, was at work. Despite difficulties with mooring and rough water, the contractor found the bar to be "a succession of hummocks and pits . . . [these were removed, despite difficulties] so that when the work was finally ac-cepted, the depth of water in the channel was at no point less than that required by the contract [thirty feet]."[66] The first steamer to take advantage of the new depth was the liner *Oceanic*, which entered the harbor on 9 May 1893.

The three old wharves that had been recommended for removal in 1888 were replaced with two larger wharves and furnished with sheds. Another significant improvement was the construction of a pile-driver barge with a hammer lift of thirty-nine feet, enough to permit the construction of longer and heavier wharves.

Perhaps the most significant new element was the construction of a fumigating plant with a chamber large enough to accept carts with six trays for disinfecting clothing and other materials. The problem of plague and fever was a major one in Honolulu. Epidemics had always come to Hawaii aboard ships, and the speed of the new steam vessels removed the safety factor of the longer voyage of the sailing ship and thus the opportunity to identify infected persons.[67]

The uncertainty of conditions generated by the overthrow of the monarchy in 1894 was reflected in the financial insecurity of the government. The ambitious plans for harbor expansion had to be put into the context of that problem. Even with the list of improvements, the harbor "had hardly kept pace with the increased demand for wharf space." The plan to provide two wharves in a slip for large steamers at the foot of Richards Street (the site of old tow path into the harbor) could be divided, it was decided. "If this is too much to provide for in one period, half of the excavation can be made and a wharf built on one side." A public derrick capable of handling at least fifty tons was needed to facilitate repair and replacement of ships' boilers.[68]

In 1884, the news that the Oceanic Steamship Company steamers would replace the Pacific Mail Steamship Company's Honolulu–San Francisco service touched off a new demand for harbor improvements. The proposed Richards Street slip was undertaken in 1896, involving a dredging to thirty feet and the building of two large wharfs in the slip. The harbor was to be expanded by dredging and filling the area around the Quarantine Station, making the harbor a uniform depth of thirty feet.[69] In 1898, the work was still in progress, and hard coral rock had been encountered.

> The dredging of the Honolulu harbor and rockcutting to deepen the site at the Waikiki end of the Pacific Mail wharf, selected for the special needs of the big steamers of the Orient line, has been pushed, and

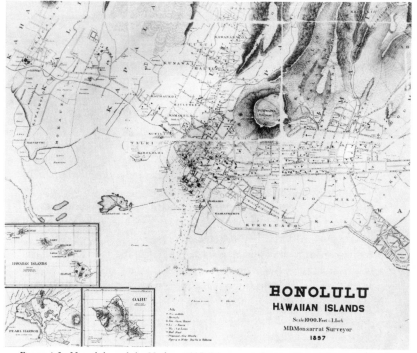

Figure 4.2 Honolulu and the Harbor, 1897 (Monsarratt Survey, Hawaii State Archives).

considerable progress has been made in filling in the Aala and other tracts adjacent to the Nuuanu stream.[70]

In 1899, the work was still being slowed by the difficult coral rock, but now the expectation was that the incoming American administration would turn all this work over to the Army Corps of Engineers. As Hawaii would discover, this often meant some rather drastic changes in local planning. The report of 1900 made the point: "Harbor deepening continues. . . . Additional to the work of our own dredger, a new one of different pattern has been constructed for the U.S. Government for completing coral excavation found necessary in the wharf facility formerly planned for the Pacific Lines, but now within the area of the Naval Reserve."[71] In effect, there were now new sets of concerns and needs to be addressed.

Notes

1. Alexander Starbuck, *A History of the American Whale Fishery From Its Earliest Inception to 1876* (Waltham, Mass.: The Author, 1878), p. 104.

2. Theodore Morgan, *Hawaii: A Century of Economic Change, 1776–1876* (Cambridge: Harvard University Press, 1948), pp. 142–144, argues that "opportunity costs" and sharp depletion of the whale stock raised the costs above more attractive investment opportunities.

3. *The Friend* (September 1872): 73.

4. Walter MacArthur, *Seaman's Contract, 1790–1918* (San Francisco: James H. Barry Co., 1919), p. 24. 1790 Act, *U.S. Statutes at Large,* I, 131–135, C.xxix.

5. *The Friend* (July 1844): 61.

6. *The Polynesian* (1 January 1848).

7. *Pacific Commercial Advertiser* (25 March 1857).

8. Ralph S. Kuykendall, *The Hawaiian Kingdom,* 3 vols. (Honolulu: University of Hawaii Press, 1957), vol. 2, 136–140; Morgan, *Century of Change,* pp. 142–153; Edward Beechert, *Working In Hawaii: A Labor History* (Honolulu: University of Hawaii Press, 1985), pp. 58–61.

9. Beechert, *Working In Hawaii,* p. 21–22.

10. Kuykendall, *Hawaiian Kingdom,* vol. 2, p. 138.

11. Robert Wyllie, Minister of Foreign Affairs, sent out a questionnaire to all of the missionary stations in 1846, asking a long list of questions as to the welfare of the Hawaiian commoner. The responses, published in his 1848 report to the legislature, revealed an interesting pattern of Hawaiians busy working at a wide variety of activities— supplying butter, milk, fire wood, vegetables, and the like to nearby urban areas, but primarily ignoring the foreign community. Nearly all of the respondents complained of the Hawaiian refusal to work for "reasonable wages." Hawaii State Archives, Kingdom of Hawaii, Department of Foreign Affairs, *Report, 1848,* "Answers to Questions: A Survey of the Missionaries of Hawaii," pp. 9, 14.

12. *The Friend* (December 1844).

13. See Robert C. Schmitt, *Historical Statistics of Hawaii* (Honolulu: University of Hawaii Press, 1977), p. 8; Beechert, *Working in Hawaii*, pp. 36–37.

14. *The Polynesian* (5 January 1850); Beechert, *Working in Hawaii*, p. 38.

15. *Pacific Commercial Advertiser* (17 July 1856).

16. Ibid.

17. Gavan Daws, *Honolulu* (Ph.D. dissertation, University of Hawaii, Honolulu), pp. 528–530. See *Thrum's Annual* (1906), pp. 55–62 for a short summary of the development of the system.

18. Harbormaster Files, 1857–1900, H. J. Holdsworth, Hawaii State Archives; Daws, *Honolulu*, p. 541. On the start of improvements, see *Minister of Finance Annual Report*, (1856), pp. 3ff.

19. Daws, *Honolulu*, p. 533.

20. Josephine Sullivan, *History of C. Brewer and Company* (Boston: Walton and Company, 1926), pp. 111–113.

21. William L. Worden, *Cargoes: Matson's First Century in the Pacific* (Honolulu: University of Hawaii Press, 1981), p. 57.

22. Jesse Conde, *Sugar Trains* (Felton, Calif.: Glenwood Publishers, 1973), p. 33; Mifflin Thomas, *Schooner From Windward: Two Centuries of Hawaiian Interisland Shipping* (Honolulu: University of Hawaii Press, 1983), p. 64.

23. "Notes on the History of Rice Culture in the Hawaiian Islands," *Thrum's Hawaiian Almanac* (1877), pp. 45–49; John Wesley Coulter and C. K. Chun, *Chinese Rice Farmers in Hawaii*, University of Hawaii Research Publication No. 16 (Honolulu, 1937).

24. Morgan, *Century of Change*, pp. 179–182.

25. John Haskell Kemble, "Pioneer Hawaiian Steamers, 1852–1877," *Hawaiian Historical Society Report No. 53* (1946), pp. 7–27, is a detailed report on these early ventures. The *Constitution* was clearly an unsatisfactory steamer. After the Hawaiian voyage, the engines were removed and the ship rebuilt as a bark in 1860.

26. Kemble, "Hawaiian Steamers," p. 13. See also, Thomas Thrum, "Brief History of the Steam Coasting Service of the Hawaiian Islands," *Thrum's Annual* (1889), p. 71.

27. Henry L. Sheldon, "Reminiscences of Honolulu Thirty-Five Years Ago," in *Saturday Press* (1881–1882); Kemble, "Hawaiian Steamers," p. 13; *The Polynesian* (2, 8 September 1854).

28. Daws, *Honolulu*, p. 541; Kuykendall, *Hawaiian Kingdom*, vol. 2, p. 14, cites several dispatches by Commissioner Gregg to this effect. Pauline King, (ed.), *The Diaries of David Lawrence Gregg, 1853–1858* (Honolulu: Hawaiian Historical Society, 1982), pp. 208–209.

29. Hawaii State Archives, Kingdom of Hawaii, *Laws of 1856*, p. 28.

30. Kuykendall, *Hawaiian Kingdom*, vol. 2, pp. 15, 166–167; Kemble, *Hawaiian Steamers*, pp. 16–17, 20–21; Daws, *Honolulu*, pp. 542–543.

31. U.S. Postmaster General, *Annual Report for 1866*, (Washington, D.C., 1866), pp. 67–70; John Kemble, "A Hundred Years of the Pacific Mail," *American Neptune*, 10 (April 1950): 123–143.

32. Charles D. Varigny, *Fourteen Years in the Sandwich Islands, 1855–1868* (Honolulu: University of Hawaii Press, 1981), pp. 242–243.

33. Kuykendall, *Hawaiian Kingdom*, vol. 2, p. 171; F. W. Hutchinson to Charles de Varigny, 7 September 1867, Hawaii State Archives, Interior Department Letter Book, vol. 8, p. 173; *Pacific Commercial Advertiser* (21 September 1867).

34. Daniel Smith to Wm. F. Allen, Collector of Customs, 10 October 1874, Collector of Customs Letter Book, Hawaii State Archives.

35. Kuykendall, *Hawaiian Kingdom*, vol. 2, p. 37; Jean I. Brookes, *International Rivalry in the Pacific* (Berkeley, University of California Press, 1941), p. 348.

36. King, *Diaries of David Lawrence Gregg*, pp. 62–63.

37. Ibid., p. 228.

38. Kuykendall, *Hawaiian Kingdom*, vol. 2, p. 41.

39. Jean I. Brookes, *International Rivalry in the Pacific Islands, 1800–1875* (Berkeley: University of California Press, 1941), p. 273.

40. The details of the treaty and the prolonged and complicated negotiations involved in both treaties is covered in detail in Kuykendall, *Hawaiian Kingdom*, vols. 2 and 3. Vol. 2, pp. 247–259 details the issue of Pearl Harbor in 1873 and the "secret" mission of General Schofield to survey Pearl Harbor and the withdrawal of the offer of that cession. Vol. 3, pp. 17–46 covers the final ratification. See also, Daws, *Honolulu*, pp. 602–612, 646–652 for the local political effects; Morgan, *Century of Change*, pp. 209–216 for some of the economic arguments for and against. Morgan concludes that "The arguments of both sides were right. The final affirmative vote showed that Congress felt political gain weighed heavier than commercial laws" p. 212. J. Laurence Laughlin and H. Parker Willis, *Reciprocity* (New York: Baker & Taylor, 1903) and Sylvester K. Stevens, *American Expansion in Hawaii, 1842–1898* (Harrisburg: Archives Publishing Co., 1945), pp. 46–140, cover the diplomatic and political problems involved.

41. Kuykendall, *Hawaiian Kingdom*, vol. 2, p. 248; Brookes, *International Rivalry*, p. 346, relates the survey to Samoa and Pago Pago harbor negotiations.

42. Schofield and Alexander to Secretary of War Belknap, 8 May 1873, U.S. Senate, 52nd Cong., 2nd Sess., Executive Documents, No. 77, pp. 150–154; *American Historical Review*, 30 (1925): 561–565.

43. William Taylor, *The Hawaiian Sugar Industry*, (Ph.D. dissertation, University of California, Berkeley, 1936), app. 1.

44. *Pacific Commercial Advertiser* (1, 8, September 1877).

45. Interior Department, Miscellaneous, Shipping, 16 April 1871, sketches of proposed wharf facilities, Hawaii State Archives.

46. Hawaii State Archives, Minister of Interior, Bureau of Public Improvements, *Biennial Report* (1880), p. 24.

47. Hawaii State Archives, Minister of Interior, *Biennial Report* (1882), p. 15.

48. Ibid., p. 16.

49. See, for example, Hawaii State Archives, Minister of Interior, Superintendent of Public Works, *Report to the Minister of the Interior*, 1860, 1862–68.

50. *Pacific Commercial Advertiser* (15 March 1879).

51. Hawaii State Archives, Letter to Capt. Jacob Brown, Interior Department, Letter Book No. 15, 11 February 1878, p. 6.

52. Hawaii State Archives, Minister of Interior, *Biennial Report* (1888), pp. 339–340.

53. Hawaii State Archives, Minister of Interior, *Biennial Report* (1890), p. 274.

54. Ibid., p. 273; *Biennial Report* (1880), p. 17; *Biennial Report* (1882), p. 21.

55. Hawaii State Archives, Minister of Interior, *Biennial Report* (1882), "Report of the Harbor Master," pp. 25–26.

56. Hawaii State Archives, Minister of Interior, *Biennial Report* (1886), p. 7–8.

57. Hawaii State Archives, Bureau of Public Improvements, *Biennial Report* (1886), p. xci.

58. Ibid., pp. 31, 33, 36.

59. Hawaii State Archives, Minister of Interior, *Biennial Report* (1888), p. 184.

60. Hawaii State Archives, Minister of Interior, *Biennial Report*, (1890), pp. 299–300.

61. Ibid., p. 300.

62. Hawaii State Archives, Minister of Interior, *Biennial Report* (1892), p. 301.

63. Ibid., p. 263.

64. Ibid.

65. Hawaii State Archives, *Biennial Report of the Minister of the Interior* (1892), p. 263.

66. Hawaii State Archives, Minister of Interior, "Report to the President and Members of the Executive and Advisory Councils of the Provisional Government of the Hawaiian Islands" (1894), p. 127.

67. Hawaii State Archives, Minister of Interior, *Report* (1895), p. 41. Epidemics had disastrous results in Hawaii. In 1848–49, one tenth of the population was lost to measles and whooping cough. Smallpox came in 1853, 1872, and 1881. *Thrum's Hawaiian Almanac* (1897), "Hawaiian Epidemics," pp. 95–101.

68. Hawaii State Archives, Minister of Interior, *Biennial Report, 1895*, pp. 49–54.

69. *Thrum's Hawaiian Almanac* (1896), p. 143; 1897, pp. 126–127. No reports of the Minister of Interior were issued in these years.

70. *Thrum's Hawaiian Almanac* (1898), p. 158.

71. Ibid. (1900), pp. 162–163.

5

The Territorial Port

Annexation

Annexation to the United States finally arrived, speeded along by the Spanish-American War. It was hoped that the struggle to expand and maintain the port could be turned over to the U.S. Army Corps of Engineers and the U.S. Navy, both of which were presumed to have much better access to money than the Hawaiian governments. The backing and filling that marked the period from the overthrow of Queen Liliuokalani in 1893 and the frustration of efforts to annex Hawaii during the Cleveland administration were resolved with the election of President McKinley. In March 1898, the Senate Committee on Foreign Relations passed a favorable resolution of annexation. The declaration of war on Spain came in April. An unusual motion in the form of a resolution of annexation was passed and signed on 7 July 1898. There probably was not the necessary two-thirds majority in favor of annexation by way of a treaty. The Newlands Resolution provided a way out by a simple majority.[1] Prior to annexation, the fleet of Commodore George Dewey refueled at Honolulu. The question of Hawaii's neutrality was immediately pushed aside and the refueling accomplished. Those in control of the revolutionary government were enthusiastic about the opportunity, as was the architect of the Philippine assault, Assistant Secretary of the Navy Theodore Roosevelt.[2]

Lorrin A. Thurston was assigned in Washington, D.C., by the Republic of Hawaii as Annexation Commissioner and Minister from 1893 to 1895 and again in 1897 as Commissioner, during which time he published in the *Washington Evening Star* a series of articles portraying the opponents of annexation as representing sugar beet growers and promoting Hawaii as a naval base against Japan. The question of annexation was related to the question of sugar. The passage of the

Figure 5.1 Panorama of the Harbor, 1902 (Hawaii State Archives).

McKinley Tariff (1891–1894) no doubt played a part in persuading the business community to take action for annexation. A near revolution in 1887 had resulted in the forcing of a constitution on King Kalakaua, which reduced him to a figurehead. The move by Queen Liliuokulani to revoke that constitution and replace it with one of her drafting and the passage of a lottery bill were the immediate events that precipitated the armed overthrow. The participation of the U.S. Minister, John L. Stevens and the marines from the U.S. warship *Boston*, were the factors that tipped the scales toward the revolutionists. [3]

The new territorial government consisted largely of the people who had made up the government of the Republic. The change from the independent, authoritarian style of government established after the overthrow of the monarchy to a territorial government operating under the U.S. Constitution was slow in coming. When a U.S. Senate subcommittee came to Hawaii to inquire into the state of affairs in the new territory, they were somewhat surprised to find a monarchical style of government prevailing. Although not surprised that there had not been a complete transition from nondemocratic forms in the short time since annexation, the committee was disturbed to find among the island leaders "a strong disposition to adhere with a strange degree of pertinacity to these old forms and practices which existed under the monarchy which were transmitted to the Republic, and are still apparent in the present government."[4]

The arrangement by which Hawaii became a territory maximized the tendency criticized by the Senate. On passage of the Newlands Resolution, the U.S. Government assumed immediate control of the office of Collector of the Customs and thus control of the port. The immediate reason was to put a stop to the importation of Chinese labor, which had risen to a high volume during the years of provisional government and the Republic. [5]

The local expectation was that the administration of the port of Honolulu would be turned over to the respective U.S. agencies. The superintendent of public works submitted a request to turn over all of the existing lighthouses to the U.S. Light-House Board. At the same time they requested that additional lighthouses be built. No action was taken on those requests. When he appeared before the Senate Committee in September, 1902, the Territorial Secretary complained that when in Washington the previous year, he had obtained the approval of the Light-House Board and the Secretary of the Treasury for the new facilities, but no action was forthcoming, despite requests made in 1900 and 1901. In both cases, the Rivers and Harbors appropriation omitted the Hawaii requests.[6]

The Harbor Lines: A Difficult Question

The slowness of the process of appropriations and the complex path through the Army Corps of Engineers, the Navy Department, and the various agencies having to do with rivers and harbors, not to mention the complexity of congressional committees, was a new experience for the power brokers of Hawaii. The establishment of harbor lines is a good illustration of the process.

A request by the Oahu Railway and Land Company (O.R.&L.) and various other owners of tide lands to clarify the ownership of tide lands raised the issue of harbor lines that had never been formally established. The letter explained that the owners and lessees of "large tracts of tide lands and harbor frontage in the harbor of Honolulu" desired to increase wharf space to handle the increasing volume of sugar. The letter was to "officially call attention to the over-crowded condition of the harbor . . . and the imperative need of immediate harbor improvements." The "lack of wharf room" had led to excessive demurrage charges.

> To meet this condition of things, the government, several years ago, made arrangements for extensive improvements in the harbor, but has delayed carrying them out largely through certain litigation pending between your petitioners and the local government. . . . The local government is now ready, regardless of the litigation, . . . to enlarge the harbor and the petitioners . . . are now ready to spend at least $250,000 upon wharf improvements. . . . But conditions have now changed through annexation and the local government no longer feels justified in fixing a permanent harbor line. . . . Enclosed you will find a memorandum of the improvements contemplated by the petitioners, as well as those by the local government.[7]

John A. Wilson, Chief of Engineers, responded, pointing out that the resolution of annexation had specified that all powers of the previous government should continue until Congress acted to create a governing mechanism. "I am therefore, of the opinion that the time [January, 1899] has not arrived for the War Department to undertake the establishment of harbor lines in this important harbor."[8] Subsequently, the Judge Advocate General ruled that because of the importance of the harbor, the Secretary of War could act under the authority of Section 12 of the River and Harbors Act of 19 September 1890.[9]

The sudden prospect of major improvements in the harbor stirred considerable activity on all sides. The long tradition of informal, power-broker style resolution of difficult issues would now be replaced by a formal proceeding. The territorial government found new energy to assert its claims to harbor lands that had lain dormant for many years. A particular bone of contention was the Sumner tract, which included what had become the Quarantine Station. The territorial government claimed that only the land portion of the Sumner claim was valid. The water portion was held to be a fishing right and did not carry permission to fill and build. The U.S. Army Board that convened to draw harbor lines highlighted the conflicting claims. They found on the one hand that the original grant specified "one portion of dry land connected with said fishing ground." This clearly did not include what had become known as Quarantine Island. On the other hand, the Hawaiian government "paid rent for Quarantine Island for thirty years and left its rights in abeyance for sixty years. Not long ago it asserted its rights to the Quarantine Island and its surrounding waters and now holds possession of Quarantine Island."[10]

The important issue, the board concluded, was the urgent need to expand wharf space in the harbor. "The harbor of Honolulu is small and the shipping much crowded. The present wharf room is entirely inadequate, and ships often have to wait two weeks or more before being able to unload or ship their cargos."

The establishment of harbor lines radically changed the picture for the northern portion of the harbor. The argument over the land and tidal waters of the Sumner tract was substantially altered by the establishment of the harbor lines. Before the lines were set, the Oahu Railway and Land Company had no harbor rights on the portions of the Sumner tract.

Before [they] could build its wharf or make any encroachment on the harbor, it was compelled to lease from the Hawaiian Government a strip of land or water one hundred feet wide, extending along the whole Southern front of [their] holdings. The new harbor lines put the O.R.&L. tract inside the 100 foot strip and along the land of the Company, thus giving them access to the harbor along all their Southern border.[11]

The board recommended transferring to the O.R.&L. the necessary rights in order to get on with the building of the proposed wharfs and slips. "The Hawaiian Government . . . have shown their desire to relinquish any benefits that may accrue to them from the Tracts A, B and D, in return for the wharves and slips they will receive in exchange."[12] The promise of extended litigation also spurred the board's desire to get on with the building.

A variety of proposals for harbor lines were soon submitted to the board, reflecting the intense local interest in shaping the harbor future. Hackfeld, the large sugar factoring firm, endorsed the O.R.&L. plan in March. In 1899, this plan was incorporated by John Mott-Smith, one of the leaders in the Republic and a former Minister to Washington, into a proposal to President Dole to extend the harbor on the north end, modifying the War Department plans to fully incorporate the O.R.&L. wharves. This would have, in effect, eliminated the contest over the Sumner and Dowsett tract claimed by the Republic.[13]

The hopes of local interests that the arrival of the federal government would bring quick improvements were soon dashed. The agreements on harbor lines reached in 1900 did not hold up. Even as agreements were being reached in Honolulu on the harbor lines and the Dillingham proposals of exchanging lands, doubts were being raised as to the wisdom of the proceedings. The Honolulu Special Harbor Board expressed strong reservations about the plans. Given the inadequacy of the harbor, the Special Harbor Board argued that "the permanent improvement of the harbor which shall provide for the future as well as present needs, is a work too seriously affecting our national and commercial needs and interests to be entrusted to local Government."[14] The Harbor Board especially argued that although the joint plan worked out with the territorial government was adequate, they objected that "transferring Government titles (now Federal titles) to tracts of land or water should be disapproved. The Dowsett and Sumner tracts referred to is [sic] very extensive, and covers the whole reef and water front of the sea side of the harbor, including the Quarantine Station."

The view from the private sector was more expansive. Ben Dillingham, always confident of his ability to work out solutions, wrote his manager in Honolulu from Washington, D.C. about the outcome of the proposed transfer. "On Iwilei: Still I believe our claim to the tide water land will hold in good, in which case we have no end of room for a coal yard, lumber yard, warehouses, etc."[15] Optimistic about the eventual demand for wharf space, Dillingham planned to move slowly. He advised his manager that although the Dearborn Steamship Company was counting on them to provide dock space for their steamers, he held off signing a firm agreement with them because, "the financial conditions were so appalling at the Islands I preferred to wait awhile. Before I get home I think I shall call them again and tell them that we shall look out for them and try to be prepared with a good dock for their second ship, and will do the best we can for their first one with our 400 foot wharf."[16]

Confusion continued to plague what seemed in 1899 to have been a simple matter of establishing the harbor lines. By 1904, the lines were in doubt. The quartermaster pointed out to the chief of engineers in January 1904 that the lines approved in May 1904 did not correspond with those being used by the territory and the U.S. Quarantine Station in improving facilities. The problem was that "the harbor line as established by the Secretary of War shoud have the necessary permanent stations or marks, so as to avoid any excuse for encroaching on the harbor lines as established."[17]

The modifications of 1900 were rejected in Washington, and agreements reached in 1902 and 1905 on the issue of exchange of land around the Sumner tract and the Quarantine Station were not formally adopted. The Secretary of War announced in 1909 that "The lines now proposed are satisfactory to all interests and coincide with the lines established in 1899, except where changed to accord with agreements involving land titles, and at a few other places where minor changes appear to advisable."[18]

Pearl Harbor

The attraction of Pearl Harbor as a naval base was no less after annexation than when David Gregg had first promoted the annexation of Hawaii to secure the harbor. The report of the secret investigation carried out by General Schofield in 1873 contained a prophetic statement on the issue. His concluding recommendation proved to be accurate: "In case it should become the policy of the Government of the United States to obtain possession of this harbor for naval purposes, jurisdiction over all the waters of Pearl River with the adjacent shores to the distance of four miles from any anchorage should be ceded to the United States by the Hawaiian Government.[19]

The Rivers and Harbors Act of 1899 appropriated money for the dredging of the harbor bar and entrance channel. Soon the issue of

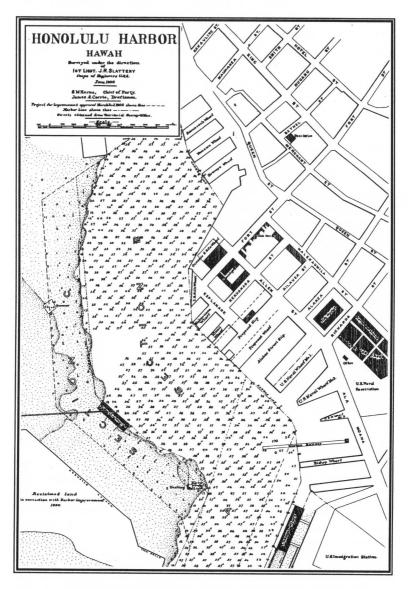

Figure 5.2 First Corps of Engineers Survey, 1906 (from U.S. Army Corps of Engineers *Annual Report* for 1906).

harbor lines arose. There were expansive commercial plans for Pearl Harbor, once it became accessible. The land surrounding Pearl Harbor was concentrated in the hands of two owners: the Campbell Estate and Dillingham. The annexation boom included the launching of no less than eight sugar plantations by Dillingham alone, including a major one on lands bordering both East and West Lochs of Pearl Harbor. Three large sugar plantations bordered the harbor and all expected to ship their sugar from that point. Dillingham controlled two of the largest, the Ewa Plantation Company and the Oahu Sugar Company.

Dillingham envisioned a major commercial port served exclusively by his railroad and piers on his lands. A major urban development was foreseen at Pearl City, where by 1900 he had already laid out town lots. His plans for the harbor were sweeping, if somewhat vague. "The opening of Pearl Harbor will, of course, concentrate a large amount of business there, especially the shipping of sugar, and perhaps it would be best for us to consider the erecting of coal bunkers, a coal wharf, machinery, etc, down there, although that point is not quite clear to me yet."[20] Dillingham moved to acquire control of the Dowsett Estate, which held land not only in the Honolulu Harbor area but in the Pearl Harbor (Puuloa) area as well. The Puuloa property was especially valuable.

> That property will pan out all right under our management. The U.S. Government will have to pay a good price for what they propose to take from Puuloa under condemnation proceedings. The carrying out of their proposed plan . . . will greatly increase the value of all surrounding property. I think we may do well to hold on a little longer to our Pearl City lots; the demand will be great for land there when the U.S. begins work in the harbor.[21]

The condemnation proceedings referred to were the initial moves by the U.S. Navy to begin the establishment of the naval base. The official letter advised that the navy wanted the area known as Walker Bay and a "plot of land on the waterfront and extending back sufficiently far, to place batteries for the defence of the channel. This land, . . . belongs to the Dowsett Estate."[22]

Dillingham went ahead to ensure the necessary facilities for his railroad. He negotiated a right of way with the Bishop Estate through the area of Halawa "to gain access to the entrance of Pearl Harbor . . . and also for necessary terminal facilities on the water front."[23]

The Honolulu Engineers Office moved methodically to acquire the needed land. Lieutenant Slattery reported that he had met with the owners of the west side of Pearl Harbor where the owners [Dillingham and Dowsett] "had laid out lots along the beach front of this property . . . they claim to regard the water front as exceedingly valuable and are anxious to save as much of it as possible."[24] He declined "to consider any price above actual cost. They have now agreed to sell at this figure." The total value of the lands of the three principal owners on the west side was set at $79,335 for 310 acres and 17 lots.

Pearl Harbor, like Honolulu Harbor, would become a source of contention between the Corps of Engineers and the U.S. Navy. Technically, Pearl Harbor was treated as a civilian works project in the Rivers and Harbors Appropriation Bill of 1899 and in subsequent years. In 1912 the Secretary of War approved harbor lines for Pearl Harbor because private land bordered the harbor. The Navy strongly disagreed, contending that "Pearl Harbor is a closed port intended solely for development as a Fleet Base." From 1913 until the lines were revoked by Secretary of War Woodring in 1936, the Corps of Engineers maintained their position. Congress appropriated no funds for further civil works projects in Pearl Harbor, thus effectively closing off the issue.[25]

A Fanciful Plan

If one of the principal landowners of the area between Honolulu and Pearl Harbor had been successful, Honolulu would have been relegated to the status of a suburb on the edge of the magnificent new city, Moanalua. Samuel Mills Damon was a banker and owner of a vast tract of land known as Moanalua Valley. His notion was to link Pearl Harbor, the Kalihi Basin, and Honolulu Harbor with a series of three canals. One channel from the sea into the Kalihi Basin would be 1,000 feet wide. One channel, 700 wide, would connect the basin with Pearl Harbor and a similar channel to the east would link up with Honolulu Harbor (figure 5.3). At the intersection of these canals would be a semicircular harbor with a radius of 4,000 feet, offering 17 slips, 250 feet wide and 1,300 feet long. The wharves were 400 feet wide at the entrance of the slip, tapering to 140 feet at the head, and opening onto an esplanade 200 feet wide. Pearl Harbor and Honolulu would be connected to this new city by a drive 500 feet wide in a straight line. A uniform, rectangular city with streets 100 feet wide was laid out behind the harbor. Damon refined the plan between 1895 and 1908. As the principal land owner, along with the Bishop Estate, of the territory involved, the plan was feasible from a land utilization point of view.

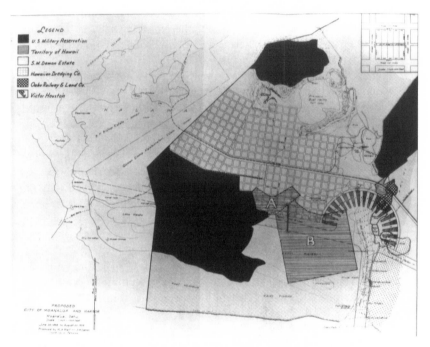

Figure 5.3   Moanalua Harbor Proposal (from *Sales Builder*, June 1940).

Damon countered all objections by pointing out the level terrain and
ease of dredging the canals, and claimed that there would be no silting
problems as there had always been with Honolulu Harbor. Needless to
say, Banker Damon and his cohort, surveyor and architect William A.
Wall, brought no maritime or engineering experience to this plan.[26]

Harbor Improvements, 1905–1920

The bureaucratic and political shuffling was finally overcome and
work began in earnest on the improvement of Honolulu Harbor. The
chief engineer summed up the history of the harbor improvements in a
short sentence: "The channel and harbor proper were dredged from
time to time by the monarchical, republican, and Territorial governments of Hawaii prior to July 1, 1904."[27] This work resulted in a harbor
with an entrance channel 200 feet wide and a depth of approximately
35 feet. The harbor featured a turn at the end of the entrance channel
that was "so sharp as to be somewhat difficult for large vessels to get

around." A majority of the harbor area had a depth of only 27 feet at low water, "making it impossible for the largest vessels calling at the port to enter the harbor when at all heavily laden. The narrowness of the harbor made turning difficult for all ships."

The first major project, approved in March 1905, called for the widening of the entrance to 400 feet and a depth of 35 feet to the lighthouse. There the lighthouse would be removed and the sharp turn into the harbor reduced by cutting off the point. The resulting harbor would be widened to 1,200 feet, with a depth of 35 feet overall.[28]

Two significant projects were commenced that would contribute both to the calmness of the harbor and its size. The fringing reef, of which the harbor is a part, extended seaward more than 1,500 feet on the west side of the entrance channel. During heavy seas, the turbulence extended into the harbor, washing past Quarantine Island from a northwesterly direction.[29]

Major steps were taken in 1906 to reclaim the area of the Quarantine Station, originally built in 1872. It was little more than a raised platform of sand and pilings to house the station, with walkways leading to the harbor edge wharf, where a concrete sea wall had been constructed. With the widening of the harbor, ample material was available to begin the reclamation of the low and submerged portions. The work was approximately three-fourths completed by the end of fiscal 1906. After a year of work and 158,214 cubic yards of fill, the island was found to be largely below grade and large cracks developed in the dredged material. A program of employing a scraper and dragging up material in front of the sea wall was put into effect.[30]

The goal of constructing a harbor of 1,200 feet in general width was slowly being accomplished. The widening of the harbor raised anew the problem of general maintenance. Serious shoaling in the entrance channel and at the Nuuanu (northern) end of the harbor necessitated maintenance dredging to obtain the goal of thirty-five feet of depth in the general harbor basin.

Problems of administration and execution were reflected in some of the early disputes between the Honolulu Engineers office and local interests, and, later, between the Corps of Engineers and the U.S. Navy. The local political community was long accustomed to doing things "their way." The attorney general of the territory explained to the Senate Investigating Committee that local traditions had always involved strong government. "There is a government in this Territory which is centralized to an extent unknown in the United States, and probably almost as much centralized as it was in France under Louis XIV."[31]

It came as no surprise to find the newly established Honolulu Engineers Office in conflict with one of the most powerful men and companies in the Territory—Benjamin Dillingham of the Oahu Railway and Land Company and his son, Walter, of the Hawaiian Dredging Company. The Hawaiian Dredging Company objected strongly when contract specifications were rigidly applied, particularly in regard to progress payments. In one particularly acrimonious squabble, Captain Otwell, the Honolulu Engineer, stopped the harbor dredging when the Hawaiian Dredging Company refused to remove a superintendent who was dumping the dredge spoil in defiance of the contract. Otwell had earlier permitted the contractor to deposit the fill where he chose. The dredge had, for example, deposited some 40,000 cubic yards on private land when the contract called for only 5,000. On being notified of his impending transfer to another duty station, Captain Otwell reduced the previous oral agreements to writing to guide his successor. The company refused to accept the new agreement, claiming that the United States was protected by the surety bond and that the work would be finally done as per the original contract. When Hawaiian Dredging refused to comply, Otwell ordered the removal and later, the arrest of the two supervisors of the dredges. The problem was that one of the supervisors was a member of the board of directors of the dredging company.[32]

Otwell not only removed the supervisors, he withheld progress payments on the contract, escalating the issue to a new level. In a complaint to the San Francisco Engineers Office, Walter Dillingham charged that they were owed some $107,000 in progress payments for the 60 percent completion of the contract. "Because of our refusal to agree in writing to perform outside of the contract, Capt. Otwell has endeavored to force us to meet his ideas by putting all manner of obstruction in our way. . . . He and his assistant have a grudge against our Mr. Lord. They ordered me to discharge Mr. Lord . . . and because I cannot discharge the vice-president and Director of the Company . . . we are declared in default.[33] As a leading figure in the political elite, Dillingham and his cohorts were accustomed to dictating their wishes to government officers. Strict adherence to contract terms was a novelty. The San Francisco office concluded that Otwell probably had been overly zealous in his office and should have merely withheld payments until the contract "was properly carried out . . . in any case, the United States was well protected."[34]

Some of the problems involved in carrying out the plans were located in Washington, D.C. The Quarantine Island work was held up because the Corps of Engineers in Washington had insufficient funds to send a cabled response to an urgent question from Honolulu. A dispute arose as to how close the dredge was to work in the vicinity of the Treasury Department wharf on Quarantine Island. The Engineer's Office ordered the dredge to work to within fifteen feet of the wharf being built. The Treasury Department contractor had ordered the dredge to remain forty feet away, threatening a law suit if the piers were damaged. The Treasury Department in Washington was persuaded to accept the fifteen-foot figure. The Honolulu office had to be notified by mail "because the Cable Company is refusing to accept telegrams unless paid by the sender." The office budgets were so low that the notification had to proceed by mail, thus arriving after the dredge had moved, making the issue moot.[35]

Another part of the problem can be laid to the fact that Hawaiian Dredging was the sole firm in Hawaii. It was difficult to get reliable bids from the mainland, particularly if the work involved any serious complications. In 1912 bids were invited to correct shoaling in the outer entrance channel to Honolulu Harbor. No bids were received for this obviously difficult job in rough waters.[36] The Chief of Engineers recommended that the next appropriation include an additional sum of $100,000. "The United States will be in a position to buy or build a plant and do their own work if a satisfactory price is not bid for dredging."

A persistent problem in the development of the port was the fixing of the responsibility for expansion, maintenance, and harbor operation. Historically weak in funding, the territorial government persistently sought to put projects into the hands of the Honolulu District Engineer to save money. An early example of that situation was the request by the harbor commissioners to have the old Quarantine Wharf area removed from Sand Island as part of the Section C work of the Corps of Engineers. The Washington headquarters emphasized that dredging inside "duly established lines with River and Harbor improvement funds is specifically prohibited."[37]

Ambitious plans to expand the harbor led to an examination of the possibility of using the Kalihi Channel and Basin to connect with Honolulu Harbor. This would both provide a second entrance to the

harbor and greatly expand its area. The idea stemmed from the settlement of the Quarantine Island title disputes. In the settlement,
O.R.&L. was granted rights to a channel, known as the Reserved
Channel, which was to be 600 feet wide. This area, the partially
submerged land separating Quarantine Island from the mainland, was
ceded by O.R.&L. to the United States, "to be used only as a navigable
channel."[38] In return for the cession, O.R.&L. was to have full and
unobstructed wharfage privileges on its northern portion.

When the Kalihi Channel Survey was proposed in 1913, the District
Engineer said, "It does not appear that the harbor of Honolulu is at
present crowded or congested" or that wharf space was inadequate. Yet
the *Pacific Commercial Advertiser* in December 1914 featured stories on
the "congested harbor."

The survey arose from the fact that Honolulu Harbor wharf space
was almost exhausted. "Outside of Sand Island, the entire harbor front
is now occupied by wharves, with the exception of about 800 feet just
north of the 'Reserved Channel.' Further work under the present
(1905) project will not increase the harbor frontage, but is necessary to
render the harbor safe and convenient for the maneuvering of vessels."[39]

The level of activity in the harbor had increased significantly since
1905, when the project began. Vessel tonnage had increased from
665,000 to almost 1.9 million tons, and with the impending opening of
the Panama Canal, the increase could be expected to continue. The
harbor could not "be enlarged toward the east. It can only be enlarged
by extending it toward Kalihi." A further attraction to working in the
Kalihi direction was that rail facilities, factories, and oil storage tanks
had been constructed in that area. More important, at the Kalihi end
of the Reserved Channel was a basin "about the size of Honolulu
Harbor, known as 'Kapalama Basin.'" Originally the depth of the basin
was twenty-five or thirty feet. It had in the past twenty years of
development silted up to a depth of only eight to ten feet. That, it was
argued, would make for easy dredging at minimum cost. The requested
survey was made and the project was authorized in 1915.[40]

To match these basic harbor improvements, the Territorial Board of
Harbor Commissioners was carrying on an ambitious program of improvements. The board had been created in 1911 and removed the
jurisdiction of the harbor from the Superintendent of Public Works to
the appointed board, where, it was hoped, the harbor would receive
more careful and direct attention. Before gaining territorial status,

questions of jurisdiction and responsibility under the Minister of Interior were not handled adequately, and the Territorial Public Works Office was not effective.[41]

An early action by the new board was to purchase the site of the old marine railway that had sunk badly and become unusable. The board also began to acquire other private sites as funds and the opportunity arose, looking toward the eventual acquisition of private wharves and waterfront property by the territory. Related to the acquisitions was the plan to construct a belt railroad around the harbor, connecting with the O.R.&L. system from Nuuanu Stream, along Queen Street and Ala Moana to the Channel Wharf.[42]

Long-neglected maintenance work on pier substructures was also put into motion. A small increase in port revenues in 1915 due to the opening of the Panama Canal was seen as a harbinger of future increases in traffic and hence a need for an expansion of harbor facilities. In anticipation, the board undertook an extensive revision in port regulations and fees. That optimism faltered somewhat in the ensuing two years. World War I, frequent landslides in the Panama Canal, and the withdrawal of the Pacific Mail Steamship Company from Hawaii resulted in a decline in harbor usage. Ship traffic continued to decline slowly over the next several years.

Enthusiasm did not decline. The appropriation for the Kalihi Channel was hailed as insuring "practically unlimited" development and was a project that could continue on a unit by unit basis, "as the necessary funds are made available. When completed [the project] will provide a beautiful, landlocked harbor, with ample berthing and storage facilities to take care of Honolulu growth for years to come."[43]

The old marine railway was removed. Made obsolete by age and the building of a floating drydock by the Inter-Island Steam Navigation Company, the space was devoted to a new slip. The board arranged a transfer of a strip of land next to the old marine railway and the Immigration Station and constructed the Channel Wharf, dedicated to the use of lumber schooners that arrived in a near continuous stream from the Pacific coast. Wooden pilings were being replaced gradually with concrete piers to end the problem of perennial replacement.

In an important move to free up space in the harbor, the sampan fishing fleet was moved from piers 15 and 16 to the newly refurbished Kewalo Basin to the east of the harbor. This reduced congestion in the harbor entrance and freed up two piers for development.[44] Pier 15 was designated as a 900-foot lumber pier, as it was better located for land transportation than the earlier lumber pier at the Channel Wharf. Piers 8, 9, and 10 were reconstructed as first-class passenger and freight piers, able to handle the largest vessels calling at Honolulu.

A notable improvement was the placing of an oil fuel line at pier 16 to service the sharp increase in oil-burning vessels. This in turn led to a new problem—oil spills in the harbor. The extent of the oil spills created a fire hazard, and debris and flotsam, also were reaching alarming proportions.

Symptoms of an old Hawaii problem reappeared. The Hawaiian economy, always narrowly based, was subject to sharp fluctuations in response to events and conditions occurring on the mainland. Ship traffic continued to fluctuate, frequently showing declines. By 1921, war-time inflation and the post-war depression had combined to create serious problems for the Harbor Commission. They summed up the situation: "There has been a marked decrease of vessels calling at Honolulu during the year, particularly noticeable during the first six months (1921), due to the fact that many vessels of the U.S. Shipping Board were laid up at the termination of the War, and also a decrease in Trans-Pacific vessels calling for fuel and supplies."[45]

A remedy was proposed to attract new trade: The creation of the Aloha Tower complex, built around the newly reconstructed piers, 8, 9, 10, and a proposed pier 11. The complex would occupy nearly six acres. A central feature of the new passenger-freight terminal would be the Aloha Tower, some 200 feet tall. "The proposed tower will not only be ornamental, but will be a utility as well, as it is planned to have offices for the various departments requiring them on the waterfront and on the top will be provided a pilot lookout."[46]

Hawaii, as always, was looking for a providential ship of change to come over the horizon and drop anchor in the harbor.

Notes

1. Lorrin A. Thurston, Memoirs of the Hawaiian Revolution, Andrew Farrell (ed.) (Honolulu: Pacific Commercial Advertiser Press, 1936) pp. 571–572.

2. Thurston, Memoirs, p. 574.

3. See Ralph S. Kuykendall, The Hawaiian Kingdom (Honolulu: University of Hawaii Press, 1967), vol. 3, pp. 568–570, 582–590, for the details of events such as the Lottery Bill and Minister Stevens' actions. It was the landing of troops and Stevens' statements that persuaded Cleveland to reject the offer of annexation; pp. 620–622.

4. U.S. Senate, Subcommittee on Pacific Islands and Porto Rico, Report on General Conditions in Hawaii, 3 vols., (1902) vol. 1, p. 8.

5. Edward Beechert, Working In Hawaii: A Labor History (Honolulu University of

Hawaii Press, 1985), pp. 117–118. The U.S. Customs Officer turned away a group of Hawaii Chinese residents with re-entry permits issued by the Republic, in December, 1898, citing the Chinese exclusion laws of the United States.

6. U.S. Senate, *Report on General Conditions*, Vol. 2, pp. 14–15. The amounts requested totaled $49,000.

7. W. A. Kinney, attorney to Henry S. Pritchett, Superintendent of U.S. Coast and Geodetic Survey, 28 January 1899, National Archives, Record Group 77, General Correspondence, 1894–1923, No. 29777/1, Office of Chief Engineer (hereafter, RG 77, OCE).

8. John A. Wilson, Chief, OCE to Asst. Ajd. General, San Francisco, Honolulu Harbor Board, 18 April 1899, RG 77, OCE, No. 29777/6.

9. Report of Honolulu Harbor Board, San Francisco, 6 February 1899, RG 77, OCE.

10. Proceedings Of A Board of Officers Convened At Honolulu. Special Order No. 28, 8 February 1900, RG 77, OCE, No. 29777/15.

11. Ibid., p. 4.

12. Ibid., p. 5.

13. President S. B. Dole to Harbor Board, 4 December 1899, RG 77, OCE, No. 29777/18. Hackfeld endorsement, 7 March 1899, No. 29777/19. Chamber of Commerce endorsement of O.R.&L., 14 March 1899, No. 29777/20.

14. Special Agency, Honolulu, H. M. Sewall to Secretary of State, 21 December 1899, RG 77, OCE, No. 29777/14.

15. Ben. Dillingham to Elmer Paxton, 24 May 1900, Oahu Railway and Land Co., Dillingham Papers, Box 1, Honolulu, Bernice P. Bishop Museum.

16. *Ibid.* The enthusiasm generated by annexation led to a temporary boom in the Hawaiian economy, a boom that soon collapsed and produced a small depression by 1902. See U.S. Bureau of Labor, *Report of Commissioner of Labor on Hawaii 1902*, (Washington, D.C., 1903).

17. Quartermaster, Honolulu, to Chief of Engineers, U.S.A., 22 January 1904, RG 77, OCE, NO. 29777/40.

18. Secretary of War to Chief Engineer, U.S.A., 21 July 1909, RG 77, OCE, No. 29777/57.

19. J. M. Schofield & B. S. Alexander to Wm. W. Belknap, May 8, 1873, Confidential Report on Pearl River Survey to the Secretary of War, U.S. Senate, 52d Cong., 2d Sess. Exec. Doc. No. 77, pp. 150–154, reprinted in *American Historical Review* 30(3) (1925): 564.

20. B.F.D. to Elmer Paxton, 24 May 1900, Dillingham Papers.

21. B.F.D. to Paxton, 27 April 1900, Dillingham Papers.

22. J. L. Emory, Commandant, U.S. Navy, U.S. Naval Coal Depot, Honolulu, 18 February 1900, Dillingham Papers.

23. O.R.&L. Co. to Bishop Estate Trustees, 19 June 1901, Dillingham Papers, box 3.

24. Lt. J. R. Slattery to Col. W. H. Heur, San Francisco, 1 August 1904, RG 77, OCE, No. 50640/13.

25. Erwin N. Thompson, *Pacific Ocean Engineers: History of the Army Corps of Engineers in the Pacific, 1905–1980* (Honolulu: U.S. Army Corps of Engineers, Pacific Ocean Division, 1985), pp. 45–46.

26. "Mudhooks or Moorings: Safe Harbor for Ships From the Sea," *Sales Builder,* 13(6) (June 1940): 11–14.

27. U.S. Army Corps of Engineers, *Annual Report of the Chief of Engineers, 1906,* Part 1, p. 788, hereafter Corp of Engineer's Report.

28. Corps of Engineers, *Report* (1905), Pt. 2, p. 2564.

29. Corps of Engineers, *Report* (1906), Pt. 1, pp. 788–789; Map of 1906 work, Part 2, p. 2050, reclaimed area.

30. Corps of Engineers, *Report* (1907), Pt. 1, p. 804; Pt. 3, p. 2236. The Chief Engineer estimated the final cost of the projects to be $982,832. The contract was awarded to San Francisco Bridge Co., p. 2234.

31. U.S. Senate, *Report on General Conditions,* 1902, vol. 1, p. 10.

32. Lt. Riddle, San Francisco Engineer's Office to Chief of Engineers, Washington, D.C., 8 September, 1980, RG 77, OCE, No. 64183/65.

33. Walter Dillingham to Capt. John Hackett, San Francisco Army Engineer's Office, 25 August 1908, Dillingham Papers, Hawaiian Dredging Co. Files, folder 44.

34. Lt. Col. Riddle, 8 September 1908, RG 77, OCE, No. 64183/65.

35. 15 May 1906, RG 77, OCE, No. 38027/53. A similar problem arose in 1911, when authorization to Otwell to accept a bid had to be sent by mail because the telegraph company "refused to handle the message unless the charges therefore were paid in advance." 11 October 1911, No. 64183/11.

36. Corps of Engineers *Annual Report* (1913), Pt. 1, p. 1409.

37. Chief Engineer to Honolulu District Office, 16 August 1916, RG 77, OCE, NO. 38027/156.

38. District Engineer Officer Major W. P. Wooten to Chief of Engineers, 5 June 1913, RG 77, OCE, No. 38027/103.

39. No. 38027/103, p. 2.

40. Reserved Channel Improvement, U.S. House of Representatives, 64th Cong., 1st Sess., House Document No. 392 (1915) p. 6. The channel was to be 35 feet deep, 800 feet wide and 1,000 feet long.

41. From 1850 to 1900, the Minister of Interior was responsible for the Harbor. The Superintendent of Public Works assumed the sole responsibility in 1900. Territory of Hawaii, *Session Laws,* 1911, Act 163. The five member board was appointed by the governor and confirmed by the Territorial Senate.

42. Harbor Commissioners, *Biennial Report,* 1914–1915, p. 3.

43. Harbor Commissioners, *Biennial Report,* 1919–1920, p. 12.

44. Harbor Commissioners, *Biennial Report,* 1918–1919, p. 54.

45. Harbor Commissioners, *Biennial Report,* 1921–1922, p. 54.

46. Harbor Commissioners, *Biennial Report,* 1922–1923, pp. 10–11.

6

The Quiet Years

The Hawaiian Economy

There were very different perceptions of the needs of Honolulu Harbor. Local business tended to the view that the harbor was congested and in constant need of expansion, hoping that business would somehow increase in the immediate future. Delays in loading and unloading cargo tended to be blamed on lack of sufficient wharf space, rather than on the distribution and transportation systems involved. The Corps of Engineers saw a different harbor—one that was only a part of a Pacific network, responding to changes in commerce and shipping on a national scale.

Persuading Congress to allocate Rivers and Harbors monies among the many competing interests was no easy task. In answer to repeated requests for expansion of the Corps' projects in Honolulu Harbor, the Chief Engineer reported to the Secretary of War in 1920 that beyond the existing (1905) project, "improvement by the U.S. of Honolulu Harbor is not deemed advisable at the present time." Widening the entrance channel to 400 feet and a depth of 35 feet in both the channel and the harbor was estimated to cost $2,300,000 in federal funds. Since 1900, the territory had expended $2,656,162 for sea walls, wharves, bouys, and dredging slips.[1]

The completion of the Aloha Tower complex of piers in 1926 brought an end to the development of the old harbor for many years to come. The harbor commissioners reported in 1924 that they "had developed Honolulu Harbor facilities as far as it is practical to do so." If there were to be "adequate facilities for the increasing shipping that is bound to come, the development of Kapalama Basin is the only means of providing on a large scale for this increase."[2]

Looking toward the future, the harbor commissioners had moved to eliminate the conflicting claims to the basin by negotiating a settlement with the Bishop Estate, which gave the board a clear title to the area. The basin encompassed a number of ancient fish ponds, the title to which conflicted with the modern harbor use.

The report of the harbormaster for 1925 was typical of the forward-looking perspective. The tonnage increase for the year of a little over 300,000 tons having "been about an average annual increase during the last ten years," he drew an optimistic picture of the future:

> With settled conditions and future development of the Orient, it is logical to presume that the shipping in the Transpacific trade will increase correspondingly, and the geographical position of Honolulu, will naturally make it a port of call for the majority of vessels engaged in that trade. Under these conditions it does not need an ultra optimist to predict that Honolulu Harbor will be too small take care of the shipping.[3]

Two elements common to most predictions of the future stand out in this estimate. First, change in the outside world is ruled out and a tranquility or "normality" is assumed. Second, under the conditions of sailing ships and the need for water and provisions, Hawaii was indeed a Pacific centerpoint. The advent of steam, and more particularly, the advent of oil-fueled ships, put more emphasis on the economies of great circle navigation. Hawaii lies far to the south of such routes to Asia.

The realities of the Hawaiian economy dictated a somewhat different pattern for the port. As had been the case in the early period of Hawaiian history, there tended to be a concentration of political and economic power in a few hands. The sparse nature of the Hawaiian hinterland left few meaningful economic resources for development. The whaling industry had promoted a few firms to considerable size and importance in Honolulu. The slow development of sugar in the nineteenth century followed a pattern of steady absorption of the plantations as Honolulu mercantile firms assumed control and direction of the industry.

By the 1920s, the pattern had been clearly established. A large export economy was based upon sugar and pineapple and the importing of almost all merchandise needs through these same firms. The plantation workers—the bulk of the population—had a comparatively low level of consumption. Although it was frequently said that Hawaii's agricultural workers were paid more than such workers elsewhere, the fact remains that the level of consumer consumption was far below

United States' working class standards. This meant that the importation of consumer goods was at a lower level than one might have expected from the population size.[4]

Table 6.1 illustrates clearly the small size of the Hawaiian population and the dominance of its agricultural produce. Once the sugar industry came under the U.S. bounty system in 1876, Hawaii's exports exceeded its imports by steadily widening margins. Sugar and molasses were generally 90 percent or more of the exports. Horses, mules, vehicles, and agricultural supplies were the major imports. Following World War II, the steady growth of the tourist industry was reflected in the rise in imports and consumer goods, building supplies, and food items. The volume of sugar, if not its value, remained steady at one million tons per year. Fixed by the various sugar acts since 1936, Hawaii has met the quota by intense use of chemicals and fertilizers and mechanization of the agricultural processes. Facilities for bulk shipping of sugar, begun in 1941 and completed in 1954, reduced the number of interisland ships, as well as the number shipping from Honolulu.

The narrow economic base, matched by a narrow political base almost identical in composition, had a major effect on the business of the port and thus on its development. The impact of this circumstance exacted a heavy toll on Hawaiian business. Gavan Daws described it exactly:

> The Big Five controlled 75 percent of the sugar crop by 1910 and 96 percent by 1933. By a kind of inevitable extension they came to control as well every business associated with sugar; banking; insurance; utilities; wholesale and retail merchandising; shipping between the islands and between the islands and California. The agencies, established in the nineteenth century to serve the plantations, had become the tail that wagged the dog.[5]

Three conditions always underlay Hawaii's economic problems: (1) the interlocking control and ownershiip between Matson and its major customers; (2) the absence of "arm's length" dealings with Matson and its four principal owners on payments for agency, stevedoring, and terminal services; and (3) the restraint on newcomers seeking to enter the shipping trade because of an inability to have equality of access to return cargoes.[6]

Antitrust legislation in the United States seems to have had very little impact on the Hawaiian economy. Interlocking directorates specifically were forbidden by the Clayton Act of 1914. By 1959, four of

Table 6.1. The Trade of Hawaii, 1840–1980, Five-Year Averages (In thousands of dollars).

Year	Imports	Exports	Exports to U.S.
1840–44	179.0	—	—
1845–49	650.8	271.2	—
1850–54	1,304.4	462.2	—
1855–59	1,257.6	509.2	—
1860–64	1,174.0	905.6	—
1865–69	1,974.6	1,842.6	—
1870–74	1,323.0	1,848.4	—
1875–79	2,567.4	2,791.6	—
1880–84	4,691.8	5,572.6	27,881.0
1885–89	4,726.8	10,927.4	10,797.8
1890–94	6,029.0	10,284.2	10,210.0
1895–99	10,485.6	15,997.4	15,917.6
1900–04	13,417.0[a]	14,657.0[a]	23,732.0
1905–09	18,054.4	35,033.6	34,828.0
1910–14	30,421.8	45,788.6	45,171.8
1915–19	50,537.2	71,861.4	69,946.5
1920–24	75,030.8	111,217.2	109,408.4
1925–29	87,980.0	108,838.6	106,709.4
1930–34	74,815.0	95,177.0	93,990.4
1935–39	101,976.8	114,526.0	112,827.0
1940–44	171,190.8	104,431.4	101,978.6
1945–49	287,660.0[b]	150,841.0[b]	147,717.3
1950–54	369,740.0	246,540	241,660.0
1955–59	453,560.0	273,050.0	256,540.0
1960–64	582,580.0	300,500.0	271,820.0
1965–69	930,860.0	360,360.0	316,680.0
1970–74	1,468,200.0	520,080.0	450,900.0

Source: Calculated from Schmitt: *Historical Statistics of Hawaii,* Tables 21.2, 21.3.
a. Data for three years only.
b. Data for two years only.

the Big Five firms, American Factors, Ltd., Castle and Cooke, Inc., Alexander and Baldwin, Ltd., and C. Brewer and Company, Ltd., owned 73.58 percent of Matson stock. Nine directors of these factors held 105 positions in sixty-five companies besides Matson. "Thus most of Matson's direct interlocking [was] through its relationship with its four principal owners."[7]

The Matson Line

In 1882, William Matson took the schooner *Emma Claudine* to Hilo on a joint venture voyage. Hilo provided a unique opportunity for Matson in that the other major islands were reasonably well served by the Inter-Island line; Hilo was not. A lack of roads and railroads meant that sugar cargoes could not be consolidated in Hilo for larger ships.

Captain William Matson was associated with the Spreckels sugar family in his early days in San Francisco. It was favorable charter arrangements for Spreckels' ships that launched Matson on his rapid rise to wealth and power in the shipping business. Spreckels' entrance into the Hawaiian market after the Reciprocity Treaty of 1876 brought large amounts of capital and enabled Spreckels to quickly assume a position of dominance in both Hawaiian politics and sugar production.[8]

From this beginning, Matson brought a variety of goods to Hilo and took out sugar, hides, and passengers.[9] By 1887, the line had four ships in the trade. In 1902 the line included its first steamer, the *Enterprise.*[10]

The concentrated sugar-pineapple base of the Hawaiian economy resulted in a single dominant shipper to and from the islands. By 1907, Matson, already a major ship operator and prominent in the oil industry of California, moved his center of operations from Hilo to Honolulu. To accomplish this he switched his business from W. G. Irwin & Company to Castle and Cooke. Affiliation with the largest sugar factor and with the operators of two of the largest sugar plantations, gave Matson a large piece of the sugar hauling business. Matson Navigation quickly came to be controlled by the sugar factors who supplied the cargo for Matson ships.

In 1911, Matson became the first shipper to fit tanks in his ships to carry molasses. For many years, molasses was a problem product, because there was no practical way to ship it. When fuel oil began to be imported into the islands to replace coal, Matson moved into this business by converting several sailing ships to oil tankers. Vessels carried oil to the Islands, cleaned the tanks with steam and loaded molasses for cattle food or distilleries on the mainland.[11]

Emerging from World War I as the dominant carrier between Hawaii and the Pacific coast, Matson Navigation moved to consolidate its hold on shipping. Matson freighters served not only Honolulu but each of the other island ports, Hilo, Kahalui, Port Allen, and Nawiliwili, as well as some private landings.

The growing tourist trade of the 1920s was seen by Matson as a lucrative business. Not only did they put new ships into service, but construction was begun in 1925 on the first luxury hotel, the Royal Hawaiian.[12]

The developing tourist industry elevated an old Hawaii tradition to a new level. The arrival of ships in the harbor had, from the earliest days, been a signal for Honolulu people to swarm to the harbor for the latest news, supplies, or just to see the new arrivals. When regular steamer service began in the 1870s, Boat Days became established events. Ships were greeted with crowds, bands, lei sellers, newspaper reporters, photographers, friends and relatives, and the merely curious. With the advent of Matson's weekly sailings, Boat Day became an elaborate ceremony and brought a significant number of people to the central harbor.

When the ship rounded Diamond Head, it was met by small boats bringing out hotel representatives and all those who had purchased tickets to join the ship on its entry. The Royal Hawaiian Band, accompanied by dancers, marked the arrival and departure of each liner. Boys surrounded the ships, diving for coins thrown by the passengers. Lei sellers lined the dock with their fragrant offerings. Taxis crowded the narrow streets leading to the Esplanade. World War II put an end to these festive occasions. Although resumed after the war, the increasing number of air travelers diminished the importance of the traditional Boat Day.[13]

The increasing size of Matson's passenger liners began to make outer island calls impractical. Matson turned to the Inter-Island Steam Navigation Company in 1925 to round out its passenger service to the outer islands. Inter-Island Steam Navigation Company had been the principal interisland carrier since its formation in 1883 through the merger of three interisland shipping companies. Schooners and small steamers had long picked up the sugar of isolated Hamakua plantations from landings and off-shore lighters.[14] Matson had already made serious inroads into the freight business of Inter-Island, as had an independent meat company that successfully shipped its cattle in its own vessels. Inter-Island was faced with the problem of replacing its aging fleet and

was generally in a weakened position. The principal sugar and pineapple companies began to shift shipment of their rapidly expanding
production to Matson.

The "merger" was accomplished Hawaiian style. Inter-Island simply
put out a new stock issue of $1.25 million and sold the issue to Matson
Navigation. Major shareholders in Matson already owned large
amounts of Inter-Island stock. The board of directors was enlarged from
nine to eleven. Two veteran directors resigned and four new directors
from the four principal Matson owners were elected to the board. By 1
January 1926, Matson controlled virtually all of the shipping to and
from Hawaii and the outer islands.[15]

The economic structure of Hawaii was moving rapidly to that awesome level of concentration so often remarked. The entire sugar crop of
Hawaii for 1919 was carried in Matson ships. Of course, that gave
Matson the advantage on incoming cargo; in 1920, 75 percent of the
incoming cargo, almost one million tons, was carried in Matson
ships.[16]

One of the principal elements in maintaining the tight control over
the Hawaiian economy was the fact that there was little cargo going
east except sugar and pineapples. Ships plying between the mainland
and Hawaii faced an expensive eastward voyage largely empty. The
sugar industry owned the California and Hawaiian Sugar Refinery in
California and a ship to carry the sugar. Four Matson ships completed
the fleet necessary to carry all of the sugar and pineapples leaving
Hawaii. Military cargoes going east, personal effects and the like made
up the bulk of available cargoes.[17] Considering that more than 90
percent of Hawaiian consumer goods is imported from the U.S. mainland and more than half of everything produced in Hawaii is shipped to
the mainland, the lack of competition takes on a major significance.
The demand for commodities essential for daily activities varies only
slightly with price increases related to freight charges. Consequently,
Hawaii faces a constantly increasing cost of living, second in the
United States only to Fairbanks, Alaska. On the other hand, the sales
of Hawaii's principal products, sugar and pineapple, show a marked
sensitivity to increasing prices.[18]

Although William Matson died in 1917, his company continued to
scoop up all opposition. The Los Angeles Steamship Company
(LASSCO) entered the Hawaii trade in 1922, after successfully running ships between San Francisco and Los Angeles. Backed in part by
the Chandler family of the *Los Angeles Times*, the new competitor

Figure 6.1 Honolulu Harbor (west view), 1930. (Hawaii State Archives).

offered worrisome competition to Matson. LASSCO made a consider-
ble dent in Matson's passenger traffic. The competition was a spur to
the building of new ships by Matson.

The Depression of 1930 put an end to the worry. Pineapple magnate
James Dole was confronted with a cash flow problem when the canned
pineapple market collapsed. With three million cases of pineapple
awaiting shipment and a new crop maturing, Dole tried to use the
Isthmian Steamship Line for shipping his pineapple. When the crunch
came, he was "rescued" by Castle and Cooke, who moved Dole out of
control of the company and put the Dole cargo at Matson's disposal.

A fire on the Los Angeles Steamship Company's *City of Honolulu* at
its dock in Honolulu made the company receptive to an offer to merge.
Although allied with the Dillinghams, the Los Angeles company recognized that they could not break into the lucrative cargo business, even
though they were holding their own with pasenger traffic. In May 1930,
the Matson line announced the merger with its rival, without any cash

outlay. Matson simply exchanged shares of its stock for those of its rival.[19] The stage was now set for the emerging tourist industry.

Tourism

The era of upper class affluence that marked the 1920s also impacted Hawaii. In 1924 the first move was made to open a luxury hotel. For Hawaii, "the commodity of the day was the tourist who could afford about what he wanted. For him there must be great ships and great hotels."[20]

Castle and Cooke took the lead in establishing the Territorial Hotel Company, Ltd., in 1924. The directors of Matson Navigation were the principal organizers and promoters. A 400-room hotel, the Royal Hawaiian, opened in February 1927, to tap the prosperous tourist. To match the luxurious hotel, Matson ordered a new flagship, the *Malolo*. Matson now had what it expected to be a "complete commodity-handling system."[21] The optimism that produced this system was greater than the economic reality. The Royal Hawaiian Hotel operated

Figure 6.2 Honolulu Harbor (east view), 1931. (Hawaii State Archives).

Figure 6.3 Aloha Tower Passenger Terminal, 1931 (Hawaii State Archives).

for years at a very low level of occupancy. Hawaii's tourism was not ready for the volume projected by the Royal Hawaiian Hotel and passenger capacity of Matson's ships.[22]

A familiar pattern quickly emerged in this sector of activity to match the long-standing Matson record. The Territorial Hotel Company was liquidated in 1934 and turned over to a firm called Hawaiian Properties, Ltd., with the same partners. This in turn was transformed into the Hotels Division of Matson Navigation in 1941.[23]

The Matson Company lost none of the enterprise displayed by its founder. Matson moved into aviation in 1929 through its subsidiary Inter-Island Steam Navigation, which incorporated Inter-Island Airways, using two "flying boats" between Honolulu and the outer islands. Several years later, when Pan American sought financing for its proposed trans-Pacific air service, Matson and Inter-Island invested half a million dollars each in the new service. The arrangement continued until it was disallowed in 1941 by the newly created Civil Aeronautics Board. At that time, Matson and Inter-Island bowed out of aviation.[24]

Traffic in the Harbor

Although the territory did little to the harbor beyond maintaining the deteriorating wharves, the Corps of Engineers continued to make basic improvements. A long-discussed and petitioned-for project was the elimination of the point of land to improve turning conditions for entering ships. Strong winds frequently threatened to put ships down on the west side of the entrance channel as they slowed to make the turn into the harbor basin. The chief engineer explained:

> Owing to the narrow width of the entrance channel and its relatively short length, the larger vessels entering or leaving Honolulu Harbor must operate at reduced speed. At times when strong winds prevail this creates a very unsatisfactory navigating condition, which will become more serious with the expected increase in the size of vessels.[25]

A proposal long-supported by the Chamber of Commerce Maritime Committee and the harbor commissioners was for a widening of the entrance channel to 600 feet to allow vessels to pass in the entrance, thereby speeding up entry and exit. The chief engineer recommended that the entrance be maintained at 500 feet, which would "be adequate to serve present and prospective traffice." The extra width, he said, would create surge and wave problems within the harbor.

Given the overall depth of the harbor at thirty-five feet, there was "scant clearance" for the larger steamers with drafts of thirty-two feet. Hawaii's very small tidal action of approximately two feet did not offer much in the way of clearance. The depth was "entirely inadequate during storm periods, when wave actions cause[d] the ships to pitch or 'sound.'" A straight channel with a depth of forty feet would enable vessels to use the channel in any weather and at any stage of the tide.

Another favorite local project, also long-recommended, was a second entrance, a back door through the Kalihi Channel and Kapalama Basin, as a means of relieving congestion and providing a measure of safety in the event of a ship blocking the harbor entrance. The response of the chief engineer was "available records show that the number of entrance-channel passages in one day rarely exceeds a total of 15 arrivals and departures, which is considered conclusive evidence that no congestion exists at the present time."[26]

Removing 320 feet of Sand Island would expand the basin to provide adequate maneuvering room. This would entail the removal of the Public Health Service wharf and the relocation of the lighthouse facility. In addition, it was agreed to dredge and widen the Reserved Channel to 400 feet at a depth of 35 feet. This would create the second entrance and dredge the Kalihi Channel to navigable depth.

As the outer islands developed better transportation facilities, more of their agricultural production went directly to the mainland. Production on Oahu increased apace. Sugar shipped at Honolulu rose from 107,870 tons to 248,152 tons by 1930. Pineapple production skyrocketed from only 1,803 cases shipped in 1902 to 8,786,999 cases in 1930.[27]

The depression took its toll on Hawaiian shipping, when the rosy projections of increased traffic and tourism failed to materialize. The exceptions to this were pineapple and sugar. Following Dole's ouster from his pioneering business, the sale and distribution of pineapple increased sharply from the bottom of the depression in 1932. One of the principal exports was pineapple juice, the product Dole had introduced in 1930, just before he lost control of the company.

The essentially flat activity of the port is reflected in shipping statistics (table 6.2). Behind the array of numbers lies the fact that the Hawaiian economy in the decades of the 1920s and 1930s remained heavily agricultural, almost entirely dependent on two crops. A workforce that reached 44,000 at the peak of expansion in 1929 made up the bulk of the population. The non-plantation economy of Honolulu expanded more slowly. The details of imports into Hawaii during this time period reflect the heavy agricultural balance. Fertilizers, lumber, hay and feed, tin plate and cans for the pineapple industry, and automobiles were the dominant imports. Sugar and pineapples made up three-fourths of the exports to the United States.

The territorial government was hampered in its harbor development plans by low revenue and a generally poor economic pattern. The board reported to the legislature in 1938 that the biennial funding requirement "made it impossible to take up the slack in lean years," because excess revenues reverted to the general fund.[28] In 1939 the board experimented with reducing the tariff base rates in the hopes of stimulating more revenue." A 10 percent reduction in certain of the tariff base rates on September 17, 1938, accounts for a substantial portion of the lessened revenues but an expected increase in business failed to materialize. On the contrary, there was a falling off in over-seas business." Part of the problem was the use of private piers. Inter-Island Steamship transferred its two passenger ships to its own terminal, and

Table 6.2. Shipping Statistics, Honolulu Harbor, 1904–1940.

Year	Steam Vessels	Sailing Vessels	Registered Tonnage
1905	364	372	1,808,218
1906	549	363	2,236,576
1907	526	194	1,982,152
1908	476	267	2,088,101
1909	553	290	2,171,672
1910	570	257	2,666,780
1911	545	232	2,589,067
1912	1067	234	4,664,317
1913	578	129	3,489,057
1914	673	91	4,413,277
1915	777	91	5,089,783
1916	759	115	5,075,722
1917	703	144	4,377,061
1918	645	151	3,800,954
1919	748	145	3,460,205
1920	986	83	5,430,976
1921	946	56	6,580,551
1922	871	61	6,090,145
1923	874	53	6,580,557
1924	924	42	6,899,681
1925	1037	31	7,993,137
1926	841	10	7,037,074
1928	858	7	7,163,148
1930	896	7	7,595,827
1932	796	5	7,246,731
1934	669	5	6,888,178
1936	716	3	7,271,711
1937	715	2	6,588,435
1938	793	—	7,175,345
1939	694	—	6,623,458
1940	870	—	7,434,241
1941	1142	—	8,799,141

Source: Corps of Engineers, *Annual Reports, Waterborne Commerce of the United States,* 1906–1942; Territorial Board of Harbor Commissioners, Biennial Reports, 1910–1942. No commercial sailing vessels entered after 1938.

the U.S. Army leased three private piers for its expanded Corps of Engineers work. Any effort to raise rates was defeated by the private piers.[29]

The harbor was under pressure from the expansion plans of Matson, American President Lines, Theo H. Davies, and Nippon Yusen Kaisha, which involved a minimum of five new ships and possibly seven. When the board asked the legislature in 1939 to authorize the issuance of bonds to build a new pier 15 to handle this projected increase, the legislature refused, citing the poor financial condition of the territory.

A major political controversy developed around this expansion plan. Opponents argued that it was unwise financially. Supporters of the pier proposal charged the Oahu Railway and Land Company and private pier operators with attempting to protect their hold on the more lucrative cargo business. Piers 13 and 14 were too small and shipping companies refused to use them. They were, in fact, being used as a skating rink and car parking areas. Only Pier 10 could handle the largest ships coming into the harbor without overhangs of up to 100 feet.[30] Each of the Hawaii ports showed a significant decrease in the number of ships in 1939, reflecting the delayed effect of the military buildup.

The value of port commerce declined by $38 million and there was a decline in tonnage of over one million tons from 1938 to 1939. The impact of the military build-up had not yet been felt. Very likely the sharp recession of 1937 was a major factor in the decline of east-bound traffic. The data for 1939–1941 were harbingers of what was to come with the sharp increases in military preparations launched in 1938 by the Roosevelt administration. Pearl Harbor was one of the principal targets of that expansion.

Notes

1. National Archives, Record Group 77, Office of Chief Engineer, 27 March 1920, No. 38027/173; COE, Annual Report, 1920, pp. 1934–1935.

2. Harbor Commissioners, *Biennial Report*, 1924–25, p. 11.

3. Ibid., p. 65.

4. Edward Beechert, *Working in Hawaii: A Labor History* (Honolulu: University of Hawaii Press, 1985), pp. 143–144. See also U.S. Bureau of Labor, *4th Report on Hawaii*, Bulletin 94, 1911; James Shoemaker, *Labor in the Territory of Hawaii, 1939* (Washington, D.C.: G.P.O., 1940), pp. 39–40, 201–202.

5. The Big Five firms were: Castle and Cooke, American Factors, Alexander and

Baldwin, C. Brewer, and Theo H. Davies. Gavan Daws, *A Shoal of Time* (New York: Macmillan, 1968), p. 312.

6. Vernon A. Mund and Fred C. Hung, *Interlocking Directorates in Hawaii and Public Regulation of Ocean Transportation* (Honolulu: Economic Research Center, University of Hawaii, 1961), p. 34.

7. Ibid., p. 14; see also pp. 4–5. Directors of the fifth Big Five firm, Theo H. Davies and Co, were also investors in smaller amounts.

8. Worden, *Cargoes*, pp. 5–6.

9. Worden, *Cargoes*, pp. 8, 12, 19. See also Jacob Adler, *Claus Spreckels, The Sugar King in Hawaii* (Honolulu: University of Hawaii Press, 1966) for details on Spreckels' career.

10. Ralph S. Kuykendall, *The Hawaiian Kingdom* (Honolulu: University of Hawaii Press, 1967), vol. 3, pp. 105–106; Worden, *Cargoes*, p. 25.

11. Worden, *Cargoes*, p. 41.

12. Ibid., p. 59.

13. Robert E. Van Dyke (ed.), *Hawaiian Yesterdays: Historical Photographs by Ray Jerome Baker* (Mutual Publishing Co., Honolulu, 1982), pp. 65–72.

14. Mifflin Thomas, *Schooner From Windward: Two Centuries of Hawaiian Interisland Shipping* (Honolulu: University of Hawaii Press, 1983), p. 63.

15. Ibid., pp. 167–168.

16. Worden, *Cargoes*, p. 58.

17. Ibid., pp. 23–24. The Commerce Act of 1920 restricts United States coastwise shipping to domestic carriers, thus limiting competition from east-bound freighters from Asia.

18. Mund and Hung, *Interlocking Relationships*, pp. 29–32.

19. Worden, *Cargoes*, pp. 69–71.

20. Ibid., p. 59.

21. Ibid., p. 63.

22. Bernard J. Stern, *The Aloha Trade: Labor Relations in the Hawaii Hotel Industry* (Honolulu: University of Hawaii Center for Labor Education and Research, 1989), pp. 1–2.

23. Worden, *Cargoes*, p. 72.

24. Ibid., p. 84.

25. Report of the Division Engineer, San Francisco, 21 July 1931, House of Representatives, 73rd Cong., 1st Sess., House Document No. 54 (1932), pp. 12, 16. The entrance channel had a bend of eleven degrees in its length and a turn of sixty-five degrees into the harbor basin. The project had been recommended in the 1905 project report. Corps of Engineers, *Annual Report* (1905), app. XX, p. 2565, and in subsequent reports.

26. House Document No. 54, p. 14.

27. House Document No. 54, pp. 22–23.

28. Board of Harbor Commissioners, *Report* (1938), p. 5.

29. Ibid., p. 6; Corps of Engineers, *Report* (1938), p. 1926.

30. Harbor Commissioners, *Report* (1939), p. 10; Pier 10, *Report* (1936), p. 21.

31. Harbor Commissioners, *Report* (1939), p. 5.

7

The War Years: 1941–1950

The Mobilization Boom

Hawaii had always been seen by Washington as an important factor in the nation's military strategy. This was not always reflected in the level of activity in Honolulu. Since General Schofield's secret assessment in 1873, the many recommended projects for Honolulu Harbor and Pearl Harbor had to work their torturous way through the mechanism of the U.S. House of Representatives' Rivers and Harbors Committee allocation schemes.

The development of Honolulu harbor during the 1930s resulted in what amounted to three harbors. The northwest end was in private hands with seventeen piers and all of the rail facilities (Fig. 7.1). Federal agencies owned five wharves, with the remainder, nineteen, in the hands of the Territorial Harbor Commission. Revenue to maintain the harbor had to come from the fees for pilotage, moorage, wharfage, and tenant fees collected by the Harbor Commission. The commission had no power of taxation, and until 1939, could not issue bonds. Surpluses, when they existed, reverted to the general fund at the end of the biennium.

Between 1930 and 1941, the privately owned cargo space had increased from 230,380 square feet to 710,340. The territorial facilities were handling only 37 percent of the freight in 1940, as compared with 59 percent in 1930. To meet the problem of the shift to private piers, the commissioners reduced the tariff base rates in September 1938 by 10 percent, hoping to stimulate a great use of territorial piers. "[B]ut an expected normal increase in business failed to materialize. On the contrary, there was a falling off in overseas business of 702,629 tons of inward and outward cargo."[1] If the harbor was to be maintained in

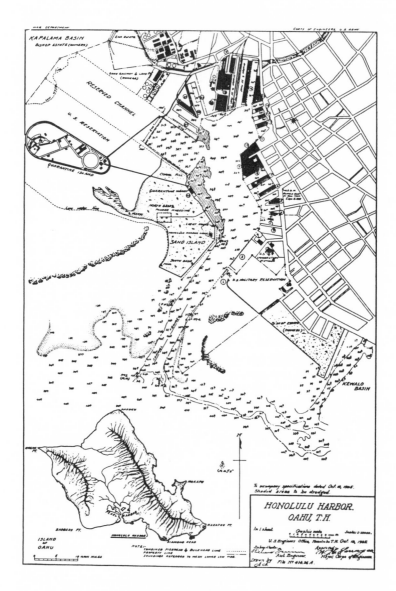

Figure 7.1 Corps of Engineers Survey, 1925 (from U.S. Army Corps of Engineers *Annual Report* for 1925).

adequate fashion, new facilities would have to be constructed and financed by other than direct appropriation.

When President Roosevelt visited Hawaii in 1934, army and navy commanders took the opportunity to impress the president with the importance of the military aspects of Hawaii. The opportunity was not wasted. The first visible results were appropriations in 1936 for coastal artillery improvements. In 1937, the army adopted a Defense Mobilization Plan for Hawaii.[2]

This mobilization plan charged the district engineer with maintenance of all transportation, utilities, and harbors, control of lumber, operation of the Honolulu Iron Works, allocation of all structural steel, construction of prisoner of war cages, and making provision for blackouts. The plan also gave the governor of the territory the right to suspend habeas corpus and declare martial law, using the authority of the Hawaii Organic Act of 1900.[3]

Partly in response to the poor economic situation, the legislature set the Harbor Commission free in 1939 to arrange bond financing and to deal with maintenance costs and operating charges. The fact that the military paid nothing for the use of piers did little to help matters. The federal agencies claimed exemption under Section 89 of the Organic Act. The harbor commissioners had long objected to the exemption. They argued that no wharves or landings in Honolulu Harbor existed that were constructed or controlled by the Republic of Hawaii.

In May of 1939, the military initiated practice blackouts for Honolulu. In 1940 and 1941 the blackout drill was extended to the entire territory. The military staged a mock air battle after the third practice blackout to demonstrate the invulnerability of Pearl Harbor to an air attack. The U.S. Navy announced that, thanks to the cooperation of the people of Oahu, aerial defenses of Pearl Harbor were complete.[4] The fever pitch of war preparations was reflected in the newspaper stories of the preparations. Ironically, just one month before the attack on Pearl Harbor, on 7 November, the *Honolulu Advertiser* carried a headline: "Japanese May Attack Over the Weekend!"

The Honolulu City Council fell into the spirit of the times by creating a Major Disaster Council in 1940 and an Emergency Disaster Plan in April 1941. The Major Disaster Council was to "administer essential civilian activities in the event of of war." In effect, the plan placed civil authorities on the Island of Oahu at the disposal of General Walter C. Short. A medical mobilization was also established that planned to train some 3,000 civilians in first aid treatment. The level of awareness of the tense international situation was moderated by the fact that the legislature adjourned without appropriating funds for the training plan, leaving the American Red Cross to provide the financing. The head of the Red Cross in Hawaii explained the situation:

> While the United States is not actually at war, and there is no occasion for war hysteria . . . the time has come *now*—not tomorrow—for intelligent, adequate, civilian defense preparedness. . . . The Army and Navy are not here to protect the population of Honolulu; their duty is to defend Hawaii as one of the most vital parts of the American Defense system.[5]

Military strategists tended to think of Hawaii as an unapproachable bastion. With the granting of independence to the Philippines in the Tydings-McDuffie Act of 1934, it was conventional wisdom to assert that the Philippines were strategically indefensible and that the American bases would be abandoned. The United States, it was thought, would organize a defense based upon Hawaii, Guam, and Wake Island.[6]

The Board of Harbor Commissioners had long operated under the requirement of being self-financing through fees for service. This requirement, in addition to a prohibition on the issuing of bonds, meant that harbor projects were slow to develop. When the New Deal Public Works Administration (PWA) was created in 1933, the commissioners eagerly sought funds for a variety of projects, particularly those in the outer island harbors, where the scale of the needed projects was small. In 1934, PWA money was obtained for a cattle pier at Kawaihae.

Even with the Corps of Engineers' work in Kapalama Basin, the maintenance dredging was falling behind. Piers 1 and 2 in the basin had less than twenty-five feet of water in 1937. The revenue problems of the early years of the depression were now manifest.

The impact of the military preparations finally had a visible effect on the harbor traffic in 1940.

> The vast naval and army expansion programmes recently approved by the Congress will undoubtedly have a stimulating effect upon business in general; and since large sums have been appropriated for use in Hawaii and other Pacific areas, it is felt that this will help to offset the loss in shipping sustained as the result of the European war, and it is hoped that by the end of the current biennium there will be a sufficient gain in our revenues to wipe out this year's deficit.[7]

Table 7.1. Harbor Traffic, 1936–1945.

Year	No. of Ships	Gross Tonnage	Tons of Cargo
1936	715	6,588,435	2,254,172
1938	793	7,175,345	2,365,631
1939	649	6,623,458	2,443,908
1940	870	7,434,244	3,353,844
1941	1,142	8,799,141	4,328,318
1942	1,006	6,752,450	2,116,212
1943	1,318	8,273,143	2,194,348
1945	1,736	11,705,115	6,506,528

Source: Board of Harbor Commissioners, Biennial Reports. (1937, 1944 not reported.) Cargo tons, U.S. Congress, 79th Cong. 2d Sess., House Doc. No. 705, 9 July 1946, p. 7.

In fact, within six months, the board was reporting a shortage of cargo handling space as a result of the defense build up. Because of army preemption, only piers 27 and 28 were being used for overseas cargo. Always a relatively small harbor, Honolulu was now bursting at the seams (table 7.1).

By mid-1940, the congestion of traffic and the piling up of cargo reached serious proportions. In July, the army and navy formed a committee to work with the stevedoring firms to see what could be done to relieve the congestion and to perhaps increase cargo handling facilities.[8] No report was ever made.

By the end of November 1940, the local papers were carrying stories on the increasing congestion and the apparent failure to reach any effective, short-term solutions. It was in this context that the Harbor Commission urged the replacement of pier 15 and the upgrading of others. Some of the crowding was blamed on the labor shortage created by the military draft and the military construction program, then going full speed.[9] Despite all of the pressure and the obvious need, the projected pier expansion plans failed to make it through the territorial legislature. At the close of the session on 5 May 1941, the plans were buried in the House Ways and Means Committee. Once again, the political influence of the private wharf owners overrode the Harbor Commission.

In an effort to deal with the growing problem, the administration of the harbor was turned over to the U.S. Navy, effective 1 December

1941. This was done in good part to resolve the obvious lack of coordination between the territorial administration and the private sector. "Since December, 1941, all shipping between the Territory and over-seas ports as well as that between island ports has been operated by agencies of the Federal Government which have been paying no charges to the Territory."[10] The board had a deficit of $188,624 for the fiscal year of 1942. They attempted to negotiate with the army and navy for appropriate payments. They argued that the deficit was "a loss directly attributable to the war . . . it is felt that the burden of the losses should be spread over the entire nation."[11]

The issue was resolved by congressional action in 1943 that suspended for the duration of the war the operation of Section 89 of the Organic Act, which had permitted the free use of territorial wharves by the federal government. Federal agencies were authorized to pay the territory "reasonable value for use."[12]

War in the Pacific

The attack on Pearl Harbor completed the transformation of Hawaii into a war economy. By midday on 7 December, Governor Poindexter had invoked the Hawaii Defense Act and at 3:30 P.M. declared martial law as provided in the Organic Act of 1900. The governor added a provision not anticipated in that act. He transferred all civilian authority to the commanding general of the Hawaiian forces. This provision was ultimately held to be unlawful, in effect making the entire period of martial law, to 30 June 1944, a misuse of power.[13]

This extreme action was initiated by the army and navy who had argued for many years that the large Asian population of Hawaii posed a threat to national security. They urged a replacement of civil government with a military commission ruling Hawaii. By 1917, the Japanese in Hawaii and on the West Coast were a major concern of both navy and army intelligence. The Bureau of Investigation (after 1921, the Federal Bureau of Investigation) linked the Japanese with the radical political and labor movements of the time.[14]

The principal justification for the transfer of civil authority and the closing of the courts was the threat of Japanese invasion, but even when that threat diminished, the military rule continued. The immediate strategy for the now global war was to focus on Europe, with the Pacific as a secondary concern. This was based upon the decisions reached in 1940 as to the appropriate division of responsibility between the United States and Great Britain. "In general, the Americans felt that the Far

East, except Japan itself and areas to its north and east, was a British and Dutch sphere of responsibilities. . . . The Americans . . . indicated that no strengthening of American forces in the Far East was contemplated."[15]

Hawaii's role in the Pacific war was as a forward supply base and a link to Central Pacific strategy. By 24 December 1941, the general staff had concluded that beyond a sporadic shelling or air attack, the Japanese posed no threat to Hawaii, so the territory was assigned a priority in shipping below that of Australia.[16] In a short time, even this priority was changed to put Hawaii below the so-called "ferry islands," the air ferry routes to Australia, which had begun to be developed in 1936. Beyond Hawaii, Midway and Wake had embryonic air stations. Engineers were in the process of building airfields at Christmas and Canton islands and naval facilities at Palmyra and Johnston islands. "In the grand strategy laid down at the *Arcadia Conference* on 31 December 1941, the security of the main air and sea routes in the Pacific were listed as an essential part of the 1942 program."[17]

An immediate result of this change in strategy was to create a scarcity of shipping to Hawaii. Naval insistence on the use of convoys for all Pacific shipping delayed sailings dramatically. General Emmons, commander of the Hawaiian Department, complained bitterly in January 1942 about the idle shipping on the West Coast and the sometimes strange loading priorities that resulted in Hawaii receiving a shipload of beer at the expense of other badly needed items. Chief of Staff Marshall replied that Hawaii would have to make do with the slower ships and denied that there was any idle shipping capacity. Exotic items sometimes were added as last minute efforts to fill all available cargo space.

In good part, the problem was that the army in Hawaii had all of the authority, but no practical experience in the administration of a complex economy and society. General Emmons, for example, in January 1942, ordered a quantity of sulfanilamide greater than the total capacity of the U.S. pharmaceutical industry. He wanted 37,000 new Garand rifles to arm the civilian population and rocket guns to defend fifteen air fields. The rocket guns were still under development and not yet manufactured.[18]

All of these complaints finally surfaced in Washington and provoked an investigation by the War Production Board. The investigation charged that by the end of March 1942, the army supply system had "broken down completely in Hawaii." Gasoline had fallen to an eighteen day supply, even essential air craft spare parts were exhausted. The shortage of cement, it was charged, had become so acute that it would take "seventy-three freighters, plying continuously for three months, to remedy it."[19]

At the base of the problem were two factors: the low priority assigned to Hawaii and the competition between the army and navy and their refusal to cooperate. In addition, the problem was aggravated by the special character of Hawaii's economy. The extreme concentration of economic power produced a powerful group with very close ties to the military. Their ability to bring pressure to bear through unofficial channels often created contradictory policies. The business community strongly supported the military takeover and worked intensively to protect the plantation system, gaining priorities in equipment and supplies to maintain their output. Sugar and pineapple were declared essential to the war effort, ensuring a good position in priorities for essential supplies. The military governor relied heavily on the business community for his appointments, such as that of Walter Dillingham of the Hawaiian Dredging Company as director of Food Production.[20]

The absence of any overall plan of operation for the global war effort and the inexperience of the military led to a great deal of confusion. The tendency of area commanders to view the war from their theater's perspective was "a recognized and well-nigh universal malady."[21] As the U.S. Supreme Court found in its examination of the military rule, military inexperience in government produced many anomalous situations. Ruling by the issuance of general orders, the military governor frequently contradicted basic U.S. law. Instead of confining itself to matters affecting military functions, the military government issued a steady stream of general orders that attempted to govern the civilian sector, written by military officers with no civilian experience in such matters.[22]

By March 1942, the combined chiefs of staff and the combined staff planners had assigned priorities for the various theaters and responsibilities for particular assignments. This helped to reduce some of the confusion. Hawaii was placed in category B, except when involved in "major operations."[23] No amount of central planning could overcome the shifting fortunes of the Pacific War. Victory at the Battle of Midway did not subsequently prevent the Japanese from occupying two islands in the Aleutians. Hawaii was still weakly defended, and as the army was granted an additional bomber group, Admiral Chester Nimitz was given a greater freedom to move planes from Hawaii to the South Pacific.

Within these changing strategic plans, the army retained the responsibility for supplying both the civilian and military needs of Hawaii. During much of 1942, tonnage shipped from San Francisco was high as a result of the effort to halt the Japanese advance. By September, tonnage shipped to the Pacific dropped sharply as the European focus of the war effort came into play. The air of urgency that had characterized early operations faded. Thereafter, Hawaii was in a role of static defense.[24]

Some improvement came in the form of the creation in 1943 of the Army Port and Service Command. The new command combined the functions formerly handled by ports of embarkation and service commands. It directed all port operations in Honolulu and the outer islands, all rail transport, as well as all of the army posts, camps, and stations. One of the first tasks the new command undertook was the completion of piers 39 and 40, which the Army Construction Quartermaster Corps had commenced in early 1941.[25] The first was completed in December 1943 and the second in January 1944. These two piers, with a connected complex of warehouses, were capable of handling six Liberty ships simultaneously. This relieved some of the severe congestion in the harbor. In the last three months of 1943, the new command discharged a total of 518,193 tons of cargo and 36,505 troops.[26]

Coordinating army and navy functions and jurisdictions was a never-ending problem. The creation of the Army Port and Service Command was accompanied by yet another change in the overall command. General Emmons suggested far reaching changes that would center logistical and strategic control under his command. The outcome was the creation of the Joint Overseas Control Office in November 1943, under the control of Admiral Nimitz. General Richardson, nominally in charge of logistical support for army forces in the Pacific Ocean Area, was unable to allocate shipping, which was fully under Admiral Nimitz.[27]

The nature of the problem became apparent almost immediately in the Gilbert Islands campaign. Beginning in October 1943, the army-operated piers in Honolulu were "partially stripped of the cargo handling equipment and vehicles to supplement equipment for the Navy."[28] This cut severely into the cargo handling capacity at Honolulu Harbor for some time. On the whole, the system probably represented the best compromise in the different roles of the two services.

The Pan American Clipper service, begun in 1935, had been using

Pearl Harbor for its Oahu landing. With the expansion of Pearl Harbor naval facilities, it became necessary to find another site. Keehi Lagoon was the logical choice and in 1940, three runways and a seaplane basin were authorized.[29] After the attack on Pearl Harbor, the navy wanted the seaplane runways completed as soon as possible, regardless of cost. With the wartime situation, the usual constraints of authorization by Congress through the Rivers and Harbors Appropriation Bill were no longer present. A seaplane basin and two runways were completed in October 1944. The facility joined the Territorial Airport and the rapidly expanding Hickham Air Force Base. With victory at the Battle of Midway, however, the focus shifted to creating facilities to support the coming offensives. The Keehi seaplane basin was abandoned, and Kapalama Basin became the focus of development, with the enlargement of Sand Island. Kalihi Channel was to be enlarged as a second entrance to the harbor, cutting across one of the seaplane runways. This plan was put aside with the defeat of Japan. The second entrance and bridge were abandoned in August 1945 as no longer militarily justifiable.

Sand Island became the headquarters of the Army Port and Service Command and the center of greatly enlarged military activities. Dredged material from Kapalama Basin and the Reserved Channel and a turning basin doubled the acreage of Sand Island. A ship repair basin was constructed. Adjacent to pier 40, a small harbor was constructed to handle small vessels. Eleven wharves were built on Sand Island for military use.[30]

Despite the rapid changes in planning and strategic aims, Honolulu Harbor, for all of its divided commands and overlapping authorities, functioned with amazing efficiency. It was rated the top port in the world in October 1943, and for the next year and a half was ranked in the top three by the Army Port and Service Command. All of this was accomplished with a consistently smaller work force per ton of cargo than other major ports.[31] Stevedores put in ten-hour days, seven days a week, for months on end to launch the various offensives. It required a monthly average of 35,000 tons of food and 50,000 tons of civilian cargo to maintain the war economy, in addition to the military cargo, which at its peak reached 538,000 tons for the army and 150,000 tons for the navy.[32]

The Honolulu Chamber of Commerce urged President Roosevelt to turn aside any efforts to restore civilian authority when the newly appointed governor and his attorney general went to Washington in

December 1942 to seek an end to military rule. The governor and the Hawaii delegate to Congress were able to secure return of eighteen functions, including the reopening of the civil courts, except in cases involving the military or violations of the military's general orders.[33] "Restoration Day" was proclaimed on 10 March 1943, and martial law officially expired on 24 October 1944. Under the rubric of military security, the port and harbors remained under military control until July 1945.

The Aftermath

Honolulu Harbor emerged from World War II well used, even battered, and unfinished. The second entrance project, hastily begun in 1941 as a military necessity, was abandoned in an early stage of construction. Piers were in poor condition for lack of maintenance and lack of replacement parts such as roll-up doors. The intensive use of piers and almost complete lack of repairs and skilled labor for maintenance left the territory with only three structures—piers 2, 8–10, and 15—"in fair repair" at the end of the war.[34]

In 1946, the Corps of Engineers presented a plan for bringing the harbor up to standard and to improve the facility. Of the thirteen piers owned by the territory, two were in a state of collapse. The harbor would have to be dredged to a depth of 35 feet in the two basins, the Reserved Channel would be dredged over its 600 foot width to a depth of 35 feet and the turning basin in Kapalama Basin was to be made 1,000 feet wide and 3,000 feet long.[35] The harbor, the corps reported, was "considered inadequate for normal commerce."

The process of returning to a peace-time economy presented many difficulties for Hawaii. The small size of the economy in relation to the war effort had produced many significant changes. A sharp increase in population, many new business firms, and heightened expectations combined to create pressures to sustain or even to increase the economic growth of the war years. The economy continued to expand, albeit somewhat erratically, as it was converted into a service-oriented economy in which federal expenditures and service functions would replace agriculture as the dominant force.[36]

The enlarged commercial sector resulted in a worsening of Hawaii's balance of trade as imports soared over the relatively stable sugar and pineapple exports. Coupled with a sharp decline in federal expenditures, the concern of both the harbor commissioners and the community was the need to plan for development. The obvious imbalance in the economy, and its clear threat to the standard of living, touched off a flurry of planning, which sought to find a solution before Hawaii's population again dwindled because of poor employment prospects and declining investment.

To add to the woes of the harbor commissioners, peace brought only more bad news. The struggle between the territorial-run portion of the harbor and the private piers continued. Matson Navigation, the only shipper of significance, announced in 1946 that it would send the larger part of San Francisco and Los Angeles freight over piers 31, 32, and 33 of Oahu Railway and Land Company as soon as they could be made ready. This further exacerbated the revenue crunch. Such a move would result in a serious loss of revenue and would probably necessitate a sharp increase in tariffs throughout the territorial ports. The commissioners sadly concluded, "We are no longer competitors to the private sector."[37]

Although the Harbor Commission succeeded in persuading the federal agencies to pay for their use of the harbor facilities, the old problem of the private piers draining off the lucrative portion of the trade remained. Faced with the need of a massive overhaul of all of the territorial ports, the revenue of the harbors seemed grossly inadequate. Raising tariffs would likely only increase the use of private piers. Once again the commissioners asked that a port authority be created to operate all of the harbor. It would be some years in the future before the problem was resolved. Meanwhile the commissioners were faced with the mandate of recovering all of their operating costs from the fee schedule.

A review of the condition of the port by the territorial legislature in 1943 revealed serious deterioration and a very shaky financial structure. Piers built with public funds had long been used by private concerns. Bonded indebtedness had not been redeemed from the revenues collected from these piers. Pier 6 constructed in 1911 at a total cost of $104,764 still had bonds outstanding worth $36,644 in 1943. As the special committee remarked, "It is of interest to note that the amount of bonds now (1941) outstanding constitutes the exact amount originally issued."[38] The pier in question could no longer be used for vessels or cargo. Piers 35 and 36 were built in 1931 at a cost of $924,874. Bonds outstanding in 1941 amounted to $726,343. Both piers were used exclusively by the three pineapple canning companies. The annual loss on the piers, paid from general funds, was more than $39,000 per annum.

A significant difference between the territorial piers and the privately controlled piers emerged in a comparison of the handling of cargo. The private piers were able to handle 3.14 tons per square foot of wharf space compared to only 1.04 tons per square foot on the territorial piers. These figures reflected the sharp differences in cargo handling facilities and the deterioration of the territorial piers. The joint committee recommended a wholesale reorganization of the harbor and its methods of operation and the return of the harbor to civilian control at the conclusion of the war.

The war postponed what promised to be a major development for the harbor. The Hawaiian Sugar Planters' Association announced plans in 1940 to build bulk sugar loading facilities. Tate and Lyle, the English sugar giant, had already moved to bulk shipping of its sugar from the Caribbean and even forced the militant labor forces in Cuba to acquiesce after they had for many years prevented its full utilization. As the commissioners put it in 1940, when the news was announced: "[B]ulk sugar shipments which when put into effect will over-night cause our present equipment to become obsolete . . . [most of the] improvements to the present type of conveyor . . . will have to be written off if the new system is put in. . . . [T]he bond service charges go on regardless whether the equipment is used or not."[39]

The bulk loading method was installed at Kahului, Maui, just before the war broke out. Kauai and Oahu followed as materials became available at the war's end.[40] Hilo's bulk plant was delayed by a severe tidal wave in 1946. Around $1.3 million in damages had to be repaired before the bulk plant could be installed.

There remained the issue of the charges to be paid by the military for use of the harbor from 1942 to 1946. Negotiations produced gradual settlement. In 1946, the fees for the year 1944 were agreed to by the army, but the navy balked at the sum levied. The claims were settled in 1948 at $1,126,203.

The war experience led the Board of Harbor Commissioners to rethink their role and the organization of the harbor. Looking ahead in 1944, they concluded that a new, modern freight terminal would be required, preferably to be located at the sites of piers 4, 5, 6 and to be designated as pier 2. The long depression in the 1930s and lack of maintenance and replacement during the war was evident. The 1916 pilot boat No. 1 needed to be replaced and pilot boat No. 2 needed a new engine. The appearance of the longshore union shortly before the war now meant that the commissioners had to meet their demand for washrooms and toilets on the piers. New diesel fuel lines were also needed to replace the older, corroded fuel oil lines.

As early as 1941, the principal competitor with the territorial wharves, Walter Dillingham, testified to the legislature that a wharf at the Waikiki end of the harbor would reflect the movement of business and the population. Like most predictions about population movement and growth, the sentiment was accurate, even if the predictions were not. He said, "there is no reason to suppose that private freight going Ewa [west] of the [Nuuanu] stream will ever increase materially. . . . Not only has the population of the city moved toward Waikiki, but so has business."[41]

In 1945, shipping agents demanded a faster discharge of their cargo, arguing that obsolete cargo handling methods and labor practices were costly. This reinforced the arguments put forward in 1941 by Walter Dillingham and the presentations of the chairman of the Harbor Commission, Benjamin Rush, to the legislature.[42] In 1947, the legislature acted on the suggestion and promptly touched off a struggle identical to that which had surrounded pier 15 in 1938 and 1939.

The next step was taken when the Honolulu Chamber of Commerce president, Randolph Sevier, withdrew support for the new terminal on 26 April 1948. This was followed by the introduction of a bill in the territorial Senate to delete all funding for the proposed terminal. A committee of shipping agents announced their opposition to the terminal, which they deemed "unnecessary."[43] Despite all the maneuvering, the Harbor Commission went ahead with the planning and arrangements for land transfers. The Senate passed legislation deleting the terminal from the appropriations bill. One senator issued a minority report detailing opposition by the Oahu Railway and Land Company to the terminal and charged them with being responsible for the introduction and passage of Senate Bill 155, which effectively killed the terminal proposal.[44] The effort to cut off the terminal failed in the House of Representatives. The outcome was the construction, beginning in 1951, of the Diamond Head Terminal.[45]

Another prediction commonly made at the war's end was the need for more and better passenger terminal facilities to handle the hoped-for boom in tourism. As the commissioners put it in their 1948 report, "it is believed that [the number of passenger vessels] will resume at a later date when other shipping companies get their passenger ships in operation." They noted that the population of Oahu had more than doubled from the 1927 level—from 171,250 to 371,649. The outer islands showed little or no change over that period, reflecting their largely agricultural population. Planning, accordingly, was necessary for the expansion of traffic at Honolulu Harbor.[46]

A significant change in harbor management came in 1945, when the legislature gave the harbor commissioners the authority to retain all earnings in the Harbor Board Special Fund. Previously (1941) the board had been allowed a maximum of $100,000, with amounts above that reverting to the general fund.[47]

The long sought and often frustrated plan for a second entrance, the "back door," through the Kalihi Channel surfaced again. One of the basic arguments had been that the narrow entrance channel was in danger of being blocked by a ship wreck or, in earlier days, by hostile powers. A Liberty ship, the SS *Britain Victory* went on the entrance channel reef in 1946, blocking the harbor. The *Honolulu Advertiser*, long a promoter of the second entrance, immediately proclaimed that the harbor would be closed indefinitely.[48] One week later, the ship was floated off the reef and the harbor reopened. This episode renewed the effort to resume work on the Kalihi Channel. The chief of the Corps of Engineers recommended approval of the work to Congress in 1949, but it was not until 1954 that the funds were approved.[49]

A glimpse of the future was in the 1948 report of the newly appointed harbor manager and chief engineer.

> Much of the passenger traffic between the mainland U.S. and points West is now going by way of the air. This has decreased the number of passenger vessels necessary to handle this type of service. . . . It is impossible to predict what the future of passenger travel through the Port of Honolulu will be. However, if present prices for passenger travel of ships prevail, and the lower fares on air passage can be maintained, it is almost certain that surface carriers of passengers will never reestablish the volume of traffic existing before the war.[50]

The development of the new freight and passenger terminal authorized in 1946 went ahead. Withstanding a severe challenge that came close once again to sinking the project, the commissioners began construction in 1949 at pier 1, envisioning a traditional bulkhead pier with a large shedded area.

The new Honolulu Freight Terminal at the old Channel Wharf was well into the planning stage, with transfers of land between the territory, the Corps of Engineers, Inter-Island Steam Navigation, and the Immigration Station in 1949–1950. A berthing space of approximately

1,700 feet and a 1,200-foot by 250-foot shed with a large open storage area for lumber were contemplated.

Plans can be made, but events can disrupt and derail the best of plans. For one thing, the modernization undertaken in 1949 was soon overtaken by the swift pace of technological change in the maritime world. And the post-war wave of Pacific maritime labor strikes had a serious impact on Hawaii's economy and development.

Maritime labor had long played a key role in Hawaii's economy, but it began to demonstrate a new and far-reaching impact on future development plans. The more diversified, complex service economy was much more vulnerable to interruption than the old, narrow agricultural-based economy.

Notes

1. Board of Harbor Commissioners, *Biennial Report* (1939), p. 4.

2. "Mobilization Plan, 1937," U.S. National Archives, San Bruno, Hawaiian Department, U.S. Army Overseas Operations and Commands, 1898–1942, Record Group No. 395; J. Garner Anthony, *Hawaii Under Army Rule* (Palo Alto: Stanford University Press, 1955), pp. 1–2; Erwin N. Thompson, *Pacific Ocean Engineers: History of the Army Corps of Engineers in the Pacific, 1905–1908* (Honolulu: U.S. Army Corps of Engineers, Pacific Division, 1985), pp. 76–77.

3. Thompson, *Pacific Ocean Engineers,* p. 78; Anthony, *Hawaii Under Army Rule,* p. 5.

4. *Honolulu Star Bulletin* (18 May 1939), 23 April 1940, 8 May 1940, 23 April 1941, 19 May 1941, mock attack, 23 May 1941); *Honolulu Advertiser* (19 May 1939).

5. Anthony, *Hawaii Under Army Rule,* p. 2; *Pearl Harbor Attack Hearings,* "Civilian Preparedness Activities and Establishment of Major Disaster Council," Joint Committee, U.S. 79th Cong., 2d Sess. (1946), 18:3401–3421; Alfred Castle statement, p. 3416.

6. Hector C. Bywater, "Japanese and American Naval Power in the Pacific," *Pacific Affairs* (June, 1935): 170; Stanley D. Porteus, *And Blow Not The Trumpet* (Palo Alto: Pacific Books, 1947), pp. 46–47.

7. Harbor Commissioners, *Report* (1940), p. 4.

8. *Honolulu Star Bulletin* (28 July 1940).

9. *Honolulu Star Bulletin* (6 December 1940).

10. *Honolulu Star Bulletin* (10 November 1941); Harbor Commissioners, *Report* (1942), p. 6.

11. Harbor Commissioners, *Report* (1942), p. 7.

12. Ibid., 1943, pp. 5–6; Twenty-Second Hawaii Legislature, *Special Committee Report No. 29 on Joint Resolution No. 4,* Special Session Laws of Hawaii, 1941, p. 4.

13. Anthony, *Hawaii Under Army Rule,* p. 5, pp. 101–118.

14. National Archives, U.S. Army, Military Intelligence Department; Investigative Files of the Bureau of Investigation, File B.S. 202600, Reels 47–50, 1918–1921.

15. Richard Leighton and Robert Coakley, *Global Logistics and Strategy, 1940–1945* (Washington, D.C.: Department of the Army, Office of the Chief of Military History, 1955–1968), p. 54. See also, *Pearl Harbor Attack Hearings*, vol. 15, pp. 1490, 1492.

16. Leighton and Coakley, *Global Logistics and Strategy*, pp. 146–147.

17. Ibid., pp. 150–151.

18. Ibid., p. 162. (See chapter 8 for similar problems with labor.)

19. Ibid., p. 161.

20. Edward Beechert, *Working in Hawaii: A Labor History* (Honolulu: University of Hawaii Press, 1985), pp. 285–286; Lawrence Fuchs, *Hawaii Pono: A Social History* (New York: Harcourt, Brace & World, Inc., 1961), pp. 299–302.

21. Leighton and Coakley, *Global Logistics*, p. 391.

22. U.S. Supreme Court, *Reports*, "Duncan v. Kahanomoku", 372 U.S. 304 (1946); Beechert, *Working in Hawaii*, pp. 285–289.

23. Leighton and Coakley, *Global Logistics*, pp. 272–273.

24. Chester Wardlow, *The Transportation Corps: Movements, Training, and Supply* (Washington, D.C.: Department of the Army, Office of the Chief of Military History, 1955–1968), pp. 492; Leighton and Coakley, *Global Logistics*, p. 393.

25. Joseph Bykofsky and Harold Larson, *The Transportation Corps: Operations Overseas* (Washington, D.C.: Department of Defense, U.S. Army Technical Services Series, 1957), pp. 511–512.

26. Wardlow, *Transportation Corps*, pp. 512–513; for details of the Corps of Engineers reorganization, see Thompson, *Pacific Ocean Engineers*, pp. 124–126.

27. Bykofsky and Larson, *Operations Overseas*, p. 514. The Hawaiian Department of the Army went through four major changes. In August 1943, it became U.S. Army Forces, Central Pacific Area. In July 1944, it was U.S. Army Forces, Pacific Ocean Areas. Finally on 1 July 1945, it was U.S. Army Forces, Middle Pacific.

28. Bykofsky and Larson, *Operations Overseas*, p. 516.

29. Thompson, *Pacific Ocean Engineers*, p. 126; U.S. Army, Corps of Engineers, *Report* (1941), p. 2060.

30. U.S. Army, Corps of Engineers, *Report* (1946), p. 2535; Arthur D. Llewellyn, "Honolulu Harbor," *The Military Engineer*, 39 (256) (February 1947): 51–55.

31. U.S. Army Forces, MIDPAC, Army Port and Service Command, "History of the Army Port and Service Command," Honolulu, Hawaii War Records, 1945 (mimeo).

32. Gwenfread Allen, *Hawaii's War Years, 1941–1945* (Honolulu: Greenwood Press, 1950), pp. 176–175.

33. Allen, *Hawaii's War Years*, p. 301.

34. Harbor Commissioners, *Report* (1945), pp. 5–6.

35. Corps of Engineers, *Report* (1946), p. 2522.

36. John L. Hazard, *Transshipment Hawaii: Steps Toward an East-West Trade* (Honolulu: University of Hawaii, Bureau of Economic Research, 1963), pp. 12–13.

37. Harbor Commissioners, *Report* (1946), p. 6.

38. Territory of Hawaii, Legislature, *Special Joint Committee Report No. 29*, p. 7.

39. Harbor Commissioners, *Report* (1940), p. 5 (bulk shipments).

40. Harbor Commissioners, *Report* (1945), p. 6. For details on bulk shipping of sugar, see Edward D. Beechert, "Technology and the Plantation Labour Supply," in *The World Sugar Economy in War and Depression, 1914–1940*, Adrian Graves and Bill Albert (eds.) (London: Routledge, 1988), pp. 131–141.

41. Population and business moved in the Ewa (western) direction in the 1960s and 1970s. Harbor Commissioners, *Report* (1946), p. 7.

42. *Honolulu Star Bulletin* (30 December 1945).

43. *Honolulu Star Bulletin* (26 April, 18 June 1948).

44. *Honolulu Star Bulletin* (7 April 1949).

45. Ben F. Rush, "History of Construction and Development of Commercial Harbors," Honolulu, Board of Harbor Commissioners, 1956, p. 11 (mimeo).

46. Harbor Commissioners, *Report* (1948), population tables and freight tables for 1927–1948, Tables 1 and 2, pp. 8–10.

47. Territory of Hawaii, Act 142, *Session Laws, 1941*; Harbor Commissioners, *Report* (1945), p. 5.

48. *Honolulu Advertiser* (31 October 1946).

49. Corps of Engineers, *Report* (1954), pp. 1334–1335.

50. Harbor Commissioners, *Report* (1948), pp. 7–8.

8

Hawaiian Maritime Labor

Multi-Ethnic Struggle

Hawaiians who sailed on the first ships calling at Hawaii began a flow of information that continued unbroken from the 1780s to the present.[1] Many Hawaiians worked alternatively as seamen and as long-shoremen in Hawaii and on the West Coast, and were in close touch with maritime events throughout the Pacific. The logs of ships trading to Hawaii in the nineteenth century reflected a general satisfaction with the work of Hawaiian seamen. They, of course, enjoyed an advantage over their mainland fellow seamen. They could jump ship in Hawaii with relative impunity, as they were not subject to the bonding requirement for all other seamen leaving ship in Hawaii.

The Honolulu longshoremen early established a reputation for militant labor action. In 1867, they struck for an increase of fifty cents over the prevailing wage of $1.00. In what was to become a familiar pattern, Chinese workers from the plantations were hired for two days to unload the struck ship at $1.00 per day, effectively putting an end to the strike.[2]

The Hawaiian response was often simply to leave the work. In 1869, the *Pacific Commercial Advertiser* complained of the refusal of Hawaiians to accept longshore work for wages of $2.00 per day and even turning down $2.50. The editor visited his wrath upon the "lazy and hopeless" workers, warning that they could not prevail over "capital." In reality, the Hawaiians had struck demanding an increase in wages from $1.00 to $2.00 for a twelve-hour day. The strike ended with minor concessions to the longshoremen.[3]

A pattern of hiring Chinese workers who had left the plantation to work during strikes continued through the 1880s. In 1880, when the Hawaiian longshoremen struck for a wage of $2.50, Chinese were hired for a $1.50 per day, effectively breaking the strike. The following year, the Hawaiians struck again for $2.50 and for a ten-hour day. Once again an editor proclaimed that "two dollars was pretty tolerable pay for mere muscle and bone." Another editor asked, "Where in the world would such a preposterous wage be asked for?"[4]

Sometime in the early 1880s, a quasi-political organization of long-shoremen was formed, the *Hui Poola*. They apparently did not partici-pate as an organization in any of the labor struggles, but appeared in political rallies and parades with their red banner.[5]

Slowly the longshoremen pushed up their wage level. In 1886 they demanded $3.00 over their pay of $2.50. Losing that demand, they next struck in 1889 for the $3.00 wage. Once again surplus workers from the plantations were hired as strikebreakers at lower wages.[6]

The practice of employing surplus plantation workers did not lead to the displacement of the longshoremen. Employers preferred the Hawaiian longshoremen and gradually they were rehired and wages adjusted upward slightly. The important point for the stevedoring companies was to avoid the appearance of conceding to labor demands but not to lose the valuable sense of community that characterizes longshore work.

A significant change came in 1901 when the Honolulu long-shoremen organized a local of the International Longshoremen's Asso-ciation (ILA) to fight a wage cut from thirty-five cents per hour for a nine-hour day to $2.00 a day with no overtime. The stevedoring company, McCabe, Hamilton and Renney, explained that they were merely equalizing wages along the waterfront because the Corps of Engineers was paying $2.00 per day. This time the striking Hawaiian and Portuguese workers were replaced with Japanese scabs.[7]

The use of different ethnic groups to break strikes was common in this period. Where the numbers were not large, it was relatively easy to mobilize a group of strikebreakers, given the low levels of job oppor-tunities available in Hawaii, particularly in the waterfront areas. When the Japanese warehousemen of the Oahu Railway struck in 1911 for overtime pay, they were replaced with Korean workers. The steady exodus of workers from the plantations to the urban areas facilitated this practice. The flow of workers from the plantations into the urban centers was too great to contain and employers were able to hire strikebreakers with ease.

In 1911, the Longshore Association of Portland, Oregon, merged their organization in the International Longshoremen's Association as the Pacific Coast District of the ILA. A charter was issued to a Hilo local.[8] The Hilo delegate, David Ewaliko, reported on the use of Japanese and "alien" labor in Hilo and Honolulu. Conditions had improved in Hilo since the organization of the Allied Federation of Trades and Citizens' Labor Union in 1909, but conditions, he reported, were far worse in the port of Honolulu. He successfully introduced a resolution at the national convention in Ohio calling for the complete exclusion of "Asiatic" labor. The term Asiatic was not defined in the resolution, blurring over the many ethnic combinations present in Hawaii. Ewaliko was then appointed Hawaii organizer and began to organize locals in Hilo and Maui.

At the following convention, a Maui delegate to the Pacific Coast District convention was able to secure passage of a resolution to permit the admission of aliens to membership but prohibiting their transfer to the mainland locals. The motion was adopted and the author was elected to the district executive board. This was the beginning of a long struggle to achieve multiethnic unity in the work force.

In the 1916 longshore strike, the workers demanded a wage increase and a union shop. They wanted a wage of forty cents per hour for a nine-hour day, with forty cents an hour for overtime. An effort was made to coordinate the strike with the local in San Francisco to create a boycott of Honolulu cargo loaded by scab labor. San Francisco workers had just suffered a smashing defeat. The Preparedness Day Parade bombing case left San Francisco labor weak and unable to offer any assistance, despite the promises of the Sailors Union of the Pacific.

The strike produced responses new to Honolulu. The Chamber of Commerce attempted to mediate the dispute. The mayor agreed to present the case of the workers to the employers but his efforts were rejected summarily. One prominent businessman offered the novel notion that the longshoremen were entitled to at least $4.00 per day. Their wages of $2.00 per day were just what they had been thirty years before, despite sharp increases in the cost of living induced by World War I.[9]

The strike slipped into violence as a train carrying strikebreakers to the waterfront was derailed. Battles between strikers and scabs became a daily occurrence. The strike was finally settled with a compromise—thirty cents per hour and forty cents per hour for overtime, with no recognition of the union. Despite the difficulties, union membership increased from 300 to over 1500.

The special character of Hawaii's multiethnic work force was demonstrated at the end of the strike. The company refused to rehire eleven Japanese longshoremen. They offered as the reason the fact that their Japanese supervisor refused to have Japanese workers who had struck. The longshoremen, predominately Hawaiian, refused to go back to work unless their Japanese brothers were rehired. A mass rally of 5,000 workers was held in Honolulu to support the strike. Finally the Japanese members resigned from the union in order to free their Hawaiian brothers to return to work. This and other episodes point to the fact that the supposed racial hostilities of workers were more a matter of employer than worker attitudes. [10]

Hawaiian longshore workers continued to respond to the major labor movements in the Pacific maritime industry. As the West Coast labor movement regrouped in the antilabor atmosphere of the 1920s, the Hawaiians were circulating in a steady flow to and from the Pacific Coast and were part of the movement to revive the International Longshoremen's Association on the coast in 1924 and 1926. [11] These efforts culminated in the formation of a new ILA local in San Francisco. Two seamen from Hawaii, Levi Kealoha and Harry Kamoku were part of this movement. Other Hawaiian members of the Sailors' Union of the Pacific, and the Marine Firemen, Oilers, Watertenders, and Wipers had received considerable exposure to maritime labor organizing in this period. [12]

Among the Hawaiians who participated in the climactic San Francisco strike of 1934 was Harry Kamoku. He returned to Hilo determined to build a new labor movement in Hawaii. Promptly fired and blacklisted from the waterfront, Kamoku persisted in his efforts. He envisioned a territory-wide labor movement with labor temples "all around the island to make them visible in the community." [13]

Although conditions were admittedly poor on the waterfront, the alternative employment opportunities were few and far between in the narrow Hawaiian economy. The major sugar factors controlled most of the non-plantation sector, as well as the waterfront. Those who joined unions risked a farreaching blacklist from which the only recourse was to leave the islands. Matters were little better in urban Honolulu, where the control over employment was almost as great as in the outer islands.

Paternalism of the companies sometimes led to concessions to the fledgling unionists. When Hilo longshoremen walked off the job in 1937 over the brutal behavior of a dock foreman, the Hilo Port employer, a C. Brewer company, reached an informal settlement with the union, recognizing the union and offering redress for the grievance. The informality of the pact was maintained for many years.[14]

A New Deal

A dramatic change came to Hawaii in 1937 in the form of the first National Labor Relations Board (NLRB) hearing to be held in the territory. In 1936, the newly formed International Longshoremen and Warehousemens' Union (ILWU) broke away from the parent ILA on the West Coast. The ILWU promptly issued charters to the Hawaiian locals in Hilo and Honolulu. In addition, ILWU President Harry Bridges chartered a territory CIO district in Honolulu and appointed Edward Berman as Director. On behalf of Honolulu longshoremen, this unpaid director initiated unfair labor practices charges in 1937 against Castle and Cooke, Ltd., the major stevedoring company and major owner of Matson Navigation Company.[15]

The first task for the NLRB administrative judge was to orient himself to the Hawaiian economy. The intricate, carefully woven structure of companies involved in the movement of cargo and maritime activities had to be unraveled.

> The relationship [of the companies] is so close, the acts of one melt into the acts of another without lines of demarcation, that it is impractical when discussing the occurrences to separate in each case the different companies according to the time. . . . What [they] did prior to September 15, as agents for Matson Terminals, Inc. is remembered and has its effect when [they] are agents for Castle and Cooke, Ltd, and still carried over when they act as agents and officers of Hawaiian Stevedores, Ltd.[16]

The examiner, George D. Pratt, also found an interesting employer organization, the Industrial Association of Hawaii (IAH). The IAH was organized in 1935 to "combat radical unions and radical labor leadership."[17] Pratt described the mechanism of intimidation and coercion that characterized labor relations in Hawaii: "Army Intelligence cooperates with the Industrial Association of Hawaii, and the latter, in turn, is managed by the attorney for Respondent, Castle and Cooke, Ltd."

Pratt attributed these attitudes to the long history of concentrated ownership and political power that had existed in a framework of an indentured, alien work force.

> It is far from surprising that an attitude of feudal paternalism on the part of the employers has developed toward the working peoples of the islands. . . . The mores of the Territory provide no place for a union or any of its employed inhabitants, and consequently, activity in looking toward such union organization and moves toward it which are commonplace on the mainland become endowed with portentous and revolutionary significance when seen through island eyes.[18]

The NLRB investigator was accompanied by the power of subpoena and the full force of federal law. This was, in effect, the beginning of what turned into a veritable revolution in attitudes in Hawaii. Hitherto, the federal government had been remote from the ordinary people of Hawaii. Now suddenly there was an agency that could compel attention to laws and civil rights. Upholding the unfair labor practice charges, the case opened a new era in Hawaii labor relations.

The Hilo Massacre

In 1937, in a move inspired by the San Francisco ILWU's effort to organize away from the waterfront, the famed "March Inland," Harry Kamoku organized the Hilo Industrial Union Council representing nine different unions. "To consolidate the many races of workers into one solid organization is something of a miracle, which is happening here in the Port of Hilo," he wrote to Harry Bridges.[19]

Union organization was evident elsewhere. On Kauai, the Port Allen longshoremen asked for affiliation with the ILWU, hoping to extend their organization into the ranks of plantation workers. In reality, the longshoremen of most of the outports were part-time plantation workers or part-time longshoremen, depending on one's perspective. Except at Hilo and Kahului, there was not enough shipping to support a full-time longshore force. Optimism was fueled by the growing number of Hawaiian workers on the West Coast. The editor of the *Voice of Labor,* the weekly newspaper of the Honolulu labor movement, explained that "six Hawaiian boys are working as permit men for 90 days as a guests of Local 38-79 (Seattle) They will be relied upon to give leadership on their return."[20]

From this beginning, Ed Berman was confident he could organize "65,000 workers in agriculture, canneries, and allied industries," needing only $3,000 and six months to complete the task. He named

"Brothers Akau and Bert Nakano from Seattle and Brothers Amoka and Kawano from San Francisco" to begin the task of building a labor movement in Hawaii.[21]

The newfound strength and optimism, coupled with a partial recognition from the employers, was offset by the appearance of inter-union rivalry as the national conflict between the American Federation of Labor (AFL) and the Congress of Industrial Organizations (CIO) threatened the new organizing drive. The AFL issued a federal union charter to a new organization, the Hawaii Waterfront Workers Association, led by Charles Wilson, the brother of John Wilson, long-time leader of *Hui Poola,* the political waterfront organization of the Democratic party in Honolulu.

This rivalry came to a focus in the organizing effort at Inter-Island Steam Navigation Company (IISN), the sole interisland transportation available in Hawaii. Five different unions claimed jurisdiction. The Inland Boatmen's Union (IBU) was disputed by the Sailor's Union of the Pacific and the Marine Firemen. The Hawaii Waterfront Workers disputed the ILWU claim to the longshoremen. The company refused to recognize the unions and asked for a membership check and an NLRB investigation. The unions refused and struck on 4 February 1938.[22] An agreement was reached with the company to recognize the Inland Boatmens Union, shortly in advance of the arrival of an NLRB examiner. The strikers were restored to their positions. The ILWU easily defeated its rival for representation of the longshoremen, and the IBU won the election for deck and engine room personnel.

Also involved in the organizing effort was a varied group of unions made up of machinists, boilermakers, and carpenters, loosely grouped in the Metal Trades Council, representing workers at the IISN dry dock operation. The three unions presented demands to the company, which varied according to occupation, but agreed on two essentials: a closed shop agreement and comparable pay with the West Coast.

Nothing was calculated to raise the wrath of the companies more than these two demands. The hiring hall was the focal point of opposition on the West Coast by these same employers. The ILWU had won this right in the bitter 1934 strike but the maritime employers of the Pacific region were not reconciled to its spread. On the pay issue, the employers took the position that the historically low wages of Hawaii would require a lengthy period of adjustment and, in addition, the peculiar circumstances of Hawaii made it impossible to make comparisons with West Coast wages. Hawaii's maritime workers often worked seven day weeks, long days with irregular hours, making it difficult to calculate overtime pay. As for penalty cargo rates, there was no definition of this category as there was in mainland ports. Long-shoremen attempting loading offshore on either wire cables or lighters were subjected to frequent injury and the threat of death for no extra compensation.

The adamant refusal of IISN to negotiate led to a renewal of the strike in late May 1938. As the strike dragged on, the interruption of the only cargo-passenger service available to the outer islands began to have its effect. Hilo merchants pressed for a resumption of shipping, even though this meant hiring strikebreakers. Some progress was made in negotiations as the ILWU and the IBU agreed to drop the hiring hall demand. The Metal Trades Council adamantly refused and the strike continued. Charles Wilson of the Hawaii Waterfront Workers was caught in a clumsy attempt to blow up an Inter-Island ship in dry dock. This did much to set nerves on edge.

The company sent the Inter-Island steamer *Waialele* to Hilo, manned by strikebreakers. It was met with a picket line and a threat of violence. While the Chief of Police was negotiating with the strike leader, Harry Kamoku, an over-anxious police lieutenant threw a tear-gas grenade without warning. The leaders were able to control their men and violence was avoided. The ship met with further threats of violence when it called at Kauai. The company announced that no further sailings would be attempted until protection was assured. The Hilo Chamber of Commerce pressed the Big Island sheriff to agree to such protection. The company agreed to an 1 August arrival of the ship in Hilo.

The union made elaborate plans for a community demonstration that would be carried out on lines borrowed from Gandhi, a man much admired by Harry Kamoku. The mass of people would move slowly to the apron of the dock and occupy the apron, line by line, in a passive demonstration. This would effectively prevent the unloading of the ship.

Sheriff Henry Martin prepared as if for a major battle, using sixty-eight policemen in three lines. The first line of five was armed with tear-gas grenades. Behind these were nine policemen armed with shot-guns to which bayonets had been fixed. The third line consisted of firemen equipped with water hoses. The remainder of the police were inside the warehouse, equipped with shotguns and three Thompson submachine guns. As the crowd arrived, the leaders discussed with the sheriff their right to be there. After the passengers on the ship had disembarked, the crowd began its demonstration. As one line sat down on the apron, supporters would move up and sit in front of them. Women strikers from the Hilo Laundry and the Kress store were in front, much to the distress of the sheriff.

At this point, Sheriff Martin ordered the shotguns reloaded, changing from buckshot to birdshot. Subsequent events indicate that not all of the policemen obeyed the order. Lieutenant Warren confronted the crowd and began clubbing the demonstrators. Firing began and some police used their bayonets, including Warren. He later claimed that the victim he stabbed had lunged at him and impaled himself on the bayonet. This was a rather remarkable feat as the wound was in the man's back. Fifty-one people were injured, including two women. The majority of the wounded were shot in the back as they fled the scene.

In the confused aftermath, the sheriff defended his actions by asserting that there were "seventy or eighty armed special deputies" on the ship and he feared they would fire on the crowd. No evidence was found for such a fear, although plantation use of heavily armed special deputies was an old tradition in Hawaii. Newly found evidence collected at the time of the event suggests that the police lieutenant acted without orders and without regard to the damage that would be inflicted.[23]

Forced to concede the loss of the hiring hall, the unions returned to work in September to end the strike. The union had to be content with the valuable lesson of solidarity and the importance of skilled negotiations and strike strategy. One new element in the strike was the use of radio. Hawaii's newspapers had either been outrightly hostile to organized workers or vaguely neutral. Even the large Japanese language press (some fourteen newspapers) was divided in its views on labor issues. With radio coverage and ILWU radio broadcasts—eleven in all—the public had a much clearer view of the strike, which contributed to public support for the union cause. Despite the clumsy effort at dynamiting in Honolulu and the violence in Hilo, the strike and negotiations had been conducted with a surprising lack of anger and recrimination.[24]

The date of The Hilo Massacre remains as an important day in Hawaii's labor circles. The maritime unions celebrate the event with a paid holiday in tribute to the early labor movement.

Collective Bargaining

In addition to the arrival of the NLRB in Hawaii, the setting up of the Agricultural Adjustment Administration assumed considerable power over the agricultural sector as the price for obtaining federal subsidies. These subsidies required the submission of data on profits, wages, and expenses that had been totally private in Hawaii. If the Hawaii industry wished to qualify for "compliance payments," it could do so only by setting wages at "minimum annual averages." What the Japanese and Filipino workers had tried to accomplish with their strikes in 1920 and 1924 was done with the stroke of a pen on 20 September 1938 when the old bonus system was abolished and replaced by "the higher wages which determinations required."[25] The passage of the Fair Labor Standards Act in 1938 and the Social Security Act meant that pay rates in many occupations had to be adjusted, particularly with respect to overtime and back pay.

The longshore locals moved to organize all of the ports of Hawaii in 1939. The International Convention of the ILWU voted to help the Hawaiian Islands Organizing Committee by returning to the locals a portion of their per capita payments. The Hawaiians calculated that this action meant they had a total of $182 per month for the organizing effort. This was sufficient to pay three organizers at $60 a month. Two veterans of Honolulu organizing were hired, Jack Kawano and Fred Kamahoahoa, along with Bert Nakano of Hilo.

Despite the optimism, the union on the Island of Hawaii had lost three of the small outports—Mahukona, Honuapo, and Kailua—primarily because of their isolation and the lack of local leadership. Port Allen on Kauai was the only local with a contract. Even Honolulu was poorly organized.

In July 1940, the longshore-plantation workers at Ahukini Landing on Kauai walked out on strike. The strike was precipitated by the management's attempt to prevent the application of wage and hour benefits due longshore workers from spilling over to plantation workers who were exempted as agricultural workers. Workers were told to choose between longshore and plantation work. The difficulty was that longshore work was part-time—two, perhaps three, days a week at best. If they chose longshore work, they lost the plantation housing perquisite since the company would have to pay overtime rates and include the cost of the perquisites in the wage calculation.

The longshoremen offered a compromise. They would work as longshoremen for a guarantee of $15.00 per week for thirty-one weeks per year and vacate the housing. This was similar to the informal, unwritten agreement of the Hilo longshoremen. The proposal was flatly rejected by the company, American Factors. This touched off a 298-day strike, the longest in Hawaiian labor history.[26]

The strike involved a significant element of multiracial cooperation. When American Factors attempted to unload Ahukini cargo at Port Allen, the longshoremen there walked off the job. The workers at Ahukini were primarily Filipino and those at Port Allen mainly Japanese. For nine months the longshoremen closed the ports of Kauai to all except tankers and Inter-Island steamers. This brought demands for federal intervention, and Secretary of Labor Francis Perkins ordered an investigation. The Honolulu administrator of the Wage and Hour Office reported that the company had misinterpreted the Fair Labor Standards Act and that the dual employment could easily be handled with some extra bookkeeping. The company refused to accept his findings, although the union was willing to accept the offer.

Harry Bridges, in San Francisco, offered some blunt advice: give up the strike, go back to work, organize the scabs and build local leadership. He dispatched an assistant from San Francisco to bring about an end to the strike. A mediator from the Pacific Maritime Conciliation Service won a prompt settlement of the strike, although at a considerable cost to the workers. They were forced to choose between longshore and plantation work. The longshore workers won a wage increase of four cents and company recognition of the union. The settlement installed a sense of bitterness that would return to trouble the union in coming years. Some blamed the ILWU Executive Board for failing to provide significant financial support. The strike illustrated once again that racial diversity was not in itself a barrier to labor organizing.

Preparation for War

In 1941, the ILWU, having won the representation election at McCabe, Hamilton and Renney and at Castle and Cooke, was locked in contract negotiations in Honolulu. The federal mediator was unable to move the company. Clifford O'Brien, the San Francisco assistant, reported to Bridges in May 1941 that the companies spent their time in the meetings "insulting the longshoremen on the committee and, I believe, trying to provoke a strike.[27] Hanging over negotiations were the increasing military preparations taking place in Hawaii. In April 1941 the army proposed to ship a black quartermaster battalion to Honolulu to handle longshore work at their piers. The union was alarmed at the prospect of losing employment. The political and social leaders of Honolulu reacted swiftly to secure resolutions from Congress opposing the use of such labor battalions in Hawaii.

An equal threat was posed by the large number of Japanese longshoremen. O'Brien was worried that the military would pose objections to their presence when unloading military cargo. He was anxious to protect these members with a contract and was willing to make concessions. A contract was reached with both firms at the end of May 1941. The contract, unique in Hawaii's labor history, offered wages of sixty cents per hour with stipulated raises twice in 1942, a penalty cargo list of thirty items, a safety code, a grievance procedure with provision for arbitration on items relating to discharge and safety, and an equal work opportunity. This last item was all that the union could salvage of the request for a union-run rotary hiring hall. Similar agreements, with appropriate modifications were signed for Hilo, Port Allen, and Ahukini. The research director of the Hawaii Employers' Council later wrote, "The year 1941 was a year of great success for the ILWU, marking the victory of the first stage of its drive for power in the longshore industry."[28]

Several elements in the situation were new to Hawaii. Workers had struck in a determined manner, called on the parent mainland organization for assistance, and successfully invoked pressure from Washington to gain a meaningful contract. It was the first genuine victory in what would be a protracted battle to establish the principles of collective bargaining in Hawaii.

Military Rule

Hawaii had been preparing for war since 1939. By the end of 1940 some 200,000 defense workers had been added to Hawaii's population. The imposition of martial law and the creation of the office of military governor had far-reaching effects on this labor force. Federal statutes such as the National Labor Relations Act, the Fair Labor Standards Act, and the National Wage Stabilization Program were all ordered suspended on 20 December 1941 by General Order No. 38. All employees of the federal, territorial, county governments, contractors, and public utilities were frozen to their positions. All labor contracts between employers and employees were suspended.[29] The national mobilization of labor also contained job controls. Washington made a major effort to contain rapidly rising prices and wages generated by the sharp increases in production. These national guidelines were overturned by the military authorities in Hawaii. The military governor created his own War Manpower Commission, with disastrous results. In the words of the territorial attorney general, "The military orders made little or no attempt to halt the rapid increase in wages; upgrading and misgrading of employees and the pirating of labor were the order of the day."[30]

Japanese aliens were barred from the waterfront, both as construction workers and longshoremen. Curiously, these men were freed to accept higher paying jobs in the many nonmilitary construction jobs available. Stevedoring operations were hampered by the use of convoys. When large convoys arrived there was an acute shortage of skilled workers for the key jobs of winch driver, hatch tender, and ship's clerk. Military personnel were not able to fill this gap.

A curious Hawaiian situation arose in the diversion of plantation labor to the waterfront. Plantation workers were paid their regular plantation wages for this work, but the plantation collected the waterfront wage. Plantation wages at that point were approximately forty-two cents per hour plus nine cents for perquisites. As labor contractors, the plantations collected sixty-two cents per hour for each worker furnished. The difference was retained as a "legitimate reimbursement for their expenditures, overhead, and lost sugar production." The workers, under martial law, were compelled to obey. At first the union was optimistic that the plantation workers would be able to collect their just pay but such was not the case. This pettiness cost the plantations dearly in the postwar era. Workers cited this practice in their eagerness to organize after 1944.[31]

Japanese-Americans were in a peculiar situation. The threat of internment was a major restraint on union militants. The military attitude that all persons of Japanese ancestry were suspect was difficult to overcome. The harassment of the president of the Kauai longshore local, Ichiro Izuka, was a warning to other waterfront militants. Izuka was confined for four months by the Civil Defense Board of Kauai and charged with impeding the war effort and distributing leaflets advocating strikes and slowdowns at military installations. In fact, Izuka had distributed the national newspaper of the Masters, Mates, and Pilots Union. The ILWU had committed the union members to President Roosevelt's no-strike policy for the duration. The Civil Defense Board was made up of three plantation managers, including the manager of the plantation against whom Izuka's ILWU local had struck in 1940. Although interrogated extensively about Marxism and Harry Bridges, no charges were filed against Izuka, who was released after 126 days of imprisonment.[32]

Not until late in the war, when the military's power had been

drastically curtailed, did any labor leader make a public statement. Art
Rutledge of the Teamsters' Union charged the military government
with incompetence. There was, he said, "no plausible reason for a
continuance of this illegal military control over patriotic citizens."[33]

In January 1944, the longshoremen began to organize, not on the
waterfront but on the plantations. They assembled a war chest and sent
ten longshoremen to Maui and Hawaii to recruit plantation workers
into the ILWU. In good part this was a reaction of the Japanese-
Americans who had suffered during the war. They were skilled workers
who had made a significant contribution to the war effort, working
tirelessly and without complaint. Many served in the special units such
as the 100th Battalion of the National Guard and the 442d Regimental
Combat Team, made up of Japanese-American volunteers, two of the
most highly decorated units in the war. The seeming weakness of the
union during the war was converted into militant strength in the
immediate postwar period.

Postwar Struggles

Despite the seeming incongruity of longshoremen organizing agricultural workers, the move made sense when seen in the context of
Hawaii's unique economy. It was virtually impossible to know where
one company ended and another began in the movement of supplies to
Hawaii from Pacific Coast docks, in the growing of the cane, and the
processing and shipping of the raw sugar to San Francisco where it was
manufactured, distributed, and sold by wholly owned companies. Longshore work was only a part of the whole, interwoven structure.[34]

The immediate outcome of the campaign begun in 1944 was to
establish the ILWU as the bargaining agent for some 33,000 sugar
workers, approximately 6,000 maritime workers, and miscellaneous
workers in commercial service firms. What had begun with a war chest
of $1,000 in 1944 emerged as a significant political power in the
territorial legislature and a well-financed, expertly staffed labor organization.

There remained a burning issue for Hawaii's maritime workers. Pay
rates of Hawaii workers were substantially less than rates on the coast,
even when employed by the same firms in San Francisco and Honolulu.
The significant victory of the union in the 1948 Pacific Coast strike
encouraged the Hawaii locals to attempt to end what they termed the
"colonial wage pattern," made worse by post-war inflation. The union

asked for a raise of thirty-two cents per hour and a termination date of the contract identical with that of the West Coast contract.

The employers rejected all of the demands, insisting that such a contract would "upset the area wage pattern." This apparently meant that traditional low pay rates should be maintained in Hawaii, regardless of economic circumstances. The employers offered eight cents per hour only because of a recent rise in the cost of living. They made this offer despite "adverse economic conditions existing in Hawaii." Negotiations failed. The union set 15 April 1949 as the strike deadline. Recognizing the potential damage a complete maritime strike would have in Hawaii, the union announced it would (1) work all military ships and cargoes; (2) determine which ships were "hot ships" and "hot cargoes" (i.e., which were the product of strikebreaking labor); (3) work all relief ships carrying food and medical supplies; and (4) unload all perishable and food cargoes on ships in port and U.S. mail. Interisland cargo and foreign cargoes were left for further study. The union also modified its wage stand to twenty-four cents, postponing the equalization demand.

Neither management nor the union foresaw the length or severity of the strike. There was little appreciation by management of the changed circumstances of the union and union officials underestimated the resolve of the employers to resist the union. Matson ships found it virtually impossible to unload on the Pacific Coast. Gulf and East Coast longshoremen also were reluctant to break the Hawaiian strike. The territorial legislature promptly seized the docks and placed their operation in the hands of an administrator, acting through the Board of Harbor Commissioners. All seven of the stevedoring companies were seized. Actual stevedoring operations started on 15 August and continued for seventy-two days to 25 October. The combined effect of the 1948 Pacific Coast strike and the Honolulu strike meant that Hawaiian shipping was interrupted for a total of five months between September 1948 and October 1949.[35]

The solidarity of maritime workers on the mainland made the seizure of the docks less than effective. Despite alarmist stories in the press, Hawaii was in no danger of running out of food or essential supplies. During August and September considerable amounts of freight were unloaded at Honolulu. One source of the supplies was a "splinter fleet" organized by Honolulu businessmen. Typically, these were small vessels chartered on the coast. An agreement was reached with the union to pay going rates with the expected increase placed in an escrow account to be paid at the conclusion of the strike. The move was effective in maintaining essential food supplies and a trickle of commercial goods. Combined with government unloadings, an adequate supply of essential supplies was maintained.

Three factors contributed to ending the 178-day strike: (1) competition from the splinter fleet and the Big Five's growing fear of losing their grip on the wholesale business of Hawaii; (2) the rapidly mounting pile of raw sugar on the plantations, and (3) the intervention of the Federal Mediation Service. The raw sugar situation was vital to the union because the plantation workers were providing the majority of financial support for the striking waterfront workers. If the plantations were forced to stop processing cane because of a lack of storage space, there would be an end to that source of support.

The intervention of the Federal Mediation Service came through some clever strategy by John Burns, Oahu Democratic Party chairman, who was enlisted by the union to help end the strike. Burns was able to persuade Secretary of Labor Maurice Tobin that the closely intertwined companies of Hawaii could afford to settle, given their total profits.[36] Cyrus Ching of the Mediation Service brought the two sides together in New York and quickly produced a settlement—one that was proclaimed as a victory by each side, albeit for different reasons. The union was running out of financial support and their public support was badly eroded. The potential losses of the sugar companies outweighed the losses these same companies were taking in their transportation, stevedoring, and wholesaling activities.

The Harbor Commission summed up the strike effects in this manner. "In spite of the stevedore strike which started 1 May 1949 and ended 25 October 1949, and except for War years, the past fiscal year has been the most successful financially of the Board's harbor operations."[37] Total overseas cargo, in and out of the port, however, dropped from 509,910 tons in 1948 to 263,873 in 1949 and 272,477 tons in 1950.[38] The "financial success" came from increases in charges for interisland cargo and the increased shipping inward—the splinter fleet. Outgoing cargo fell drastically.

The longshore strike had been marked by intense, virulent attacks on the union and its leadership by the media. The campaign was aimed at persuading the membership to disaffiliate from the Hawaii union and the ILWU in San Francisco. It attempted to destroy the union's racial unity by dividing Filipino and Japanese workers. The leadership of the union retained the confidence of the membership of all units and successfully withstood this multipronged attack.[39]

The 1949 strike established the principle that Hawaiian longshoremen would have parity with their counterparts on the mainland. The union was secure in its recognition and did not have to contest that issue again. The focus of union activity shifted away from the waterfront to the plantation and to the political sector after 1950.

Modernization and Mechanization

After 1934, when the Pacific Coast longshoremen won the hiring hall and restrictive work practices, the ILWU had been successful in resisting or holding back changes in longshore work arising from mechanization. By 1955, this slowdown and resistance was difficult to maintain in the face of sweeping changes in cargo handling techniques. More and more cargo was being shipped on wrapped and strapped pallets, eliminating the individual handling of break-bulk cargo. In Hawaii, bulk shipping of sugar appeared in 1941 and full-scale adoption was held up by wartime shortages of material. It spread rapidly following the end of the war.

The stability that the ILWU brought to the Pacific Coast waterfront after the 1948 strike rested in part on basic agreements between Paul St. Sure, head of the Pacific Maritime Association, and Harry Bridges. When the 1958 longshore contract was up for renewal, St. Sure raised the issue of mechanization and proposed a study. The union report in 1958 produced an impressive list of the changes that had already occurred and of the changes pending in world shipping and cargo handling.[40] The union study concluded that there were two approaches that could be followed. They could fight to hold the job-sharing and work-extending practices for a time or they could relax their opposition to mechanization and demand a share in the savings to be gained. The Maritime Association offered a bonus of $1.5 million to the union while an intensive, three-year study was undertaken.

A basic agreement unleashing full and unrestricted mechanization of the Pacific Coast stevedoring operations was signed in October 1961. The agreement provided many benefits for longshoremen, including an early retirement program with ample bonuses, a guarantee of a thirty-five hour work week, and life-time job security for those remaining in the industry. The program was then extended to Hawaii.[41] Despite objections from many longshoremen and what they perceived to be unnecessary concessions from the workers, the plan was accepted by the union membership and put into operation. The plan produced many quirks and centers of opposition to the basic idea, but modernizing and mechanizing the work of stevedoring proceeded apace.

The impact in Hawaii was dramatic and visible. Hawaii longshore workers had made some significant contributions to efficiency prior to the mechanization debate. In 1956, the union made comprehensive suggestions to improve cargo handling. Maui longshoremen contributed the idea of loading cargo in plywood containers—"boxes"—before 1941. Special pallets for canned pineapple, open boxes for brick and tile and "Jensen boxes" for such items as liquor, candy, and valuable cargo. These plywood boxes, six by six by four feet were sealed with aluminum seals. They were named after the head of the Maui Matson Terminals.[42]

The containerization now pending was something that would drastically reduce the work force (see table 8.1), although it lowered cargo handling costs. SeaLand Service had pioneered the use of containers on the East Coast in 1956. Matson provided innovations to this idea, using shore-based gantry cranes and larger containers. The union and the companies agreed to shift displaced workers from Hilo to the West Coast, for those desiring to remain in maritime work. Some 320 workers were laid off when the container barges arrived in Hilo.[43] In Honolulu, 217 men were laid off by Castle and Cooke in 1964.

A new idea emerged from these dramatic changes. A state-wide pool of longshoremen was developed. Men and their gear are flown to the outer islands as needed and minimal crews are kept in each of major

Table 8.1. Longshore Employment in Hawaii.

Year	Number employed
1900	810
1910	877 (including 2 women)
1920	1580 (including 8 women)
1930	1576 (including 1 woman)
1940	1280
1950	2162 (including 4 women)
1960	1378 (including 5 women)
1970	578
1980	204 (129 longshore equipment riggers, 6 women)

Source: U.S. Census, Occupations.

ports.[44] These innovations not only dramatically altered forever the idea of the longshoreman working in the hold, manhandling the cargo, pulling it with his hay-hook to the hatch. The old camaraderie of the waterfront gang was replaced by the high speed movement of twenty-four foot containers—one man on the crane and two on the dock or the deck. The arrival shortly thereafter of new ships, with new methods of carrying cargo would further alter the work along the waterfront.

Notes

1. This chapter is based upon the author's *Working in Hawaii: A Labor History* (Honolulu: University of Hawaii Press, 1985), chaps. 7, 13, 15.

2. *Pacific Commercial Advertiser* (4 May 1867).

3. Ibid. (19 April 1869, 17 July 1869).

4. *Hawaiian Gazette* (4 May 1881); *Saturday Press* (7 May 1881).

5. *Daily Bulletin* (25 June 1886; 14 December 1889).

6. John Reinecke, *Feigned Necessity: Hawaii's Attempt to Obtain Chinese Contract Labor, 1921–1923* (San Francisco: Chinese Materials Center, 1979), p. 10.

7. *Pacific Commercial Advertiser* (16 October 1901).

8. International Longshoremen's Association, Pacific Coast District, *4th Annual Convention*, 6–12 June 1911, p. 22.

9. *Pacific Commercial Advertiser* (26 September 1916).

10. Beechert, *Working In Hawaii*, pp. 158–159.

11. Richard Liebes, "History of Hawaiian Labor Organizations" (Master's thesis, University of Hawaii, Honolulu, 1937), pp. 35–36.

12. Interviews, Pacific Regional Oral History Program (PROH), Fred Low, Daniel Haleamau Interviews, April, 1965.

13. *Voice of Labor* (27 July 1936), article by Harry Kamoku. In 1960, the ILWU headquarters in Hilo was built and named in honor of Kamoku. It has become an important community center.

14. *Honolulu Record* (29 July 1952).

15. Beechert, *Working in Hawaii*, pp. 257–259.

16. National Labor Relations Board, 12th Region, *International Longshoremen's Association and Castle & Cooke, Ltd.*, Case XX-C-55, (Pratt Report), Honolulu, 14 August 1937, George O. Pratt, examiner, p. 3. Lawrence Fuchs characterized the period 1900–1941 as "The Web of Oligarchy" in his social history, *Hawaii Pono: A Social History* (New York: Harcourt, Brace & World, Inc., 1961), pp. 153–262: "For forty years, Hawaii's oligarchy was able to conserve and expand its hold on the wealth of the Islands" (p. 258).

17. *Honolulu Star Bulletin* (28 August 1935); See also Reinecke, *Feigned Necessity*, p. 180; *Honolulu Record* (1 September 1955), Wilson Interview.

18. National Labor Relations Board, Pratt Report, pp. 6, 32–33.

19. Harry Kamoku to Harry Bridges, 28 July 1937, ILWU Organizing Files, Hawaii, 1937–1943, ILWU Archives, San Francisco.

20. Edward Berman and Maxie Weisbarth to Harry Bridges, 8 June 1937, ILWU Territorial Organizing Committee, ILWU Archives, San Francisco.

21. Berman to Bridges, 27 October 1937, ILWU Archives, San Francisco.

22. For a full examination of this event, see William J. Puette, *The Hilo Massacre: Hawaii's Bloody Monday* (Honolulu: University of Hawaii, Center For Labor Education and Research, 1988). See also, Beechert, *Working in Hawaii*, pp. 260–268.

23. Puette, *The Hilo Massacre*, contains material recently found in the state archives.

24. A contemporary report on the event concluded that while unions were treated with some respect, the factionalism had caused labor "to lose face; its poor showing in the [territorial] elections gave it no hold over the legislature. . . . Nor have industrial relations markedly improved in Hawaii." Yet despite its mistakes and losses, the Inter-Island strike remains a source of inspiration to union men. John Reinecke, *Report on the Hilo Massacre* (Honolulu: Social Affairs Committee, Hawaii Education Association, 1939), p. 149.

25. James Shoemaker, *Labor in the Territory of Hawaii, 1939* (Washington, D.C.: G.P.O.), pp. 39–40.

26. *Honolulu Star Bulletin* (19 December 1940). The company claimed that the Federal Mediation and Conciliation Service recommendations were an incorrect application of the Fair Labor Standards Act.

27. Clifford O'Brien to Harry Bridges and Matt Meehan, 29 May 1941, ILWU Correspondence, O'Brien, ILWU archives, San Francisco.

28. Phillip Brooks, *Multiple-Industry Unionism in Hawaii* (New York: Columbia University Press, 1952), p. 70.

29. For full details on the operation of martial rule, see J. Garner Anthony, *Hawaii Under Army Rule* (Palo Alto: Stanford University Press, 1955).

30. Ibid., p. 43.

31. James Shoemaker, *The Economy of Hawaii in 1947* (Washington, D.C.: G.P.O. 1949), p. 26.

32. Ichiro Izuka, "The Labor Movement in Hawaii, 1934–1949," unpublished paper, University of Hawaii, Honolulu, 1974; Beechert, *Working in Hawaii*, pp. 287–288.

33. American Federation of Labor, Teamster's Union, Memorandum on Military Control of Hawaiian Labor, 22 March 1944, University of Hawaii, Honolulu, Hawaii War Records.

34. For details on the organizational campaign, the legal issues, and jurisdictional problems, see Beechert, *Working in Hawaii*, chaps. 13–15.

35. Harbor Commissioners, *Report* (1949), p. 5; *Report* (1950), p. 12; Territory of Hawaii, *Session Laws*, 1949, Act 2.

36. Paul Brissenden, "The Great Hawaiian Dock Strike," *Labor Law Journal*, 4 (4) (April 1953): pp. 231–279; Sanford Zalberg, *A Spark is Struck: Jack Hall and the ILWU in Hawaii* (Honolulu: University of Hawaii Press, 1979), pp. 265–266. Burns, unknown in

Washington was introduced to an influential Catholic priest who took him to Secretary of Labor Tobin.

37. Harbor Commissioners, *Report* (1950), p. 7.

38. Ibid., p. 61.

39. See Edward Beechert, "Red Scare in Paradise," in *The Cold War Against Labor,* edited by Ann Fagan Ginger and David Christiano (Berkeley, Meikeljohn Civil Liberties Institute, 1987) vol. 2, pp. 447ff. For details of the Smith Act trial of the Hawaii Seven, which included Jack Hall, regional director of the union, see, Thomas M. Holmes, *The Spectre of Communism in Hawaii, 1947–1953* (Ph.D. dissertation, University of Hawaii, Honolulu, 1975).

40. Charles Larrowe, *Harry Bridges: The Rise and Fall of Radical Labor in the United States* (New York: Lawrence Hill, 1972), pp. 351–358; William L. Worden, *Cargoes: Matson's First Century in the Pacific* (Honolulu: University of Hawaii Press, 1981), pp. 143–144.

41. Lincoln Fairley, *Facing Mechanization: The West Coast Longshore Plan* Institute of Industrial Relations Monograph No. 23 (Los Angeles: University of California, 1979), pp. 176, 238.

42. Worden, *Cargoes,* p. 140.

43. *Honolulu Star Bulletin* (28 April 1960).

44. *Honolulu Advertiser* (1 November 1965).

9

The Port: Now and Future

Changes in the 1950s

In 1956, Matson Navigation initiated a program to convert six of its ships to carry the new cargo containers. These ships would carry twenty containers on deck and traditional bulk or break-bulk cargo in the hold.[1] The use of shore-based gantry cranes to handle these containers demanded radical changes in pier construction. Finger piers supported by pilings, with covered sheds, could not accommodate the great weight of the cranes and containers. In addition, ample space was needed to store and marshal the vans.

Matson's move from its traditional home in the Port of San Francisco across the bay to Oakland presaged similar changes in Honolulu. Pier sheds were an obstacle in Honolulu as well as San Francisco. At the O.R. & L. piers, the vans had to be loaded onto narrow-gauge rail cars and moved to an inland storage area away from the docks. This cumbersome and costly arrangement eliminated much of the advantage in the labor savings potential offered by the containers. Speed of loading and unloading and speed of setting the containers on trailers with a minimum of handling were essential to efficient working of the system. Matson turned to the harbor commissioners in 1956 for a solution. Modifications to the Diamond Head Terminal were undertaken and completed in 1960.

Matson severed its long-time link with Dillingham in 1948 and began operating through the Castle and Cooke terminals. In 1964, Matson severed this connection and operated its own terminal service. Land secured in trades with the Immigration Service and the army was used to create a container marshalling yard and a break-bulk station adjacent to it in the shedded area. The container yard was a public facility; the cranes and the sheds were the property of Matson.

"Through an agreement with Matson, their cranes must be made available to others on a rental rate approved by the Board." This arrangement was the first step in the long-recommended public ownershp of all port facilities.[2]

That the economy was shifting from its old, concentrated control to a broader base was clear to all. What it meant was not as clear. The two stars of the postwar economy were defense expenditures and the tourist industry. Passenger traffic in the port was regarded as an important key to development and tended to receive the majority of attention from the various investigations. Rising income on the mainland was the key to this increased tourism. The tourist industry was seen as the engine that would pull the Hawaiian economy to new levels.

The minimal effect on the economy of the nearly six-month shutdown of the Hawaiian sugar industry that began in February 1958 was cited as evidence of these changes. As one consultant put it, "[t]he economy of Oahu is today primarily based on the production of services, services to tourists, services to shipping and services to a growing population with a rising personal income. With only one employee out of fifty employed in the sugar industry, Oahu was little affected by the recent sugar strike."[3]

Although this investigation by the Law and Wilson-Tudor Engineering Company found that approximately half of the non-petroleum cargo was coming in containers, this could not be expected to increase significantly. They reasoned that the present level "would not go beyond the present commitment of deck-loaded containers on C-3 cargo ships." With the break up of the Big Five domination of wholesaling, the new wholesalers would use the "stevedoring companies to sort out the consignments in the pier shed." Successful use of containers, they argued, would require large or consolidated orders and some form of warehousing. The future lay with palletized or "unitized" cargo—glued cartons on disposable pallets.[4]

Many expected cruise ship traffic to more than offset the decline in passenger traffic lost to jet aircraft. The projection based on cruise ships and Pacific Coast-Hawaii ships was a 40 to 50 percent increase by 1962 over 1958 figures. "When jet aircraft are placed in service, it is likely that the percentage by ship will decrease, though the total number so traveling will still increase. Of an estimated 500,000 visitors expected by 1967, it was projected that 125,000 would arrive by ship.[5]

The rapid fluctuation of the economy in the 1950s created great concern. The increasing mechanization of agriculture coupled with federal subsidy programs in sugar clearly meant a stable, if not declining, output in that sector. Federal military expenditures, such an important component in World War II, were now variable and unpredictable, but likely to continue at a fairly high level. Tourism and domestic consumption seemed to be the only areas available for an expansion of the economy.

Statehood and the 1960s

The greatest change in Hawaii's circumstances came with statehood in 1959. Statehood had been a goal for the corporate and political sectors since the issue was first broached in 1854. The postwar period was marked by an intense anti-Communist movement that focused on the labor movement. Following the pattern of the mainland, the Hawaii ILWU was the focus of an intense red-baiting campaign from 1950 to 1955. Opponents of Hawaiian statehood in Congress successfully used this theme to thwart efforts to achieve statehood. The achievement of the long-sought prize in 1959 touched off an economic boom.

Statehood brought an end to the Board of Harbor Commissioners. A new Department of Transportation assumed jurisdiction over the harbor, the airport, and state highways. Little or no consideration was given to the creation of a port authority, something long-advocated by maritime interests. The change in administration was largely one of titles. The legislature and the governor remained the dominant powers in all matters pertaining to the harbor.

An old theme was boosted into prominence in this period of uncertainty. Hawaii, once an entrepôt for the Pacific-Asian trade in an era of sail, could once again assume that role. The idea was stimulated by plans of Matson Navigation to expand its operations into the Asian market with a fleet of container ships. Hawaii was to become a "transshipment center; a trans-Pacific trading center." The goal was to develop "frequent, equitable, and responsive through-shipping services, not only to and from the Mainland but to and from the East and West; to open new markets to Hawaii's export of goods and services; to discover a new set of intermediate functions which Hawaii can perform on behalf of trans-Pacific trades."[6]

All of this came down to the question of whether Hawaii could "achieve the central geopolitical prominence in trade and commercial policy that has always been inherent in its location." To accomplish these goals, Hawaii "must become easy of access and perform a set of functions that facilitates the flow of trans-Pacific trades." These visions of the future were not based on the character of Pacific trade and shipping but on the idea that economic development must be regarded as inevitable. It remained only to find the proper combination.

Honolulu Harbor certainly underwent substantial change. In the postwar period the harbor was pushed to what would appear to be its maximum potential. The Diamond Head Terminal was transformed into a modern container handling facility, capable of dealing with containers and roll-on, roll-off ships. Land was obtained in a trade from the U.S. Army and Immigration Service at pier 1 for a marshalling yard.

The entrance channel was deepened to forty-five feet and the harbor basins dredged to forty feet. The Aloha Tower passenger complex was modernized and enlarged, despite the obvious decline in passenger traffic. A second entrance and channel was proposed in 1959 by the Corps of Engineers and authorized in 1965 (see fig. 9.1). A Foreign Trade Zone was established in 1966 at pier 39. By 1967, the port had fifty-one modernized wharves.[7]

The reality behind the effort to develop continued to elude many of the participants. Matson's plans were based on what the company perceived to be a permanent lead in container shipping. In late 1963, a dramatic change in Matson's structure occurred. The directors took a bold step and voted to cancel their terminal and stevedoring contracts with Castle and Cooke, despite the fact that the company owned 23 percent of Matson. The new president, Stanley Powell, was certain that Matson could perform these services at considerable savings. At the same time the company launched an ambitious ship building program to develop a Far Eastern trade.[8]

In the midst of these plans, the U.S. Department of Justice lodged a civil suit against the owners of Matson, charging an illegal restraint of trade by four of the Big Five, Alexander and Baldwin, Castle and Cooke, C. Brewer, and American Factors, the owners of a majority of the Matson stock.[9] This confronted the company with the dilemma of whether to liquidate Matson or find a buyer. The problem was resolved when Alexander and Baldwin purchased the stock of the other three defendants in the suit, something over 40 percent of the outstanding stock, giving them a 74 percent ownership.

Matson's Asian ventures ran into a long series of difficulties and serious setbacks. An important part of the Matson plan was to offer container services across the Pacific to a land bridge traversing the United States. This combined service would enable the company to capture a large volume of the Asian trade to the United States. Asian competition, particularly that of the Japanese shipping lines, proved to be formidable. Lacking the experience of the older, established Asian firms, Matson was unable to attract the cargoes they had expected, nor were they able to deal effectively with Asian governments. The Far East service was terminated in mid-summer 1970, after steady losses. Matson settled back into its traditional role of the principal shipper between Hawaii and the Pacific coast.[10]

Passenger traffic, expected to increase in total number of passengers, failed spectacularly in the face of the high-speed, efficient jet airplanes that came into service. The decline of American flag shipping in the decade of the 1960s was unanticipated by others as well. In 1970 Matson announced the sale of its flagship, the liner *Lurline*, the last American flag passenger vessel operating without a subsidy. The companion vessels, *Monterey* and *Mariposa*, were sold to Pacific Far East Lines two months later.

The underlying reason for these failed plans was a stubborn refusal to recognize a simple fact. Hawaii is a very small place. The port had been

Figure 9.1   Second Entrance, 1964 (from U.S. Army Corps of Engineers *Annual Report* for 1964).

modernized and pier facilities developed, but the results were deemed unsatisfactory by the shipping companies, the state agencies, and the public. One investigator gave a little-noticed response to the complaints. Professor Wytze Gorter published an alternative view of the Hawaiian economy in 1964. The changes wrought by World War II and the postwar period brought the scale of activities in Honolulu to a level that raised expectations of economic development. "Some of us," he said, "are unaware that it was not until the scale of activities became large enough that certain hoped-for economic developments occurred. . . . A small market can ordinarily provide adequate income for only a few sellers; it is as simple as that."[11] The ocean transportation industry was no exception, he pointed out. Almost all of the transportation requirements of Hawaii could be met with a fleet of thirteen freighters.

In a dramatic move, the state became the owner of all piers and almost all of the Honolulu Harbor waterfront on 15 August 1967. The key to this development was the purchase from the Dillingham Corporation of eighty-five acres of land and the adjoining piers. Immediately the Department of Transportation moved to set up a Harbor Task Force to help in the development of master plan.

One of the first proposals to appear was for the construction of a dry dock facility on Sand Island.[12] The proposal, soon endorsed by the head of a marine supply company, urged that construction on Sand Island was essential to the increase of shipping that was just over the horizon. A major port required a dry dock with a minimum lifting capacity of 20,000 tons. "Honolulu is the only port in the world without even minimum facilities to adequately dry dock and repair ocean-going vessels that regularly call here. Lack of modern ship repair facilities makes this segment of the shipping industry probably the most underdeveloped segment of Hawaii's economy."[13]

A feasibility study by the Tudor Engineering Company emphasized the points made by Gorter. The proposal would "result in operational deficits under all degrees of utilization." Honolulu, the feasibility study concluded, was off-track for vessels not destined to Hawaii and ships were not likely to call at Hawaii for annual maintenance and repair.[14] Since 1944, the navy-built dry dock had been operated by Dillingham Corporation at pier 41; it was able to meet most of the required services. With a capacity of 2,800 tons, the dry dock was accompanied by a marine railway of 1,400 tons haul-out capacity.[15]

The Harbor Task Force Development Plan of 1968, shorn of some its more exotic elements, moved ahead. Sand Island was largely converted to state ownership, sharing a portion of the bulkhead pier with the U.S. Coast Guard cutters and buoy tenders. Eventually, the state hopes to assume control of the entire island. Container facilities were developed at piers 50 and 51, and a Foreign Trade Zone was set up temporarily at pier 39. The interisland cargo terminals were equipped to handle container barges.[16]

No sooner were the Harbor Task Force plans announced than Isthmian Lines announced that it was canceling its service to eastern and gulf ports because of the low volume of traffic. SeaLand lines quickly moved into the competition with plans to initiate a container service in 1970 to the West Coast. For the first time, Hawaii would enjoy the luxury of a competing, turn-around container service to the coast.[17]

A second container facility at Sand Island was planned in 1970 for U.S. Lines that would provide direct service from Europe via the East and West Coasts. The facility was completed and service began in September 1973.

Much postwar planning had been an extension of existing economic patterns, but by 1970, it was clear that some massive changes already had occurred in Hawaii's basic economic structure. The economy seemed to be expanding, but in an erratic manner. Sand Island, Fort Armstrong, and the Aloha Tower complex all seemed to have reached a climax of development. Tourism and federal spending, both defense and non-defense, had become the principal props for the economy.[18] The Federal Maritime Commission concluded in 1978 that "It is unlikely that the demand for ocean transportation services which is derived from the underlying demand for commodities will experience much growth in the immediate future."[19]

For every three incoming containers, two returned eastbound empty. For refrigerated containers, a full 75 percent returned empty. Coupled with a seasonal variation in the pattern of incoming cargo, these conditions placed sharp limits on the shipping industry.[20]

Although future planning is an important factor, attention to conditions already present can be more pressing. In 1970, the Coast Guard called attention to the growing pollution of Honolulu Harbor. Asphalt, fuel oil, and molasses commonly were spilled into the harbor. Oil spills were large enough to constitute a fire hazard. The Harbors Division had no plan for dealing with such problems. Old fuel lines had corroded to the point where the Chevron refinery refused to continue delivery until the lines were replaced. At one point all three fuel lines in the harbor

from pier 18 to pier 1 were out of service.[21] The Environmental
Protection Agency entered the scene by declaring that the Harbors
Division had failed to meet the minimum standards for cleaning up its
share of pollution in the harbor.[22]

The Harbor Today

Honolulu Harbor has been the subject of more planning efforts over
the years than most other major harbors. Dating from the 1840s, it has
operated at near capacity. The small size of the harbor clearly made it
difficult to postpone needed but expensive dredging and expansion. In
recent years, the impetus toward planning has gained strength, both
from concern over capacity to handle port traffic and economic development plans.

In 1976, a new long range plan, *The 1995 Master Plan for Honolulu
Harbor,* was adopted by the legislature. Completion of the container
facilities, including building a second facility on Sand Island, head the
list in the plan. A maritime industrial park was to be developed on
Sand Island. This increased use would necessitate the building of a
second bridge across the Kalihi Channel in 1986 or 1987 to handle the
sharp increase in anticipated traffic. Control over the bascule bridge
was transferred to the state in 1976 because of a lack of ship traffic
through the second channel. The new, wider bridge, under construction in 1988, is a fixed span that effectively closes off the second
entrance to the harbor. The increasing size of cargo ships and the
development of container facilities have made the second entrance a
relatively unimportant feature of the harbor. The heavy truck-con-
tainer traffic from Sand Island had a higher priority than a second
entrance. The narrow Kalihi Channel, with a sharp turn in mid-
channel would be difficult for the increasingly large ships employed.
The planned development of Barbers Point harbor was assumed to be
able to absorb any overload of traffic.[23]

On the practical side, the Corps of Engineers began the work of
increasing the depth of the harbor basins to forty feet and the Fort
Armstrong entrance to forty-five feet. The work was authorized in
1965, but completion was delayed until 1981 by environmental requirements.[24]

Honolulu Harbor is going through the same process that has overtaken other major ports. The changes in maritime technology and the
virtual disappearance of regularly scheduled passenger liners created
problems of harbor management. Boston, New York, Baltimore, Seat-

tle, San Francisco, and many other major maritime centers have been forced to dramatically alter the workings of their ports. So it is with Honolulu.

Honolulu Harbor still faces the problem it has had throughout the modern era—a disequilibrium of trade. In 1987, out of a total trade value of $2.21 billion passing through the harbor, only $338.8 million were exported from Hawaii. Sugar and pineapple remain the only significant exports. Automobiles and household goods of people, particularly military personnel, are the other important categories of commodities.[25]

Passenger arrivals dropped to a low of 828 in 1986, with no prospect of an increase. The only passenger vessels operating out of the harbor are two cruise ships of American Hawaii Cruises, which feature week-long cruises among the islands.

The former Matson liner, *Monterey,* operated by the Aloha Pacific Cruise Company, began weekly cruises around the island in September 1988. The ship was plagued by equipment failures and the company collapsed into bankruptcy. The American Shipbuilding Company of Virginia has been seeking financing and subsidies for two ships to add to this cruise pattern. To date the effort has been unsuccessful. Since all of the existing and proposed cruises would have weekend departures, the facilities of Aloha Tower would be seriously strained. More serious would be the lack of facilities in the outer islands to accommodate this number of simultaneous arrivals.[26]

Efforts to establish interisland ferry services have been attempted sporadically, with little success. The Department of Transportation is planning a mass transit marine ferry system for the island of Oahu between Hawaii Kai to the east of Honolulu, to Waikiki and Honolulu Harbor, and on to the airport. Bids to operate the system were opened in March 1988. A California firm has been selected to design a marine ferry vessel, that probably would operate from pier 8.[27]

With all of these limiting circumstances, the harbor remains a vital factor in the economy of the state. Almost 98 percent of the goods imported into Hawaii pass through Honolulu Harbor for distribution throughout the state. The development of container handling facilities at Sand Island by Matson and SeaLand are likely to be able to handle the trade for the foreseeable future. Some of the supercontainer ships, drawing forty-five feet of water would require modification of the basin and entrance channel, but it is not clear that the Hawaii trade would attract these vessels. Such vessels require a load of 1,500 containers per visit to be economically viable. Matson and SeaLand ships seem quite able to handle the volume with considerable margin to spare.[28]

Barbers Point Harbor

Anxiety about the capacity of the port led to the development of a second, commercial deep-draft harbor at Barbers Point in 1965. The state planning authorities also hoped to shift economic development away from urban Honolulu. A small harbor with a basin of ninety-two acres and a depth of thirty-eight feet, the harbor seems destined to serve principally as a petroleum and hazardous material facility.

Concern over the shipping of explosives and hazardous material was expressed by the Corps of Engineers, beginning in 1947. In 1957, the commander of the 14th Naval District Coast Guard announced the suspension of shipping explosives into the harbor in quantities greater than 500 pounds at any one time. The construction industry was affected seriously by the restriction. This was one of the factors fueling the demand for a second harbor at Barbers Point.[29]

Projected development of the northwestern portion of the island of Oahu as a second population and commercial center was a principal argument for the construction of the Barbers Point facility. The long range development of industrial facilities was assumed to be sufficient justification for a second deep-draft harbor. In the numerous hearings between 1958, when the idea was first proposed, and 1965, when Congress approved the recommendation to construct the harbor from the existing small private barge harbor, the argument ran that "Honolulu Harbor would not be able to effectively or economically handle the expanded future commerce of Oahu and that a supplementary port would be of general benefit." A second argument favoring the new harbor was the proposal of the chief engineer to move the bulk sugar facility from "pier 19 to the new harbor to capture the economic benefits of the shorter haul from the then four plantations still operating on Oahu."[30]

The arguments were all quite rational and carefully reasoned. The economies, in practice, do not seem realistic. Hawaii's small size would mean a high overhead for relatively small quantities of cargo split between Honolulu and West Oahu. The trucking costs from the main container station in Honolulu Harbor would be much less than the costs of splitting cargo and unloading containers in both harbors. Barbers Point suffers from a serious surge problem and is not able to handle large ships. Refinery needs are met with off-shore loading facilities. The present generation of container ships would require an increase in the depth of the basin and a considerable enlargement of the basin.

Perhaps one of the most serious flaws in the notion of a second deep-draft harbor for Oahu is the cost of splitting delivery of containers between two ports or making few trips to each port. The principal argument in the Corps of Engineers survey was that the development of West Oahu as a second population center would be well served by such a harbor with its lower trucking costs to that center, rather than moving cargo twenty-five miles from Honolulu to the Ewa Plain.

Barbers Point, planned as a reliever harbor for Honolulu, and not yet completed (1990), is still discussed in terms of a second commercial port. "Overland trucking costs will be significantly reduced for those firms on the Leeward side, once the facility is operational."[31] The assumption behind this idea is that container ships or barges will be able to divide their load between Sand Island and Barbers Point. The cost of an additional harbor call would clearly outweigh the savings in

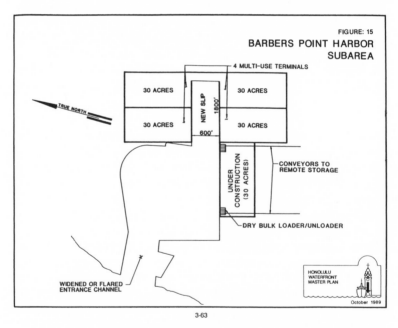

Figure 9.2 Barbers Point Harbor Master Plan, 1989 (from State of Hawaii, Department of Transportation, *Honolulu Waterfront Master Plan*, 1989).

transportation distances, which amount to a maximum of twenty-five miles.

The cost of cargo handling has been overlooked or underestimated in many of the plans, both past and present. Such concepts as trans-shipment of goods using Hawaii as a base or directing cargo to population centers tend to ignore warehousing and inventory costs, as well as the costs of unloading and loading. The conformation of the harbor, squarely facing the surf, means it is forced to shut down during adverse weather conditions. The harbor "is inadequate for the new generation of ocean-going freight vessels."

Current plans for the harbor call for a wider, deeper, flared entrance to minimize the surge problem and to handle large vessels. A dry-bulk loading and unloading facility is presently (1990) under construction. A four terminal complex with a new 600 foot by 1,800 foot slip is planned for the harbor. (fig. IX.).[32]

The principal tug and barge operator at the harbor was quoted as saying "Barbers Point will end up being a supplemental harbor . . . for grains, construction materials, and petroleum."[33] Barring dramatic changes in Hawaii's economy, the destiny of Barbers Point seems to be as a bulk commodity facility, catering largely to barge traffic and the handling of hazardous materials. As a barge and bulk facility, the harbor has a function to serve; as a container port, it is unlikely to succeed.

The Foreign Trade Zone

Perhaps spurred by the experience of the 1876 Reciprocity Treaty with the United States, the "free port" idea surfaced from time to time in Honolulu business circles as a means of stimulating the maritime commerce of Hawaii. Borrowing from the experience of European free ports, a concrete proposal was put forward in 1918 for a free port in Hawaii. "Although the islands have been annexed . . . and although they are behind the tariff wall and are looking forward to statehood as their goal . . . [they] must memorialize Congress for enabling legislation."[34] There would be, it was argued, no loss of revenue to the United States, since goods reshipped to the mainland would be dutiable at the ports of entry. The idea that shippers require a place to rearrange, repackage, relabel, or further process their goods underlies the basic idea of the foreign trade zones.

In 1957, the territorial legislature ordered a study made of the feasibility of such a zone in Hawaii. Based on legislation first enacted in 1934 and modified in 1950, there were seven foreign trade zones, of which only four had survived by 1957. The study concluded that Hawaii offered a very limited potential and would likely operate only on a limited basis, much like Seattle's zone.[35] The Board of Harbor Commissioners quickly concluded that such a zone in Hawaii would not be financially self-supporting and should not be established.

The negative recommendations deferred action until 1964, when the state made application for a free trade zone. Operations commenced in June 1966 at pier 39. The arguments were much the same as those put forth in the original 1934 legislation: the zone would create employment, expand Hawaii's role in foreign trade, increase traffic to Honolulu Harbor, attract new industries and businesses, and reduce shipping rates and thus provide Hawaii businesses with an advantage over their foreign and domestic competitors. Proponents even argued that the zone would "raise productivity levels and stimulate the entrepreneurial function in the underdeveloped regions of Asia. The State envisioned expanding the Zone to a site on Sand Island to encourage the development of new industries, particularly manufacturing activities."[36]

This 1978 Booz-Allen and Hamilton study was almost as pessimistic as the original 1959 legislative study. Local support for the concept overcame the low achievements of the zone. As the auditors pointed out, the employment effects were small and the zone operated at a loss if normal accounting procedures were used.

Although Hawaii's was one of three profitable zones of the ten operating in 1978, the prospects were not good. Two manufacturing activities had been established. Garments manufactured from Japanese printed textiles were exported from the zone to Japan at a considerable savings in customs. And a petroleum sub-zone was authorized in 1970 and began operations in 1972. This proved to be highly successful in processing and re-exporting Indonesian crude oil, and in 1974 the manufacture of synthetic natural gas.[37] Three more sub-zones subsequently were applied for and granted: a flour mill and two pineapple canneries, one on the island of Maui. Moved to pier 2, the zone expanded to a total of 500,000 square feet of which over 300,000 square feet are shedded space.

The state is fully committed to the expansion of the zone through sub-zones, whenever feasible. The leading commodities handled at the zone reflect only a modest manufacturing component, as table 9.1 suggests. The location of the principal zone at pier 2 provides adequate shipping facilities. The petroleum sub-zone is located in the vicinity of Barbers Point. That facility has become largerly a petroleum and bulk

Table 9.1. The Five Leading Commodities of Foreign Origin by Value and Weight.

Commodity	Value	Commodity	Weight (short tons)
1. Liquor	$8,840,529	1. Liquor	1,976.1
2. Wearing Apparel	2,747,242	2. Gen'l Merchandise	631.2
3. General Merchandise	2,681,709	3. Wearing Apparel	356.7
4. Machinery and Parts	1,697,376	4. Food Products	333.8
5. Electronic Products	1,144,860	5. Electronic	265.1

Source: Hawaii State Department of Planning and Economic Development, Foreign Trade Zone Report 1986, p. 5.

commodity port. The flour and pineapple facilities are adjacent to the harbor, with one of the two pineapple sub-zones located on Maui.

The foreign trade zone and its extensions are unlikely to significantly alter the volume of traffic in the harbor. Reductions in tariffs and improved packaging and transportation in foreign trade tend to eliminate many of the original reasons for such zones. As an aid to certain types of business activities, they fill a need and are likely to continue.[38]

Building the Outports

The significance of the outports shifted from their role in servicing the whaling trade to one of supplying plantations and shipping the sugar, cattle, and pineapple to Honolulu. For many years, sugar was loaded onto off-shore ships from lighters and even from wire-transport systems running out to the anchored ships. Some of that sugar went to Honolulu; in the early period, before 1900, some went directly to San Francisco. As the volume of supplies for the island populations and business grew, shipping was directed to the ports rather than the risky and time consuming process of off-shore loading.

Hilo was the first harbor to attract the attention of the Corps of Engineers. Hilo, like Lahaina, was more a roadstead than a bay. Although ample in size, the anchorages were exposed to heavy winds and poor conditions. In 1907, Hilo was authorized to build a breakwater and to dredge the entrance channel to Kuhio Bay. The breakwater was eventually extended to over 10,000 feet to protect the harbor basin. Three piers and a bulk sugar loading facility accommodate the commerce of the island.[39]

Given the static and even declining population of the outer islands until the 1960s, there was little need to develop facilities beyond those required by agricultural development. Interisland passenger traffic remained steady at approximately 10,000 to 15,000 per year for Hilo until the beginning of the war mobilization effort in 1940. The introduction of air service eventually wiped out all surface passenger traffic. These conditions meant there was little stimulus to develop facilities beyond those required for commercial purposes.

Maui, after the exciting years of whaling at Lahaina, found the locus of shipping moved to Kahului, closer to the center of agriculture and population. As in Hilo, the prime requirement was the construction of breakwaters to protect the small harbor. Beginning in 1910 with the east breakwater, the harbor expanded in 1916 when a west breakwater gave a greater protection to the basin. In 1927, the basin was expanded to accommodate expanded sugar shipments. To meet container needs, the basin was enlarged again in 1960 to provide more effective, open dock space.

The outer islands have had rather intensive tourist development since 1970. Maui, Kauai, and Hawaii, in that order, have experienced a remarkable growth in the number of hotels and tourists.[40] When the freight traffic of each of the ports of Hawaii are examined, the remarkable stability of traffic emerges as the decisive fact. Sugar has remained stable at around 1 million tons in the postwar period, governed as it is by quotas. The increases in freight figures reflect in good part the almost continuous construction of new, large hotels, as well as supplying the needs of those hotels' guests (table 9.2).

The major activity in recent years has been what the Harbors Division termed "face-lifts" for the neighbor island ports to convert them from the break-bulk facilities of the past to more efficient container handling. An unanticipated problem came in the form of the new interisland cruise ships. The occasional trans-Pacific cruise ship coming into neighbor island ports created congestion and pollution problems. A major confrontation came for two American Hawaii cruise ships, the *Constitution* and the *Independence*, when the State Health Department demanded better handling of sewage in port. The company was fined for repeated sewage discharges while in the outer island ports, particularly at Nawiliwili, Kauai, and Kailua, Kona.[41] The issue was resolved when the ships' systems were modernized.

A planning problem emerged with these ships. Long-term resolution of the congestion produced by large passenger ships calling at small

Table 9.2. Freight Traffic in Hawaii's Harbors, 1975–1985 (in short tons).

Year	Honolulu	Hilo	Kahului	Nawiliwili
1975	7,935,183	1,053,879	1,109,485	532,978
1976	7,189,535	995,544	1,276,424	460,900
1977	6,881,556	1,013,430	1,301,095	557,798
1978	7,646,270	1,272,734	1,922,112	765,877
1979	7,463,663	1,220,438	1,473,307	757,899
1980	7,646,270	1,012,019	1,441,524	785,212
1981	8,269,671	1,441,590	1,551,944	906,595
1982	7,593,097	1,381,996	1,483,955	808,153
1983	8,039,850	1,522,442	1,842,568	1,008,699
1984	8,469,971	1,570,528	1,889,204	944,770
1985	7,986,131	1,318,518	1,516,509	933,477

Source: U.S. Corps of Engineers, *Waterborne Commerce of the United States, Calendar Year 1985,* (1987), Part 4, pp. 31–26.

harbors with single berths "originally geared to handle cargo and cargo type vessels," would be a major challenge. For the foreseeable future, close coordination of sailing schedules seemed to be the feasible solution. Round-the-world ships such as the *Queen Elizabeth II* sorely tax the facilities of Honolulu Harbor. This was the largest vessel ever to dock at Honolulu (1987) and required careful planning to bring the vessel into port at the proper draft. One solution proposed at Honolulu Harbor is to develop the area of piers 12 to 15 to provide for cruise ships, charter vessels, and commercial fishing boats.[42] The outports, as well as Honolulu, probably have reached a point of near saturation in terms of accommodating large vessels in addition to the present traffic.

The Year 2010

The focus of planning for the waterfront shifted dramatically during the 1980s. A new phrase surfaced in discussions about the harbor—the "interface" of the harbor with the community. Another common phrase now heard is "waterfront revitalization." Honolulu, it was concluded, had turned its back on its harbor. Development should bring people back to the waterfront. High-rise development of the downtown section of Honolulu produced the familiar downtown spectacle of deserted streets in the afternoons and evenings. Clearly some revitalization was required. The focus was to be the conversion of the Aloha Tower complex into a tourist center by adding a hotel and shopping facilities to the passenger terminal. The waterfront would be made a vital part of downtown Honolulu.

A series of land-use regulations and agencies now control harbor development. Areas adjacent to the harbor attract planners as new combination business-residential areas that will incorporate waterfront activites. The models for much of this planning are the cities of Boston, Baltimore, San Diego, and Seattle. Several district authorities have been created, each encompassing somewhat different ideas as to the harbor and adjacent areas. Borrowing from Seattle, the legislature has defined "water dependency" as a method for sorting out the uses of waterfront. This requires three definitions: water-dependent, water-related, and water-enhanced.[43] To deal with competing claims for access to the waterfront, the definitions are proposed to enable clear, consistent decisions for shoreline management. There also are land-use regulations that blur the line between the waterfront and adjacent areas. Difficult to define with precision is the issue of economic viability. Examples of the difficulty of applying such definitions abound. A shipbuilding yard is clearly water-dependent, "but warehousing of ships' parts is not." Space on the harbor front would be assigned by these criteria. Firms in the latter two categories would be moved from the dock area to created new space. Hotels and restaurants are classified in the water-enhanced category.[44] These various regulations threaten to overlap the jurisdiction of the Harbors Division.

These new criteria for harbor development were adopted without first defining jurisdictions. The Aloha Tower Development Corporation (ATDC), created in 1981, has planning jurisdiction over the passenger terminal, extending to pier 19. The ATDC is authorized to plan for and oversee the redevelopment of approximately thirteen acres of waterfront centering on piers 8 through 11. The goals are (1) to strengthen the international economic base of the community in trade; (2) to beautify the waterfront; (3) to better serve modern marine uses; and (4) to provide for public access and use of waterfront property.[45]

The goal is to "create a major public gathering place and attractions at the historic waterfront, eliminate physical and visual barriers between downtown and Aloha Tower, maintain and enhance passenger ship operations, creating a financially self-supporting project." An agreement was signed that would create a first-class hotel, commercial and office space (150,000–200,000 square feet), a retail and restaurant complex, (40,000–100,000 square feet), parking, maritime activities (90,000 square feet), and waterfront plaza, promenade, and pedestrian overpass.

The harbor is under the jurisdiction of the Department of Transportation, but the ATDC is responsible for developing and coordinating the planning of the site. The Aloha Tower, although it functions at a much lower level than that for which it was designed, is a working passenger terminal for round-the-world cruise ships that call regularly in Honolulu, as well as for three cruise ships plying among the islands. The three interisland vessels are currently the only American flag passenger vessels operating on a weekly schedule from Honolulu. Immediate confusion over these various requirements placed the ATDC agreement in litigation. By 1987, the increased demand in the complex for maritime space, from 44,000 square feet to 248,000 square feet, had raised the cost and further restricted the amount of commercially developable space.[46] The project also is bogged down in controversy over the amount of revenues owed to the Harbors Division of the Department of Transportation. As the Director of Economic Development commented in February 1988, "it appears the statute created an entity and gave it responsibility for developing a facility without giving it the authority to resolve disputes among various jurisdictions."[47]

Immediately to the southeast of the harbor is the Kewalo Basin and the Kakaako District—a mixed industrial-residential area. This is the domain of the Hawaii Community Development Authority.[48] Kewalo Basin was intended to serve the lumber schooners and fishing vessels displaced from Honolulu Harbor in 1923. Although the lumber schooners made little use of it, fishing, and tourist boats have crowded the harbor.

The area of the basin is undergoing massive redevelopment as a first-class residential-business district adjoining the downtown area. The most likely outcome of these development activities will be to convert Kewalo Basin into a recreational-tourist facility, displacing the few remaining commercial fishermen. As commercial fishing declines in Hawaii—the only cannery in Hawaii, located at Kewalo Basin, ceased operations in 1984—the residential and park-related activities will occupy this space.[49]

Unlike the port examples most often cited by planners in Hawaii, Honolulu Harbor has little or no unused or abandoned dock space. The historical development of the city of Honolulu around the harbor perimeter has not permitted expansion. That urban proximity barred the development of a belt railroad serving all of the piers, one of the early goals of harbor planners. High-rise Honolulu, at the very edge of the harbor, limits the redevelopment potential.

In all of these plans, there is constant reiteration of the importance of the harbor to the economic life of Hawaii. The maritime activities, it is repeatedly said, must not be hampered or displaced. Although everyone seems to agree, the activities as envisioned all involve use of and occupation of harbor facilities. Most serious is a probable increase in recreational use of the harbor and the channel, creating serious problems for the increasingly large ships using the narrow entrance channel and the turn into the main basin. The examples cited by proponents of redevelopment are primarily harbors that have moved their principal marine activities from old sites to more modern facilities such as Seattle, Baltimore, Boston, and New York. There are no such abandoned areas in Honolulu Harbor. Piers 37, 38, and 42 are the only remaining unimproved waterfront areas in Honolulu under the jurisdiction of the Department of Transportation. With projected increases in vessel traffic and cargo volume, this area will have to be improved to meet that increased need.[50]

The Harbors Division views the future of the harbor somewhat more modestly than the redevelopment agencies. For pier rehabilitation, they hope to bring the berths to the recommended depth of forty feet. The expansion of marshaling yardspace coupled with an increase in shedded area probably means a shift of some shed areas away from the waterfront. Piers need to be rebuilt to withstand the increased load factor accompanying modern cargo handling. The Harbors Division will continue efforts to "improve the interface between Downtown and the Honolulu Harbor waterfront."[51]

After considerable discussion, a new proposal was made in *The Honolulu Waterfront Master Plan* in 1989. The plan includes short- and long-range plans for an area stretching from Kakaako on the east to Keehi Lagoon on the west and a new plan for Barbers Point Harbor.[52] (Fig. 9.3)

Essentially maritime activity would be shifted from the Fort Armstrong Channel and pier 2 to the Kapalama end of the harbor. The present container freight station, the Foreign Trade Zone and the Kakaako Food Distribution Center would be converted to a mix of maritime-commercial and recreational activities. Maritime activities would be shifted to the Kapalama section at the northwest corner and potentially, into the Kapalama Military Reservation when that is made

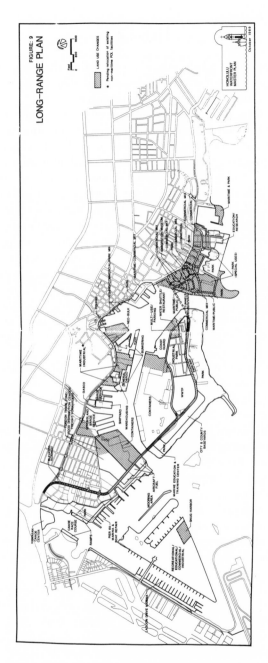

Figure 9.3   Honolulu Harbor Long Range Plan, 1989 (from State of Hawaii, Department of Transportation, *Honolulu Waterfront Master Plan,* 1989).

available. This would locate all container freight activities in one area of the harbor. The interisland barge services would move to piers 39 and 40, clearing piers 24 through 29 for other uses.

Some of the confusion in these waterfront development plans may be resolved by legislation currently pending in the Hawaii State Legislature. The Aloha Tower Development Corporation would be dissolved and the complex placed in the Kakaako Development District. The potential conflict with the maritime planning of the Harbors Division would thus be eliminated.[53]

The proposed interisland marine ferry and hoped-for interisland system are problems that will demand imaginative solutions to expand the constricted water surface of the harbor. The conflict between essential maritime needs and the desire for community access to the waterfront for recreational activities is not easily resolved.

While the conformation of the harbor is not likely to change dramatically over the near future, the fringes may see drastic alterations and a more intensive, efficient use of available dock space. This is much the same concern that has been present through all of the harbor's history.

Notes

1. William L. Worden, *Cargoes: Matson's First Century in the Pacific* (Honolulu: University of Hawaii Press, 1981), p. 143.

2. Harbor Commissioners, *Report* (1960), p. 7.

3. Law and Wilson-Tudor Engineering Company, *Report on Overseas Passenger and Freight Terminal and Development of the Port of Honolulu* (Honolulu: Board of Harbor Commissioners, 1958), pp. 44–45.

4. Ibid., pp. 7–8.

5. Ibid., p. 50. In 1967, the passenger total, including Pacific and world cruise ships, was 28,830: Robert C. Schmitt, *Historical Statistics of Hawaii*, (Honolulu: University of Hawaii Press, 1977), p. 452, table 17.13). By 1984, the number had fallen to 726. Hawaii State Department of Planning and Economic Development, *Hawaii State Data Book* (1986), p. 480.

6. John L. Hazard, *Transshipment Hawaii: Steps Toward an East West Trade* (Honolulu: Bureau of Business Research, University of Hawaii, 1963), pp. ii–iv.

7. Corps of Engineers, *Annual Report* (1968), p. 1109; U.S. Congress, 89th Cong., 1st Sess., River and Harbors Committee, House Document No. 93, (1965); Hawaii State Department of Transportation, Harbors Division, *Report*, (1970), p. 15; Corps of Engineers, *Ports of the Hawaiian Islands*, Port Series No. 50 (1970), pp. 10ff.

8. Worden, *Cargoes*, p. 146.

9. *Honolulu Star Bulletin* (21 January 1964). Theo H. Davies & Co. was the other member of the Big Five.

10. Worden, *Cargoes*, p. 153.

11. Wytze Gorter, *Another Look At Hawaii's Ocean Transportation Problems* (Honolulu: University of Hawaii Economic Research Center, 1964), pp. 24–25; See also, Federal Maritime Commission, *Hawaiian Trade Study: An Economic Analysis* (Washington, D.C.: G.P.O., 1978), p. 2.

12. *Honolulu Star Bulletin* (12 December 1967).

13. Fred Loui, "Ship Repair and Rehabilitation Requirements For the Port of Honolulu, Short and Long Term," Hawaii State Department of Transportation, no date.

14. Tudor Engineering Company, "Preliminary Dry Dock Feasibility Study" (San Francisco, 1 February 1968), p. 1.

15. Corps of Engineers, *Ports of the Hawaiian Islands* (1970), pp. 31–32.

16. Hawaii State Department of Transportation, *Report* (1969), p. 15.

17. Hawaii State Department of Transportation, *Report* (1968), p. 17; *Report* (1969), pp. 21–22; *Report* (1970), p. 23.

18. Federal Maritime Commission, *Hawaiian Trade Study*, p. 15; Hawaii Department of Economic Planning and Development, *Report* (1976), p. 1.

19. Federal Maritime Commission, *Hawaiian Trade Study*, p. 36.

20. Ibid. p. 63.

21. *Honolulu Star Bulletin* (26 August 1970; 16 October 1970); Hawaii State Department of Transportation, *Report* (1971), pp. 23–24.

22. *Honolulu Advertiser* (15 February 1972).

23. Department of Transportation, *2010 Master Plan For Honolulu Harbor* (Honolulu: Hawaii State Department of Transportation, October 1986), p. 6. This plan is a revision of the plan, *1995 Master Plan for Honolulu Harbor* (Honolulu: Hawaii State Department of Transportation, 27 February 1976).

24. Erwin N. Thompson, *Pacific Ocean Engineers: History of the Army Corps of Engineers in the Pacific, 1905–1980* (Honolulu: U.S. Army Corps of Engineers, Pacific Ocean Division, 1985), p. 326.

25. Hawaii State Department of Planning and Economic Development, *Hawaii State Data Book* (1987).

26. *Honolulu Star Bulletin*, 26 September 1988.

27. Hawaii State Department of Transportation, *Intra-island Marine Highway, Objectives* (1988), p. 2.

28. Hawaii State Department of Transportation, *2010 Master Plan For Honolulu Harbor* (1986), p. 7.

29. *Honolulu Star Bulletin* (28 May 1957).

30. U.S. Congress, House of Representatives, 89 Cong., 1st Sess. Doc. No. 93, 4 May 1964, pp. 37, 47, 78.

31. Hawaii State, Department of Transportation, *Report* (1985), p. 5.

32. Hawaii State Department of Transportation, The Honolulu Waterfront Master Plan, Barbers Point Harbor, p. 3–63, (1989).

33. University of Hawaii, Department of Urban and Regional Planning, *Honolulu Waterfront: Resource, Activity and Use Analysis* (1988), 1V-11; *Pacific Business News* (19 September 1988), pp. 1, 7.

34. William Alanson Bryan, *The Free Port Idea Applied to Hawaii* (Honolulu: Chamber of Commerce, 1918) p. 11.

35. Naomi Perlman, *The Foreign Trade Zone: Its Feasbility in Hawaii* (Honolulu: Legislative Reference Bureau, Report No. 1, 1959), pp. iv, 1.

36. Booz-Allen & Hamilton, *Final Report: Expansion Feasibility Study of Hawaii's Foreign Trade Zone No. 9* (Honolulu: Hawaii State Department of Planning and Economic Development, 1978), pp. 15–16.

37. Hawaii State Department of Planning and Economic Development, *Foreign Trade Zone Report, 1980* (Honolulu, 1981), p. 2.

38. U.S. Department of Commerce, Foreign Trade Zone Board, *Annual Reports, 1978–1988.*

39. Ben F. Rush, *History of Construction and Development of Honolulu Harbor,* Territory of Hawaii, Board of Harbor Commissioners, mimeo, 1957, pp. 31–34.

40. See Bernard J. Stern, *The Aloha Trade: Labor Relations in the Hawaii Hotel Industry* (Honolulu: University of Hawaii Center for Labor Education and Research, 1989), for details on tourism, pp. 116–123.

41. *Honolulu Advertiser* (10 January, 18 January, 6 February, 1986).

42. Hawaii State, Department Of Transportation, *Report* (1984), p. 6.

43. University of Hawaii, Department of Urban and Regional Planning, *Honolulu Waterfront, Resources, Activity and Use Analysis* (Honolulu, 1988), pp. 1X-4-5.

44. Ibid., p. X–3, citing Washington State, Department of Ecology, *Urban Waterfront Policy Analysis* (1986).

45. State of Hawaii, Act 236, *Session Laws of Hawaii* (1981), Chapter 106J, Hawaii Revised Statutes, Aloha Tower Development Corporation.

46. Clinton Tanimura, Legislative Auditor of the State of Hawaii, *Review and Analysis of the Aloha Tower Development Corporation,* Report No. 87-13 (1987), p. 27.

47. University of Hawaii, Department of Urban and Regional Planning, *Honolulu Waterfront,* pp. XIII–12.

48. University of Hawaii, Department of Urban and Regional Planning, *Honolulu Waterfront,* p. V–50. This report concludes that serious problems of aggravated traffic and congestion appear inevitable in the effort to "bring people to the waterfront" given the conformation of the road system, the highrise development, and the restricted area available, p. V-57; Michael S. Chu, "Kewalo Basin Master Plan Landside Facilities," Report to Hawaii State Department of Transportation, 1986 (mimeo); University of Hawaii, Sea Grant Extension Service, "Kaka'ako Waterfront Park Development Plan and Environmental Assessment," vol. 1, Report to Hawaii State Department of Land and Natural Resources, 1986 (mimeo).

49. Tyrone Kusao, Inc. *Environmental Assessment Report, Kewalo Basin Landside Improvements* (1986), prepared for the State of Hawaii, Department of Transportation; Sea Grant Extension Service, "Kaka'ako Waterfront" (1986).

50. Hawaii State Department of Transportation, *2010 Master Plan for Honolulu Harbor* (1986), p. 11.

51. State of Hawaii, Department of Transportation, *The Honolulu Waterfront Master Plan*, (mimeo, 1989).

52. *2010 Master Plan*, Recommendations, pp. 17–19.

53. State of Hawaii, Legislature, House Bill No. 1801, Standing Committee Report No. 1322, March 31, 1989; Senate Bill No. 1803, Standing Committee Report No. 1217, March 31, 1989. Both bills are pending before the current (1990) legislature.

Bibliography

Manuscripts and Manuscript Collections

Boit, John, Jr. "Journal of a Voyage Round the Globe, 10 October 1795." Honolulu, University of Hawaii, Hawaii-Pacific Collection (typescript).

Chamberlain, Levi. Journals, 1822–1849. Honolulu, Hawaiian Mission Children's Society Library.

Colnett, James. "The Journal of Capt. James Colnett Aboard the Prince of Wales and Princess Royal." Honolulu, University of Hawaii, Hawaii Pacific Collection. (typescript of Great Britain, Public Record Office, Adm. 55/146).

Dillingham Papers. Honolulu, Bernice P. Bishop Museum.

Mystic Seaport Museum, Mystic, Connecticut, G.W. Blunt White Library. Ships' Logs.

Pacific Regional Oral History Program. Honolulu, University of Hawaii, Department of History.

Peabody Museum. Salem, Massachusetts. Ships' Logs.

Sewall Museum, Bath, Maine. Sewall Manuscripts, Box C-22.

Sewall Museum, Bath, Maine. Ships' Logs.

"Solid Men of Boston in the Northwest." Berkeley: University of California, Bancroft Library (Microfilm).

Dissertations and Theses

Daws, Gavan. *Honolulu*. Ph.D. dissertation, Honolulu, University of Hawaii, 1966.

Healy, John. *Mapping of the Hawaiian Islands*. Master's thesis, Honolulu, University of Hawaii, 1959.

Holmes, Thomas M. *The Spectre of Communism in Hawaii, 1947–1953*. Ph.D. dissertation, Honolulu, University of Hawaii, 1975.

Liebes, Richard. *History of Hawaiian Labor Organizations*. Master's thesis, Honolulu, University of Hawaii, 1937.

Taylor, William. *The Hawaiian Sugar Industry*. Ph.D. dissertation, Berkeley, University of California, 1935.

Labor Organization Records

American Federation of Labor. Teamsters' Union Memorandum on Military Control of Hawaiian Labor, 22 March 1944. Honolulu, University of Hawaii, Hawaii War Records.

International Longshoremen's Association, Pacific Coast District. *4th Annual Convention.* 6–12 June 1911.

International Longshoremen's and Warehousemen's Union. Organizing Files, 1937–1943, ILWU Archives, San Francisco.

International Longshoremen's and Warehousemen's Union. Territorial Organizing Committee, ILWU Archives, San Francisco.

Hawaii: Kingdom, Territorial, and State Documents

Hawaii, Kingdom of. *Fundamental Laws of the Kingdom, 1841.*

———. *Laws of 1856.* Honolulu, 1856.

———. *Session Laws, 1859.* Honolulu, 1860.

Hawaii, Territory of. *Session Laws, 1911.* Act 163.

———. *Session Laws, 1941.* Act 142.

———. *Session Laws of Hawaii, 1949.* Act 2.

———. *Special Joint Committee Report No. 29 on Joint Resolution No. 4,* Special Session Laws, 1941.

Hawaii, Territorial Board of Harbor Commissioners. *Biennial Reports, 1914–1963.*

———. Law and Wilson-Tudor Engineering Company, *Report on Overseas Passenger and Freight Terminal and Development of the Port of Honolulu, 1958.*

———. Ben F. Rush, "History of Construction and Development of Commercial Harbors," 1956 (mimeo).

Hawaii, Territorial Historical Commission. *Report 1924.* Great Britain, Foreign Office, No. 58/3.

Hawaii, State of. *Hawaii Revised Statutes,* 1981. 9:46.

———. *Session Laws of Hawaii,* 1981. Chapter 206J.

———. *Session Laws,* 1981. Act 236, 9:44, Aloha Tower Development Corporation.

Hawaii. State Department of Planning and Economic Development. *Report,* 1976.

———. Booz-Allen and Hamilton, *Final Report: Expansion Feasibility Study of Hawaii's Foreign Trade Zone No. 9,* 1978.

———. *Foreign Trade Zone Report,* 1980. Honolulu, 1981.

———. *State Data Book,* 1986–1988.

Hawaii. State Department of Transportation. Fred Loui, "Ship Repair and Rehabilitation Requirements for the Port of Honolulu, Short and Long Term," no date.

———. Tudor Engineering Company. "Preliminary Dry Dock Feasibility Study. San Francisco, 1 February 1968.

———. Harbors Division. *Annual Reports,* 1968–1970.

———. *1995 Master Plan for Honolulu Harbor,* October 1986.

———. Michael S. Chu, "Kewalo Basin Master Plan Landside Facilities," 1986 (mimeo).

———. Tyrone Kusao, Inc., "Environmental Assessment Report, Kewalo Basin Landside Improvements," 1986.

———. *2010 Master Plan for Honolulu Harbor,* October 1986.

———. *Intra-island Marine Highway, Objectives,* 1988.

Hawaii. State Legislative Auditor. Clinton Tanimura, *Review and Analysis of the Aloha Tower Development Corporation,* Report No. 87-13, 1987.

Hawaii, State Legislative Reference Bureau. Naomi Perlman, "The Foreign Trade Zone: Its Feasibility in Hawaii." *Report No. 1,* 1959.

Hawaii State Archives

Adams, Alexander. Journal.

Collector of Customs. Letter Books.

Department of Finance, Kingdom of Hawaii. *Biennial Reports.*

Foreign Office and Executive. Foreign Office Letter Books.

Foreign Office and Executive. *Reports.*

Harbormaster Files, 1857–1900.

Interior Department. Letter Books.

———. Miscellaneous.

Minister of the Interior. *Biennial Reports.*

———. Bureau of Public Improvements *Biennial Reports,* 1850–1892.

———. "Report to the President and Members of the Executive and Advisory Councils of the Provisional Government of the Hawaiian Islands," 1894.

———. Superintendent of Public Works. *Reports* to the Minister of the Interior, 1860–1892.

Minister of Finance. Letter Books.

———. *Annual Reports.*

Minister of Foreign Affairs. *Annual Reports.*

Marin Papers. Historical and Miscellaneous File.

Paty, William. Journal.

Privy Council Records, 1850–1893.

United States Government Documents

U. S. Army Forces MIDPAC. Army Port and Service Command. "History of the Army Port and Service Command." Hawaii War Records, 1945 (Mimeo).

U. S. Bureau of Labor. *Report of Commissioner of Labor on Hawaii, 1902.* Washington, D.C.: G.P.O., 1903.

———. *4th Report on Hawaii,* Bulletin No. 94. Washington, D.C.: G.P.O., 1911.

U. S. Congress. House of Representatives. 28th Cong., 2d Sess., Doc. No. 92. *House Reports.*

———. 64th Cong., 1st Sess., Doc. No. 392. "Reserved Channel Improvement."

———. 73d Cong., 1st Sess., House Document No. 54, 1932. Report of the Division Engineer, San Francisco (21 July 1931.)

———. 79th Cong., 2d Sess., House Document No. 705 (9 July 1946).

———. 89th Cong., 1st Sess., House Document No. 93. "Corps of Engineers Report For Rivers And Harbors Committee," 4 May 1964.

U.S. Congress. Joint Committee. 79th Cong., 2d Sess., "Civilian Preparedness Activities and Establishment of Major Disaster Council." Pearl Harbor Attack Hearings, (1946) vol. 18.

U.S. Congress. Senate. 52d Cong., 2d Sess., Executive Documents No. 77. Schofield and Alexander to Secretary of War Belknap, 8 May 1873.

———. Senate. Subcommittee on Pacific Islands and Porto Rico. *Report on General Conditions in Hawaii* (Hawaiian Investigation), 3 vols. Washington, D.C., 1902.

U.S. Department of the Army, Corps of Engineers, *Annual Reports of the Chief of Engineers,* 1867–1989.

———. *Ports of the Hawaiian Islands.* Washington, D.C.: G.P.O., Port Series No. 17, 1935; No. 50, 1970.

———. *Waterborne Commerce of the United States, Calendar Year 1985.* Washington, D.C.: G.P.O., 1987.

U.S. Department of Commerce, Foreign Trade Zone Board. *Annual Report of the Foreign Trade Zone Board to Congress,* 1936ff.

U.S. Federal Maritime Commission. *Hawaiian Trade Study: An Economic Analysis.* Washington, D.C.: GPO, 1978.

U.S. National Archives. Hawaiian Department. San Bruno, California. U. S. Army Overseas Operations and Commands, 1898–1942. Record Group No. 395.

———. Office of Chief Engineer. Record Group No. 77.

———. National Archives. U.S. Army Military Intelligence Department. *Investigative Files of the Bureau of Investigation, 1918–1921.* File B.S. 202600, Reels 47–50.

U. S. National Labor Relations Board. 12th Region, International Longshoremen's Association and Castle and Cooke, Ltd., Case XX-C-55. Honolulu, 14 August 1937.

U. S. Postmaster General. *Annual Report for 1866.* Washington, D.C.: G.P.O., 1866.

U. S. Supreme Court. *Reports.* "Duncan v. Kahanomoku." 372 U.S. 304, 1946.

Newspapers

Daily Bulletin. Honolulu.

The Friend. Honolulu. Published 1815, ff; originally *Temperance Advocate and Seamans's Friend.*

Gentleman's Magazine. London, April 1794.

Hawaiian Gazette. Honolulu.

Honolulu Advertiser.

Honolulu Record.

Honolulu Star Bulletin.

Pacific Business News. Honolulu.

Pacific Commercial Advertiser. Honolulu.

The Polynesian. Honolulu.

Saturday Press. Honolulu, 1881–1882.

Thrum's Annual. Honolulu, 1877–1924. Title varies: *Thrum's Hawaiian Almanac* (1875–1924).

Voice of Labor. Honolulu.

Published Works

Adler, Jacob. *Claus Spreckels: The Sugar King in Hawaii.* Honolulu: University of Hawaii Press, 1966.

Alexander, W. D. "Early Improvements in Honolulu Harbor." *Hawaiian Historical Society Annual Report.* Honolulu, 1907.

Allen, Gwenfread. *Hawaii's War Years, 1941–1945.* Honolulu: Greenwood Press, 1950.

American Historical Review. 30 (1925): 561–565. J. M. Schofield and B. S. Alexander to Wm. W. Belknap, 8 May 1873, "Confidential Report on Pearl River Survey to the Secretary of War."

Anderson, Rufus. *History of the Sandwich Island Mission.* Boston: Congregational Publication Society, 1870.

Anthony, J. Garner. *Hawaii Under Army Rule.* Palo Alto: Stanford University Press, 1955.

Barratt, Glynn. *The Russian Discovery of Hawaii: The Journals of Eight Russian Explorers.* Honolulu: Editions Limited, 1987.

Beechert, Edward. *Working in Hawaii: A Labor History.* Honolulu: University of Hawaii Press, 1985.

———. "Red Scare In Paradise." In *The Cold War Against Labor,* vol. 2, edited by Ann F. Ginger and David Christiano. Berkeley: Meikeljohn Civil Liberties Institute, 1987, pp. 447–471.

———. "Technology and the Plantation Labour Supply." In *The World Sugar Economy in War and Depression 1914–1940,* edited by Adrian Graves and Bill Albert. London: Routledge, 1988, pp. 131–141.

Bingham, Hiram. *A Residence of Twenty-one years in the Sandwich Islands.* 1st ed. Hartford: H. Huntington, 1847.

Bloxham, Andrew. *Diary of Andrew Bloxham, Naturalist on the Blonde.* Bernice P. Bishop Museum, Special Publications No. 10. Honolulu: Bishop Museum Press, 1925.

Blue, George. "Early Relations Between Hawaii and the Northwest Coast." *Hawaiian Historical Society Reports, 1924.*

Bradley, Harold W. *The American Frontier in Hawaii: The Pioneers, 1789–1843.* Palo Alto: Stanford University Press, 1942.

———. "Thomas Ap Catesby Jones and the Hawaiian Islands, 1826–1827." *Hawaiian Historical Society Annual Report,* Honolulu, 1930.

Brissenden, Paul. "The Great Hawaiian Dock Strike." *Labor Law Journal* 4 (4) (April 1953): 231–279.

Brookes, Jean I. *International Rivalry in the Pacific Islands, 1800–1875.* Berkeley: University of California Press, 1941.

Brooks, Phillip. *Multiple-Industry Unionism in Hawaii.* New York: Columbia University Press, 1952.

Bryan, William Alanson. *The Free Port Idea Applied to Hawaii.* Honolulu: Chamber of Commerce, 1918.

Bykofsky, Joseph, and Harold Larson. *The Transportation Corps: Operations Overseas.* Washington, D.C.: Department of Defense, U.S. Army, Technical Services Series, 1957.

Bywater, Hector C. "Japanese and American Naval Power In The Pacific." *Pacific Affairs,* June 1935.

Calcott, Maria Graham. *Voyage of H.M.S.* Blonde *to the Sandwich Islands: 1824–1825.* London: J. Murray, 1826.

Campbell, Archibald. *A Voyage Round the World from 1806 to 1812 with an Account of a Stay in the Sandwich Islands.* 4th American edition. Roxbury, Mass.: Charleston, Duke and Brown, 1822.

Cartwright, Bruce. "The First Discovery of Honolulu Harbor." *Hawaiian Historical Society Annual Report,* 1922.

Clark, T. Blake. "Honolulu's Streets." *Hawaiian Historical Society Annual Report* No. 20, 1938.

Conde, Jesse. *Sugar Trains.* Felton, California: Glenwood Publishers, 1973.

Corney, Peter. *Voyages in the Northern Pacific: Narrative of Several Trading Voyages from 1813 to 1818, Between the Northwest Coast of America, the Hawaiian Islands and China, with a Description of the Russian Establishment on the Northwest Coast.* Honolulu: T. H. Thrum, 1896.

Coulter, John Wesley, and Chee Kwon Chun. *Chinese Rice Farmers in Hawaii.* Honolulu: University of Hawaii, Research Publication No. 16, 1937.

Daws, Gavan. *A Shoal of Time.* New York: Macmillan, 1968.

Dibble, Sheldon. *A History of the Sandwich Islands.* Honolulu: T. H. Thrum, 1909.

Dwight, Edwin W. *Memoirs of Henry Obookiah, A Native of Owyhee, and a Member of the Foreign Mission School.* New Haven: Edison, Hart, 1819.

Fairley, Lincoln. *Facing Mechanization: The West Coast Longshore Plan.* Los Angeles: University of California, Institute of Industrial Relations, Monograph Series No. 23, 1979.

Fitzpatrick, Gary L. *The Early Mapping of Hawaii.* Honolulu: Editions Limited, 1986.

Fornander, Abraham. *Collection of Hawaiian Antiquities and Folklore.* 6 vols. Bernice P. Bishop Museum Memoirs. Honolulu: Bishop Museum Press, 1916.

————. *An Account of the Polynesian Race.* Bernice P. Bishop Museum Special Publication No. 4. Honolulu: Bishop Museum Press, 1909.

Franchere, Gabriel. *Narrative of a Voyage to the Northwest Coast of America, 1811–1814.* New York: The Lakeside Press, 1854.

Frear, W. D. "Hawaiian Statute Law." *Hawaiian Historical Society Annual Report,* 1906.

Freycinet, Louis de. *Voyage Autour Du Monde . . . Pendant Les Annees 1817, 1819, Et 1820.* 2 vols. Paris: Impremerie Royale, 1824.

Fuchs, Lawrence. *Hawaii Pono: A Social History.* New York: Harcourt, Brace & World, Inc., 1961.

Gast, Ross H. *Don Francisco de Paula Marin: A Biography.* Honolulu: University Press of Hawaii for Hawaiian Historical Society, 1973.

Goldman, Irving. *Ancient Polynesian Society.* Chicago: University of Chicago Press, 1970.

"Golovnin's Visit to Hawaii in 1818." *The Friend,* 52 (1894):52–53.

Gorter, Wytze. *Another Look at Hawaii's Ocean Transportation Problems.* Honolulu: University of Hawaii Economic Research Center, 1964.

Gregg, David Lawrence. *The Diaries of David Lawrence Gregg: An American Diplomat in Hawaii, 1853–1858,* edited by Pauline King. Honolulu: Hawaiian Historical Society, 1982.

Handy, E. S. C. "Polynesian Religion." *Bernice P. Bishop Museum Bulletin* No. 34. Honolulu: Bishop Museum Press, 1927.

Handy, E. S. C., and Elizabeth G. Handy. "Native Planters in Old Hawaii: Their Life, Lore, and Environment." *Bernice P. Bishop Museum Bulletin* No. 233. Honolulu: Bishop Museum Press, 1972.

Hazard, John L. *Transshipment Hawaii: Steps Toward an East West Trade.* Honolulu: Bureau of Business Research, University of Hawaii, 1963.

Hennessey, Mark. *The Sewall Ships of Steel.* Augusta, Maine: Kennebec Journal Press, 1937.

Houston, Victor S. K., translator. "Chamisso in Hawaii." Translated from *The Collected Works of Adelbert Von Chamisso. Hawaiian Historical Society Annual Report,* 1939.

Howay, F. W. "Captain Simon Metcalfe and the Brig *Eleanora.*" *Hawaiian Historical Society 34th Annual Report,* 1926, pp. 33–39.

————. "Early Relations between the Hawaiian Islands and the Northwest Coast." In *The Hawaiian Islands . . . Papers Read during the Sesquicentennial*

Celebration, Honolulu, August 17, 1928, edited by Albert P. Taylor & Ralph Kuykendall. Hawaii State Archives Publication No. 5. Honolulu, 1930.

———. "A List of Trading Vessels in the Maritime Fur Trade." *Royal Society of Canada Transactions,* 3d series, section 2, 1932.

———. "The Ship Eliza at Hawaii in 1799." *Hawaiian Historical Society 42nd Annual Report,* 1934, pp. 103–113.

———. "The Ship *Pearl* in Hawaii, 1805 and 1806." *Hawaiian Historical Society 46th Annual Report,* 1938, pp. 27–38.

Hunnewell, James. "Honolulu in 1817 and 1818." *Hawaiian Historical Society Papers,* No. 8, 1895.

Iselin, Isaac. *Journal of a Trading Voyage Around the World, 1805–1808.* 3 vols. New York: McIlroy & Emmet. n.d.

Jarves, James Jackson. *History of the Hawaiian or Sandwich Islands.* Boston: J. Munroe, 1843.

———. *Scenes and Scenery in the Sandwich Islands . . . During the Years 1837–1842.* Boston: J. Munroe, 1843.

Judd, Bernice. *Voyages to Hawaii Before 1860,* edited and enlarged by Helen Yonge Lind. Honolulu: Hawaiian Mission Children's Society, 1974.

Judd, Laura Fish. *Honolulu: Sketches of Life in the Hawaiian Islands from 1828–1861,* edited by Dale L. Morgan. Chicago: Lakeside Press, 1966.

Kamaku, Samuel. *Ka Poe Kahiko: The People of Old.* Bernice P. Bishop Museum Special Publication No. 51. Honolulu: Bishop Museum Press, 1964.

———. *The Ruling Chiefs of Hawaii,* Honolulu: Kamehameha School Press, 1961.

Kemble, John Haskell. "Pioneer Hawaiian Steamers, 1852–1877." *Hawaiian Historical Society Report* No. 53, 1946.

———. "A Hundred Years Of The Pacific Mail." *American Neptune* 10 (April 1950).

Kotzebue, Otto von. *A Voyage of Discovery Into the South Sea and Behring's Straits . . Undertaken in the Years 1815–1818.* 3 vols. London: Longman, Hurst & Brown, 1821.

Kuykendall, Ralph S. *The Hawaiian Kingdom.* 3 vols. Honolulu: University of Hawaii Press, 1938, 1957, 1967.

———. "A Northwest Trader at the Hawaiian Islands." *Oregon Historical Quarterly* 24 (2) (1923), pp. 112–131.

Larrowe, Charles P. *Harry Bridges: The Rise and Fall of Radical Labor in the United States.* New York: Lawrence Hill, 1972.

Laughlin, J. Laurence, and H. Parker Willis. *Reciprocity.* New York: Baker & Taylor, 1903.

Leighton, Richard, and Robert Coakley. *Global Logistics and Strategy, 1940–1945.* Washington, D.C.: Department of the Army, Office of the Chief of Military History, 1955–1968.

Lind, Andrew. *An Island Community: Ecological Succession in Hawaii.* Chicago: University of Chicago Press, 1938.

Llewellyn, Arthur D. "Honolulu Harbor." *The Military Engineer* 39:256 (February 1947), pp. 51–55.

MacArthur, Walter. *The Seaman's Contract, 1790–1918.* San Francisco: James H. Barry Co., 1919.

Malo, David. *Hawaiian Antiquities* (Moolelo Hawaii), translated by Nathaniel B. Emerson. Bernice P. Bishop Museum Special Publication No. 2. Honolulu: Bishop Museum Press, 1951.

Martin, Francisco De Paula. *The Letters and Journal of Francisco De Paula Marin,* edited by Agnes Conrad. Honolulu: University of Hawaii Press for Hawaiian Historical Society, 1973.

Meares, John. *Voyages Made in the Years 1788 and 1789, from China to the Northwest Coast of America.* London: Logographic Press, 1790.

Morgan, Theodore. *Hawaii: A Century of Economic Change, 1776–1876.* Cambridge: Harvard University Press, 1948.

Morison, Samuel E. "Boston Traders in the Hawaiian Islands." *Massachusetts Historical Society Proceedings,* October–November, 1920.

"Mudhooks or Moorings: Safe Harbor for Ships From the Sea." *Sales Builder,* 13 (6) (June 1940): 11–14.

Mund, Vernon A., and Fred C. Hung. *Interlocking Directorates in Hawaii and Public Regulation of Ocean Transportation.* Honolulu: Economic Research Center, University of Hawaii, 1961.

"Notes on the Rice Culture in the Hawaiian Islands." *Thrum's Annual* 1877.

Parke, William Cooper. *Personal Reminiscences of William Cooper Parke, Marshall Of The Hawaiian Islands, From 1850 To 1884.* Cambridge: Harvard University Press, 1891.

Porteus, Stanley D. *And Blow Not the Trumpet.* Palo Alto: Pacific Books, 1947.

Portlock, Nathaniel. *Voyage Around the World, . . . 1785–1788.* London: J. Stockdale, 1789.

Puette, Bill. *The Hilo Massacre: Hawaii's Bloody Monday.* Honolulu: University of Hawaii, Center For Labor Education and Research, 1988.

Ralston, Carolyn. *Grass Huts and Warehouses: Pacific Beach Communities in the Nineteenth Century.* Honolulu: University of Hawaii Press, 1978.

Reinecke, John. *Report on the Hilo Massacre.* Honolulu: Social Affairs Committee, Hawaii Education Association, 1939.

———. *Feigned Necessity: Hawaii's Attempt to Obtain Chinese Contract Labor, 1921–1923.* San Francisco: Chinese Materials Center, Inc., 1979.

Reynolds, Stephen. "Journal of Stephen Reynolds," *Thrum's Hawaiian Almanac,* 1909, pp. 153–159.

Sahlins, Marshall D. *Social Stratification in Polynesia.* Seattle: University of Washington Press, 1958.

Schmitt, Robert C. *Historical Statistics of Hawaii.* Honolulu: University of Hawaii Press, 1977.

Sheldon, Henry L. "Reminiscences of Honolulu Thirty-Five Years Ago" *Saturday Press,* 9 July 1881.

Shoemaker, James. *Labor in the Territory of Hawaii, 1939.* Washington, D.C.: G.P.O., 1940.

————. *The Economy of Hawaii in 1947,* Washington, D.C.: G.P.O., 1949.

Simpson, Sir George. *Narrative of a Journey Around the World During the Years 1841 and 1842.* London: Henry Colburn, 1847.

Smith, Bradford. *Yankess in Paradise: The New England Impact on Hawaii.* Philadelphia: Lippincott, 1956.

Spoehr, Alexander. "Port Towns and Hinterlands in the Pacific Islands." *American Anthropologist* 62 (1960) Series 2.

Starbuck, Alexander. *A History of the American Whale Fishery From Its Earliest Inception To 1876.* Waltham, Mass.: The Author, 1878.

Stearns, Harold. *Geology of the State of Hawaii.* Palo Alto: Pacific Books, 1966.

Stern, Bernard J. *The Aloha Trade: Labor Relations in the Hawaii Hotel Industry.* Honolulu: University of Hawaii Center for Labor Education and Research, 1989.

Stevens, Sylvester K. *American Expansion in Hawaii, 1842–1898.* Harrisburg: Archives Publishing Co., 1945.

Stewart, Charles S. *Journal of a Residence in the Sandwich Islands.* Boston: H. Fisher & Son, 1839.

Stokes, John F. G. "Honolulu and Some New Speculative Phases of Hawaiian History." *Hawaiian Historical Society Annual Report,* 1933.

Sullivan, Josephine. *History of C. Brewer and Company.* Boston: Walton & Co., 1926.

Thomas, Mifflin. *Schooner From Windward: Two Centuries of Hawaiian Inter-Island Shipping.* Honolulu: University of Hawaii Press, 1983.

Thompson, Erwin N. *Pacific Ocean Engineers: History of the Army Corps of Engineers in the Pacific, 1905–1980.* Honolulu: U.S. Army Corps of Engineers, Pacific Ocean Division, 1985.

Thrum, Thomas. "Brief History of the Steam Coasting Service of the Hawaiian Islands." *Thrum's Annual,* 1889.

Thurston, Lorrin A. *Memoirs of the Hawaiian Revolution.* Editor, Andrew Farrell. Honolulu: Pacific Commercial Advertiser Press, 1936.

University of Hawaii. Department of Urban and Regional Planning. *Honolulu Waterfront: Resource, Activity and Use Analysis.* Honolulu, 1988.

————. Sea Grant Extension Service. "Kaka'ako Waterfront Park Development Plan and Environmental Assessment." Report to Hawaii State Department of Land and Natural Resources. vol. 1, 1986 (mimeo).

Vancouver, George. *A Voyage of Discovery to the North Pacific Ocean and Round the World in the Years 1790, 1791, 1792, 1793, 1794 and 1795.* 6 vols. London: Thomas and Andrews, 1801.

Van Dyke, Robert E. (ed). *Hawaiian Yesterdays: Historical Photographs by Ray Jerome Baker,* Honolulu: Mutual Publishing Co., 1982.

Varigny, Charles de. *Fourteen Years in the Sandwich Islands, 1855–1868.* Honolulu: University of Hawaii Press, 1981.

Wardlow, Chester. *The Transportation Corps: Movements, Training, and Supply.* Washington, D.C.: Department of the Army, Office of the Chief of Military History, 1955–1968.

Webb, M. C. "The Abolition of the Taboo System in Hawaii." *Journal Of The Polynesian Society,* 74 (1) (March 1965).

Westervelt, W. D. "Printed Laws Before the Constitution." *Hawaiian Historical Society Annual Report,* 1908.

Worden, William. *Cargoes: Matson's First Century in the Pacific.* Honolulu: University of Hawaii Press, 1981.

Zalberg, Sanford. *A Spark Is Struck: Jack Hall and the ILWU in Hawaii.* Honolulu: University of Hawaii Press, 1979.

General Index

Index of Ship Names

25